ELEPHANTS IN THE HOURGLASS

ELEPHANTS IN THE HOURGLASS

A JOURNEY OF RECKONING AND HOPE ALONG THE HIMALAYA

KIM FRANK

PEGASUS BOOKS
NEW YORK LONDON

ELEPHANTS IN THE HOURGLASS

Pegasus Books, Ltd.
148 West 37th Street, 13th Floor
New York, NY 10018

First Pegasus Books cloth edition January 2025

Interior design by Maria Fernandez

Library of Congress Cataloging-in-Publication Data is available.

ISBN: 978-1-63936-795-5

10 9 8 7 6 5 4 3 2 1

Printed in the United States of America
Distributed by Simon & Schuster
www.pegasusbooks.com

To

Cricket and Tony for Roots & Wings

Goldie and Anhwei, my Sun & Moon

And Dave, my Möbius

The only dream worth having is to dream that you will live while you are alive, and die only when you are dead. To love, to be loved. To never forget your own insignificance. To never get used to the unspeakable violence and vulgar disparity of the life around you. To seek joy in the saddest places. To pursue beauty to its lair. To never simplify what is complicated or complicate what is simple. To respect strength, never power. Above all to watch. To try and understand. To never look away. And never, never to forget.

—Arundhati Roy

Introduction

Midnight on the India–Nepal border. A full moon hides behind the clouds, no longer illuminating the wisp thin trail. The snowy peaks of the eastern Himalaya are shrouded in darkness. A crowd forms along the edge of a field: farmers with flashlights, boys with firecrackers and mobile phones, and young men with homemade cannons firing loud bombs that arc sparks of orange against the sky. Searchlights sweep over the rice paddy crops, ripe for harvest. They shine out from the hands of men protecting the clusters of homes behind them, where their mothers, wives, and children sleep. Aggressive shouting and static from walkie-talkies echo like a game of call-and-response. Sirens pierce from a patrol jeep, headlights flash. I feel like I am on the front line of a war zone.

A farmer casts a broad beam of light over his rice field and it lands on a massive Asian elephant with curved and piercing tusks, the sticky black secretion of musth (the elevated reproductive hormone that male elephants cycle through annually, producing aggressive, unpredictable behavior) visibly draining from his right temple as he gnaws the rice paddy. Although a male elephant in musth produces up to sixty times their normal amount of testosterone, this tusker does not appear ruffled in the least by the cacophony that surrounds him.

I am transfixed. The man next to me lights, raises, and shoots a cannon—the blast sounds lethal. It is not. Still, I yell out and almost drop my camera; it dangles from my wrist, capturing video of men's sneakers and jeans, snatches of dirt and grass, and a blur of movement. No matter, as my settings were off for shooting at night, ruining any hope of capturing decent imagery. This rare moment of documentation, lost. Who am I to tell this story? What if I have traveled across the globe, the only woman out here in the middle of the night, gifted this extraordinary access, only to squander it out of fear and inexperience?

A silence settles over the field, more chilling than calming. All shouts and firecrackers, even the sirens, abate. The tusker, known by the name Lama, continues to eat. Out from the trees rises a noise I have only heard in movies and nightmares: the resounding trumpet of a second elephant. From a different patch of trees directly to our right, a third elephant responds with an earth-shaking, full-bellow roar, followed by a steady and thunderous rumble that rattles me to my core.

This moment is why I have returned to North Bengal for my fourth journey in two years. What began as a desire to tell a single story about wild elephants and people dying in unnecessary clashes grew into a quest to unlock the secrets of the legendary "Queen of the Elephants" and, above all, to deeply understand human and elephant relationships in this region of India, what it means for our planet, and why what is happening there affects each of us.

So many misperceptions exist about elephants in India. We tend to read a headline and assume or see a photo and make a judgment. We are quick to campaign for or against things we know little about. Often we accept a singular view, depriving us of the opportunity to understand truth in the appropriate cultural and historical context. And what of truth? It is comprised of multiple layers and perspectives, of myth, bearing witness, research, and personal filter. There are many truths, and when we accept this, we are on the path to peaceful coexistence.

The truth of these elephants is my driving force. This odyssey has become my personal labyrinth. Each challenge pushing me forward into the unknown, forcing me to navigate blocked passages and ultimately find my way. With every trip, I confront my fears and shift my perspective about who we are as humans, and who I am as a woman; as a mother—moving from the ghosts of the past to an accounting of the present; from visions of the future to the growing sense of an energetic feminine force that pulses like a quiet heartbeat. That space between. Something I can feel but not quite touch.

I am an unlikely explorer. A mother of two daughters. Not a scientist or adventurer, but a woman who overcomes a lifetime of fear and lack of confidence in pursuit of a complex truth. Risk does not entice me, but a story that connects us and has the power to make change is irresistible. Somehow one story became two, then three, and eventually this book. Here is that tale. It begins with an elephant.

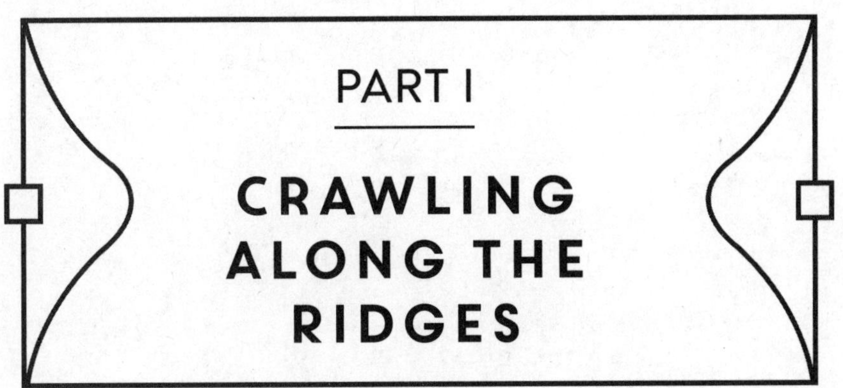

PART I

CRAWLING ALONG THE RIDGES

1

June 2013. I wake before the sun rises and walk from our bedroom into the hallway, listening for Goldie, my youngest daughter who has recently turned seven years old. She is the early riser and often I anticipate her morning call, "Mama!," moments before she yells out. Her father, still lightly snoring in our bedroom, requires his sleep. Through the tall glass windows that front the cabin, the lake is a sleek plane of blue-black. In the distance, sunlight peeps through the mounds of mountains. Goldie is stirring when I peer into the girls' room. Anhwei, my oldest daughter, is sleeping like a stone on the top bunk; she is also not a fan of being awakened.

Goldie locks on my eyes, her thick black hair wild and still damp from last night's bath. She knows the drill and silently slips from the sheets, clutching her stuffed animals, Pandy and Blankie. Thin limbs wrap around my torso, one slim hand reaches around my neck. Like a monkey mother, I carry her to the velvet cushioned daybed in the upstairs loft and deposit her in front of the television to watch her favorite movie, *Narnia*. Volume turned low, child tucked in. "I'll be right back with hot chocolate," I say before she asks. It is our weekend routine.

Down the hardwood stairs, past the built-in bookshelf, where more windows face a wraparound porch and the beach beyond. Every bit of this cabin was crafted with care, from the mahogany dining table built by a woodworking friend to the arched tilework in the guest bathroom shower covered in travertine from floor to walls. From the wide-plank reclaimed floors pulled from a barn in Ohio, to the light fixtures picked out online while the girls watched cartoons. A canvas splattered with Jackson Pollack–style paint, Anhwei's masterpiece at the age of three, hangs over the couch. Three bedrooms, all with a view of the overgrown runs at the recently failed ski resort across the open meadow.

Welcome to my dream come true.

I have a husband of eleven years, after seven years of dating and two breakups. We have two precious daughters, after adoption in China made parenthood possible. We spend summers in this jewel box waterfront home, bought during a prosperous moment. I am a mother with two master's degrees, privileged enough to leave her vibrant career to stay at home full-time with the girls. In my pockets of free time I write, and my work is just starting to win awards and get published. My husband, FH, has two daughters to ski and kayak with him, and flexibility as a business owner. The money is gone now, but we have our family.

We have. We have. We had.

The dogs shake themselves awake when I reach the kitchen. "Shhh, shhhh!" I whisper, even as it is fruitless. If he wakes up, I want him to know I was trying. I open the door and let the dogs out, hoping they don't run away.

Outside a dog barks. FH wakes up. "What the hell!?" he yells from the bedroom. "I am paddling the North Fork today—you knew that! Now I can't go! I didn't sleep! Damn it!"

It is 8:00 A.M.

"Sorry," I say. "I tried. Use your earplugs, maybe you can get in another hour."

He grumbles and pulls the covers over his head. "You know how important this is to me."

From her perch in the loft, Goldie is engrossed by the scene where the White Witch, who has turned all of Narnia into eternal winter, is casting many of the beloved animals into stone, freezing them in time. The sound is barely on, so as not to be heard beyond the room. As the characters become immobilized, their expressions twist in fear and pain, their loved ones left behind in silent helplessness.

Anhwei is now awake in her top bunk. A thick bunch of ski race medals hang from the post, representing three years of podium stands. Sleepy wide eyes, serious and not so playful. She is ten years old. Still, every morning when she first wakes, her expression looks exactly like the moment when, at eleven months, she was first placed into my arms: a brief flash of bewildered and confused, giving way to relief and contentment. That exact look is happening right now.

On that first morning, we waited in the pink Lotus banquet room in Hefei, China, among a cacophony of voices. The room was filled with nannies and orphanage staff; adoption agency guides and government officials; fourteen babies, faces stiff with fear and confusion, some wailing; and fourteen adoptive families—jet-lagged, nervous, wildly excited. A petite woman in round glasses and a close-cut bob emerged from the tangled crowd, carrying our daughter. Anhwei's thick black mass of hair had been shaved, her eyes were awestruck wide and searching, her dimpled cheeks flushed pink. This sweet, sacred child was lifted up into my grasp, a transfer forever seared into my soul. *I am a mother.*

In that instant my wish was granted. After years of trying to conceive, of doctors' diagnoses and prognoses, of endless paperwork, of waiting for permissions, for approval, for original documents, fingerprints, government stamps, clearance, the suffering of a lost dossier, the uncertainty of time frames and the SARS adoption shutdown. *Here is my daughter.*

Hope holds power. When Anhwei gripped my sweater with her plump fingers and laid her feverish cheek on my shoulder, I believed. I believed in fate and the fabled red thread. I believed in destiny, in quantum physics, and in every god that has ever been worshiped. In that moment, I understood that love and the energy in the universe is a potent force that may be impossible to understand but is clearly always at work shaping our lives.

In that moment, I vowed every vow.

Just two nights before Anhwei's adoption, I was crying on the floor of the hotel room, after a post-dinner fight. In my journal that night I wrote: *Tonight, I realize that this marriage is dead and I am broken. In this way I enter motherhood, my greatest dream clashing with my greatest sorrow.*

I believed that becoming a mother was a one-way gate. Particularly when my daughters had been abandoned by their birth family. But now, almost a decade later, we are at a crossroads. Only Anhwei does not yet know it, although she suspects, and I cannot unhear my voice, assuring her all will be well.

This is the scene that keeps me frozen in place: after a terrible argument, when FH finally left the room, after a forced cheerful bath and brushing teeth, after sitting in the girls' bedroom while we all read from our favorite books, after I said, "Close your eyes," and turned off the lights before adding, "Now open them," so their eyes would adjust more quickly to the dark, to soften any fears that came with the night. Only in that darkness did Anhwei dare speak.

"Mama?" She was nine years old at the time. "Are you and Daddy going to get a divorce?" She said it in the voice of a little girl who still believed her mother to be the truest truth teller.

And her mother, who also still believed herself to be the truest of truth tellers, replied: "No, Daddy and I will not ever get a divorce. I promise."

I had faith in this promise. I believed it to my core. In my empty bed that night, hours before my husband would come in and stare at the light of his phone until nearly dawn, I told myself: *Dig in, try harder.*

But here I am. Face-to-face with my eldest daughter, knowing I will break my vow. I hold my finger to my lips, gesturing to be silent.

"Good morning, muffin," I whisper. "Do you want hot chocolate?"

She shakes her head no.

I gather the girls, still in their pajamas, carry their shoes in one hand, my wallet, car keys, and phone in the other, and we leave the cabin. Once outside, I say, "Let's go get pastries and eat them on the dock." I load the dogs into the back of my car. The ignition will make a noise, but at least the house will be silent for a while. Maybe he will fall back to sleep and wake up happy.

On the way to the bakery, we pass the abandoned house. Peeling lime green paint on asbestos siding, windows cracked, some smashed. A few weekends ago, when we were coming home from dinner, FH had said, "Check out that house. It would be cool to photograph that." As if seeing it for the first time.

We returned the next afternoon and made our way in. Dark storm clouds were forming on the wheat-colored horizon and the wind was creating dust devils in the dirt where the front lawn used to be. FH brought his "good camera" and some beers, while the girls waited outside in the truck with activities.

"We'll be right back," I said.

"This place is creepy," Anhwei said.

"True," I said. "I won't be long."

Inside, the ceilings were falling into rooms, floral wallpaper in tatters. We walked from room to room. He was snapping photos as I studied the details—the old panes of glass wavering in the windows, the overgrown field out back. I began to sense the presence of the woman who once lived here. A woman who stared out on this landscape while she set the table for supper, with useless silver she tried to keep polished, and wedding china whose formality mocked her, wondering how she'd ended up in a godforsaken place like this. In a barely there house, just off the main road among acres of farmland, thousands of miles from her parents and the town she'd called home.

Was she a mother?

There were rooms upstairs. One was painted pink. I imagined her with a baby, rocking in the corner, staring at the shadows as they moved across the hallway until morning was afternoon, then twilight, then dawn again.

In the kitchen, the porcelain sink was black with scum, the moldy ceiling caving in, and from overhead, exposed wires dangled down. The window where the woman would have looked out while cleaning dishes was cracked into veins, distorting the view. What had she expected?

"Oh yeah, that's perfect," FH said. "Pretend you are washing your hands in the sink."

To honor and obey.

He took several photos. In them, I look like myself. Like a wife and mother who is still doing all her domestic responsibilities without realizing her home has collapsed around her.

A wind gust slammed an upstairs door. A low whistle along the cracks.

"We should go," I said. "I'm going to check on the girls."

We moved toward the exit, to the living room with its large smashed-out window. I could see the girls still in the truck drawing with new markers on pads of paper.

A gust was creating a vortex of air through the living room, a dust devil kicked up in the corner.

"Get on your hands and knees," he said. "Face the wind. Let it blow your hair back."

I did as I was told.

Down on the dirt-encrusted hardwood floor, fragments of glass scattered around my bare hands.

At first, numbness overwhelmed me. Then I felt a crystal-clear awareness, from both outside and inside of myself. The woman I had once been—confident, strong, curious, vivacious, a leader—was gone. Dead or lost, I was not yet sure.

Later that night, we fought again. As I fell asleep, I couldn't shake the feeling that I was still on my knees, trapped in a house that was rotting around me.

A fever kept me in bed throughout the next day; the flu consumed me.

Later, I learned he posted that living room photo of me on social media without telling or showing me. He'd titled it *Wind Sex*.

We eat our huckleberry pastries on the dock, too rough to row now, the water is churning with tourists in ski boats. The day has begun.

"Can we get our suits on?" Anhwei says. The mornings are chilly up here and we ran out in sweatpants, but already the sun is beating down. "I want to swim."

It's almost ten o'clock. "Yes, definitely," I say.

They run up into the house. I sip the last of my coffee and wait.

When they return, their father is with them. His eyes are swollen, the imprints of wrinkled sheets pressed on his face. He was still up when I went to bed last night, watching a movie, falling asleep, snoring then waking up again. I picked up the empty tequila glass before Goldie could see it this morning. Five years before I could even imagine exploring wild elephants in India, I am seeing our wild "elephant," the one who is increasingly taking up space in every room.

He holds his hand up to block the sun. "Oh, did you go to the bakery?" he says. "Awesome."

I hand him a bear claw and do not ask what he is going to do about kayaking.

"I told the guys I'm not going to go," he says. "I'm too exhausted, it's just not safe if you don't get enough sleep."

The girls are playing along the beach, digging holes and trails. "Anhwei," he says. "Go get your kayak. We'll practice rolls in the lake." Anhwei looks at Goldie. FH says, "Mom and Goldie will come out with us, they'll bring lunch and take the pedal boat."

Thankfully I have salami and bread, some cheese slices, popcorn with sriracha, a bar of chocolate, all in a bag with an ice pack. Sunscreen on the girls, then we are ready. We set out. It is almost noon now and FH feels better with some food. But now he is regretting that his friends are paddling and he isn't with them. "Let's go!" he yells up to the house while we are gathering the last of our things. Anhwei is dutiful. She comes down to the beach with her neoprene skirt dangling from her waist, helmet on. Her paddle in one hand and kayak hoisted over her shoulder with the other hand, just like she was taught. When she glares at me and Goldie, I can feel her simultaneously resentful and angry, and dismissive of us for being unadventurous losers. Goldie and I sit side by side in a two-person aquamarine blue fiberglass pedal boat with a blue-and-white striped canopy. Her wispy legs barely reach so I am doing most of the peddling.

FH and Anhwei are almost out of sight, yet I can hear his commands as he coaches her on her roll, her paddle strokes. While Goldie and I float in the sun eating snacks, Anhwei is out doing her duty, whether she likes it or not. My voice has nothing, is nothing, powerless to weigh in. We act accordingly.

I am so tired.

The lake stretches out into long glimmering expanse. I have stopped pedaling. We float in silence, rocking on the white caps, the rhythm is transfixing. The sound of water lapping against the small boat. Overhead, clouds are stacking up, taking turns covering the sun.

What if I lose them? What if I can't support myself? How do I even do this?

In the distance, Anhwei is lying back on her kayak, staring up at the clouds. Her boat seems so small, a red buoy bobbing on chop. She turns her head in my direction as if feeling my gaze. Her fingers lift from her paddle, and she wriggles them at me. I wave my hand and dramatically blow a kiss across our distance. A big smile, then back to paddling. They are headed back toward the house.

Soon it will be dinner and we will play the game all over again. Happy hour on the dock, dinner outside, I clean up. Anything could happen then. One night we all gathered into the boat for a moonlight cruise, some nights the music is cranked up and we are drawn out onto the floor for swings and dips to cheesy country music at full volume. Most nights end in terrible fighting over the slightest gesture or word. It's like a spin of a roulette wheel. There is one pocket with all the winnings, the kind of extraordinary found in head-thrown-back laughter, the squeeze of a hand, smiling eye contact over the heads of children, and a conversation that leaves us both feeling satiated. These glimmers of hope and faith. They are almost all gone now.

Come on!" FH yells out from across the lake.

I cannot move.

Goldie is digging through her backpack, trying to find something. I can only imagine what. Inside are candy wrappers duct-taped to create small purses holding coins or hair bands, a slingshot, two books that she won't read, markers and paper that she has already filled, a shoehorn, a noisemaker from her cousin's birthday party last fall, a plastic ring won in a vending machine, tiny rubber Japanese erasers in the shape of a panda bear and penguin. She pulls out a bathtub toy, a yellow plastic cup, looks at the lake, thinks better of it, and shoves it back in the bag, zipping it all up.

The sun breaks through a low-hanging cloud and shines rays of light among the strands of her dark brown pigtails, illuminating red and gold. Goldie turns to face me, as if just realizing I am sitting next to her. We stare at one another in silence for an uncomfortable amount of time while she studies me. Finally, she speaks:

"Mom, it doesn't have to be easy. It just has to be possible."

2

October 2015. We live full time in Ketchum, Idaho, a ski resort community of indescribable beauty high up in the Northern Rocky Mountains. It is a place where family memories are made and holidays are enjoyed, where the wealthy live an idyllic life surrounded by wilderness. It is not a hospitable place for a single mother who has given up the prime of her career to raise two daughters and be a dutiful wife now in the throes of divorce. But it is the place where my daughters and their father live, and my sister and parents. It has been my home for decades; I am determined to build back a life here.

Little is anticipated; few things are easy. After the summer in which Goldie uttered those words I most needed to hear, I moved first into my "office" in our basement, then to a small rental house in town. I share equal custody of the girls, which means I've gone from being their primary caregiver to only being with them half the time. This is a deep grief and abrupt change. It also affords me days in a row each week of alone time. In this vacant space, I begin to readjust. I fall in love with my childhood friend, David, who lives two thousand miles away. Hidden surprises of glitter and joy are woven throughout deep sadness. The divorce was not a quick one and I could have never anticipated the aftermath. My identity as a mom, now shaken to the core, is highly vulnerable.

In a small town where you and your ex have been a known couple for decades, an uncoupling and then an outside love interest who appears on the scene typically means you will be making new local friends. David is visiting me. He is making a bit of a splash because of his background. While I know him as the lanky and talkative friend that I used to lifeguard with when we were teenagers, the boy who inspired my love of old jeeps and introduced me to the Jason Bourne series, he is better known out in the world as one of the few explorers to dive to the *Titanic* and the man who led the search and recovery of the Apollo F-1 rocket engines. In 2015, shortly before this visit, he accepted the role of vice president of the Explorers Club in New York City. It is now his job to lead the process that determines who may carry the Explorers Club flag on worthy expeditions (like every Apollo mission to visit the moon), and to recognize outstanding feats of exploration at the club's annual events.

Most of the residents of this ski town do not know anything about the Explorers Club, nor does David fit their idea of an explorer. A town obsessed with Hollywood-style glamour and adventure sports, David's cerebral tendencies and lack of passion for competitive activities that take all day make him somewhat invisible to the local "dudes."

But not to our dinner companions.

We have recently been introduced to two dynamic couples by the magazine publisher for whom I work. A female filmmaker and her partner, who is an internationally renowned whitewater kayaker; and a Red Bull–sponsored paragliding endurance racer, and his *National Geographic* photographer wife, Jody.

"We were out at sea for a decade," says Gavin, the paraglider. His physique is taut with more dynamism than seems containable at this table. "Jody was seasick for most of it, but she never complained, never stopped documenting."

Jody is a superhero. She has taken photos underwater in Tonga while free diving, in the sky over islands off Africa while paragliding, from the tops of desert trains, the bottoms of Indigenous fishermen's boats, and seemingly from every angle and surface of the planet. A traveler since her earliest memories, she prefers living out in the world to within a single identified home, solo journeys to companions, and adventure beyond most people's imagination.

Jody gives a distracted smile. "I don't mind suffering. It makes me feel alive."

"Wow. You *are* tough," David says. He is holding my hand under the table.

Younger by a decade, with sun-streaked beachy hair and eyes the color of an angry sea, Jody has an easy glamour and confidence that borders on arrogance. I am simultaneously repelled and captivated by her. She leans back in her chair like a partygoer who stays in one place knowing the attendees will eventually seek her out.

The waiter delivers the drinks: beer, sake, a glass of wine. A server follows with bowls of steamed edamame and a black rectangular dish with rows of ahi sushi. There is an ease to the sharing. Chopsticks are diving, laughter between the four who have known each other for years. Outside the tall windows people are bundled up in puffy down jackets; a woman wearing a fur coat kisses the cheeks of another woman as she steps out of her Range Rover. They make their way into the restaurant. My jeans are too tight, they are cutting into my stomach. In fact, my entire outfit feels dumpy, overdone, and constraining at the same time. I should have washed my hair.

The conversation swirls around me. I have little to contribute. There is an exchange of who knows whom. Names of people I have read about in magazines, but this group knows them personally . . . as does my companion. This feels suddenly strange. Up until now, David was simply my first male friend. I was seventeen, he was eighteen and already at university. I had a mad crush on him. Years later, we ran into each other in a parking lot—he was leaving for The Hague to study international law, I had just applied to graduate schools. It had been six years since we lifeguarded together, but our conversation picked up as if it were yesterday. He was worried he would lose a clerkship with a judge if he accepted the prestigious and rare international opportunity. His peers thought he was crazy. I thought he was making the right decision and ever after I thought of David's risk-taking and saying yes to the exciting unknown.

Many times throughout my life, when faced with a choice between standing still and going forward, I thought of David. Maybe that is why his name floated into my head as I was struggling through moving out of my marriage. I found him on LinkedIn. He was newly divorced and deeply suffering, my email to him a timely lifeline. Thirty years had passed, but our comfortable friendship was immediate. We began helping each other through each of our difficult life changes.

I still have, stuffed in an envelope for decades, a birthday card, three-page letter, and a newspaper clipping—a drawing of a dashing, hip, young man. All from David as a college sophomore. His note told me that the sketch was a self-portrait in case I might want to tape it to my wall. And now the boy in the sketch is the man sitting next to me, squeezing my hand with empathy and encouragement as if to assure me he is the same guy I knew all those years before.

"We are filming." Gerry, the whitewater paddler from Scotland, is talking now. "I'm embarking on a journey across the Himalaya on an Indian motorcycle."

His fiancée adds: "I'll go for the latter half and meet up with him. I just can't leave my son for the entire month, he has school. We're doing a Kickstarter campaign now, but I'm excited to produce the film."

David and Gerry talk about motorcycle journeys. David tells about traversing Iceland; Gerry discusses the potential pitfalls of the Indian bike versus other brands.

"Gavin," Gerry asks, "when do you leave? How is the training going?"

Gavin tells us that he is training for the most extreme paragliding race in the world. He is up at four o'clock every morning, hiking up the ski mountain in preparation. "I'm trying to figure out my magnesium intake," he says. "My nutritionist says it's off-balance."

"Jody," David says, "what's next for you?"

"Headed to India next week," Jody says. "I have an assignment there. Then I'll go check on our property in Bali. After that I'm going to Summit at Sea—it's pretty amazing. I went last year. It's the largest gathering of creatives and disruptors, explorers, thinkers, tech guys. All together on one massive boat. There are think-tank sessions, insane food, all these incredible bands and speakers. Amazing networking. Last year they surprised us by secretly helicoptering in Snowden—he gave a riveting talk and we got to hang out with him afterwards."

"That sounds incredible," I say. Incredible and inconceivable. Jody's life seems to be at the opposite spectrum to my own. I was feeling proud of my new job as the local lifestyle magazine editor but now it feels small. I'm a mom of two and an emerging writer with little influence. I feel insignificant and invisible. But my curiosity is insatiable. How do you even become the kind of person who gets invited to these kinds of opportunities?

She glances at me as if I've suddenly materialized and she can read my mind. "It's invitation only. Actually, David," she says, "I could probably get you in. With your experience, you would definitely fit the guest list. It's spectacular and you would meet a lot of people. If you're interested, let me know."

"Yes, definitely," he says, squeezing my hand again under the table as if to let me know that he is not going to jump on a boat with strangers without me.

"Kim," Gavin says. "I read your article last month about the Hunger Coalition. It was great. You have a gift for storytelling."

"Thank you," I say. "That means a lot to me."

"Maybe you could write about something one of us are doing? I'm a terrible writer."

Jody says nothing, nor looks at me. I want her to see me, to agree. But she turns to David and asks him questions about the Explorers Club.

On our way home, David is flushed with excitement. It has been a hard road for him in this town. Everyone knows me, my daughters, and ex-husband, but mostly they ignore his presence entirely with typical resort-town rudeness, reserved for tourists or temporary residents.

"That was amazing," he says. "They were so interesting and accepting. A rarity here. Jody is really cool. I think she would make a good friend for you."

"I don't think she even registered that I was at the table. But the entire group, they're doing so much out in the world. I can only imagine what that would be like."

"You can do those kinds of things. You have the talent and the skills. Don't sell yourself short. Why don't we do an expedition this summer, together," David says. "I know a team diving to the *Britannic* to determine why she sank three times faster than the *Titanic*, even though she was supposed to be 'more unsinkable.' There's a good story to be told there. Why don't we see if you could write it?"

There is a difference between support and encouragement. If you are lucky, you will give and receive both. David is an encourager. He is opening a door and inviting me in. It's up to me to walk through and make the most of it.

Determined to get to know Jody better, I reach out and ask her if she would be up for meeting over a casual dinner. I've just returned from interviewing Oliver Stone for our local film festival feature, and Jody is keen to hear the details. We meet for dinner, the first of what will become our ritual, at the bar of a local restaurant. We stay for three hours, discovering unexpected parallels, our metaphorical mountains and our vision for our best selves. An authentic friendship begins to grow.

Overall, life seems to slowly be righting itself. My daughters are adjusting to the back and forth; laughter dominates our little house. David still lives two thousand miles away but is carefully transitioning his work and home to be with us. Every morning he opens his eyes and asks me to marry him, whether on Skype or in person. Every day I say yes.

It will take four years, but eventually we overcome the barriers, and he makes his way permanently to us out west. We marry and buy a home up the street from the girls' father, where it is easy for them to move back and forth.

When my job as an editor at the magazine runs its course, I turn to freelance writing and editing. David is attending multiple Explorers Club events across the country, and I tag along with him when I can. Within this international exploration community, I meet many scientists, explorers, and photographers that are engaged in groundbreaking field work, but not often sharing their stories with a broader audience. I begin collaborating with some members.

With each story I tell—the female anthropologist traversing across the Siberian tundra in a sledge with a pregnant Nenets woman; the *National Geographic* photographer, documenting in Arctic waters, who encountered a curious sea leopard that tried to feed him penguins; the pain and redemption discovered by a French photographer during his odyssey through Mongolia—my curiosity becomes increasingly unearthed and stimulated. Imagining myself within each situation awakens a new kind of restlessness. Could I ever have the extraordinary qualities needed to accomplish such an expedition?

In a stroke of ideal timing, wildlife photographer Paul Nicklen hires me to write the text for his photography book, *Born to Ice*. Nicklen is well-known for the audacious risks he takes in the most extreme climates to document our rapidly changing planet. I write these paragraphs, in his voice, by tapping into all that he has shared with me and imagining myself within his psyche:

> *Fear and fascination are often two sides of the same mind, and in an internal standoff, one will ultimately prevail. Even as fear fights a robust battle within me, fascination almost always tends to win. I am driven to spend weeks and months in the most extreme places on earth—deep under the icy Antarctic seascape and alone in the vast swirling blizzards of the Arctic. I was born to do this. My mind, body, and soul are more at home here than anywhere else. Through the risks and challenges, my innate comfort on sea ice has become my strength, allowing me to open a window into the rarely seen world of both polar regions.*

My own words, through his experience and honed like polished stone, create a mantra for me. Fear and fascination—which one will win out?

While researching for a story, I find this quotation by Confucius: "We all have two lives, the second one begins when we realize we only have one." It stops me in my tracks.

3

Jody has just returned from one of her many trips to India and we are hiking on a wilderness trail next to our house. "You won't believe this," she says. "A photographer I met over there took me to the border of Nepal to see wild elephants. The government and NGOs have built an electric fence to keep the elephants out of the Nepal side crops. Now they are trapped. It was crazy. Every day around the same time, this herd came out from one clump of trees, where they hang out and eat, and moved to the next patch of trees on the other side of the village, so they could sleep in a protected place. Because they move around the same time every day, all these people have started gathering to see them. The crowds got bigger each day we were there. The strangest thing was these guys started pushing each other out of the way, trying to get closer to the elephants so they could take pictures with their phones. They knew the elephants would come at the same time each day, so more and more people came on their bikes, motorcycles. Mostly men. They were yelling at the elephants, then trying to get selfies with them. Being idiots really, getting so close and trying to get a reaction out of the elephants with noise, or even firecrackers."

As we walk around a bend, towering pine trees sway in the breeze that kicks up through the valley in the late afternoons. In the near distance, granite mountain peaks are topped with the meagre holdouts of last winter's snow. Somewhere in these woods right now, waking to the impending dusk, are black bears, coyotes, mountain lions, elk, moose, fox, and wolves. We often see any combination of them out on the trail, along the river, crossing the highways on the way into town, and eating neighborhood garbage on trash night. Last spring, a bear came down after hibernating, began tipping trashcans, and someone reported it to Fish and Game so the bear could be moved to safety. They killed the bear, calling him a "nuisance." I didn't even know that was allowed. The animals in my backyard, most people only see in a zoo. I try to imagine what it would feel like to see an elephant as we come through the clearing. One of the few animals left on earth whose outrageous size renders them giants from the days of dinosaurs, or movies, or fantasy books from our childhoods.

"It was incredible and terrible," she says. "The elephants—there were like twenty-five of them trying to cross from one tiny patch to another. I worried about the geotagging. I mean, each day people were tagging their location and so more people showed up. It felt like only a matter of time until the village charged money like a tourist attraction. I've never seen anything like it."

Engrossed and at a loss for a proper response beyond "Wow. That's intense," I try to visualize this outrageous scenario. Everything I know about elephants at this point is specific to Africa—I am currently unaware that Asian elephants are a varied species, smaller, with distinctive features, including females not having tusks. In this moment, neither of us know that people are actively living with elephants, caught in a war over the diminishing resources of food and water throughout many parts of India. We have no idea that in India elephants are killing over four hundred people a year, or that the Asian elephant is rapidly becoming extinct—not so much because of poaching, but from shrinking habitat and death resulting from the navigation of human-made barriers such as trains, highways, army barracks, and tea garden troughs. It does not seem there is a similar outcry for protection of these elephants as their African cousins. Where is the Western media coverage about the Asian elephant?

A familiar feeling, long buried under the layers of routine life and strata of comfortable daily existence, begins to agitate out from where it has lain dormant within me. That night, I scour the internet for information about Asian elephants in India. Unlike their African cousins, Asian elephants are endangered, according to the International Union for Conservation of Nature (IUCN) Red List of Threatened Species. More than one hundred thousand elephants existed at the beginning of the twentieth century, but now there are fewer than fifty thousand. Sixty percent of all Asian elephants live in India.

I learn that elephant herds are led by the oldest females, known as matriarchs, who have the deep memory of where to locate water and food as well as protect the herd from danger. When male elephants in the herd reach adolescence, they leave, living on their own or sometimes in small groups of other males. In India, where most wild Asian elephants live, habitat fragmentation is the biggest issue, forcing herds to attempt crossing human-dominated landscapes. It's hard to fathom eating almost six hundred pounds of food and twenty-five to fifty gallons of water up to sixteen hours per day. This is why Asian elephants migrate along ancient routes with a range of edible food—bamboo, grasses, bark, fruit, etc. They are so adaptable; they have learned that human crop fields such as maize and rice can offer seven times the nutrition in a fraction of the time. No wonder they seek it out. It's no wonder they are beloved around the world; elephants create rich biodiversity as they traverse on their old routes. New plants thrive from their dung and seeds disperse throughout their journey. The photographs of wild Asian elephants compel me further. They have these little tufts of head hair, pink mottled dots on their ears and foreheads. Their heads have a unique rounded shape, kind of like a butt, and none of the females have tusks. Seeing Asian elephants online—mothers, aunties, and calves, seem somehow softer, smarter, and less intimidating than the footage I've seen of African elephants. Somehow, I can't quite picture these sweet-looking animals as human killers and house destroyers, but immediately ache for how they must have to fight daily to protect their family.

Fulfillment lies at the intersection of satisfying pursued curiosity and making a positive difference in other's lives. There is an intoxication to being valued, beloved.

I was taught by my father to dream and reach my vision by setting goals. My mother guided with wisdom: "Choose your job carefully. Because almost every day of your life you will wake up and go to work. Make sure you do something you love."

When I first became a mother, I sought to balance my commitment to my daughter, responsibilities at home, and an expanding career. It did not take long before I realized that instead of excelling as I hoped, I had become mediocre both at home and work. One day, while I was struggling to lead a conference call, I heard the nanny in the room below my office exclaim: "Anhwei! You did it! Good girl!" Whatever milestone my daughter had just accomplished, I had missed it. That was it. I had already lost nine months in utero and the first eleven months of my daughter's life; I was unwilling to miss another moment. Gone was my vision of standing on the statehouse steps, leading a protest with a baby on my hip. The truth was, I could not be my best self at either job—mom or activist. I left my career to stay at home full-time with my children. A choice that was only possible from a place of privilege. I knew we would be okay financially. My daughters would not need childcare and I no longer would be creating a system of quality early childhood education for others. This twisted irony became my hidden shame. Not only had I been unwilling to put my children in the system I had spent a decade working to improve but, in staying home with the girls, I removed my impactful leadership from the cause just as headway was being made. But I had made my choice.

By the time my girls started preschool and kindergarten, I turned to a long-ago shelved dream and began a new path, with new goals. After decades of secreted writing, I now decided to get it out in the open. I started taking online classes, crafting poems and stories in the early mornings, a few hours each day. Hungry for more and encouraged by mentors, I applied and was accepted to my top choice of graduate schools, this time for a master of fine arts. If the pen is mightier than the sword, perhaps I could make change from the domestic center of my life.

For years, my careers remained in separate compartments. Both had begun as a calling, a passionate desire compelling me to devote my energy toward ambitious visions for the impact of my work. But the seeming disparity between the two had felt uneasy. Now my collaborations began opening a conduit for a new kind of wholeness. Projects that could combine my loves toward a meaningful outcome were wildly appealing. Jody's experience watching wild Asian elephants struggling for peace and food drew me in.

Questions turn in my mind like a small bit drill, burrowing a new opening for possibility: *Could I go to India and create this story with Jody?* This question means different things at various times: Can I take this time away from my family? Will Jody be willing to partner with me? Can I see myself in India, a place far from the comforts that surrounded me? After a month of cultivating this growing idea, it becomes real. Only, I have not asked Jody if she would partner with me. I desperately want to go to India and tell this story, yet doing it alone seems such an impossibility that I do not even consider it. My only hope is for Jody to agree to do it with me.

July 18, 2017. I send my request through text: *Hi—I've been thinking a lot about the elephant social media story in India. I want to write it with you. What are your thoughts? What would we need to do? Have you travelled with a writer before? Do you think this would be a fit? If yes, what would be our next steps? Be honest—I know you will.*

A week goes by with no response. I am crushed.

Then, one day: *Sorry, I just got back from doing a plane delivery to Alaska. The elephant project . . . ya, let me get my shit together this week and put some thought into it . . . the next steps. I'd love to do a project with you.*

With those words, the earth shifts beneath my feet.

It is all I can think about. September turns into October, trips and new opportunities pile up for each of us. We decide to apply for a grant application to help fund the story. When we meet to write the grant, Jody mentions an article she read once about a mahout (elephant caregiver) who was a former princess.

"She's the only female mahout in the world," Jody says. We look her up and read the little we can find. Parbati Barua, elephant whisperer, caught her first wild elephant with a lasso at the age of fourteen. She lives in Assam. "It would be so cool if we could find her. Maybe we can do a side story about her." Jody says what I am thinking.

"Definitely. How can we find her?"

"I have a friend, the photographer who showed me the elephants, Avijan. I can ask if he knows how to get a meeting with her."

Later that night, scouring the internet for clues to Parbati Barua, I discover Mark Shand, the British travel writer and conservationist, who traveled by elephant across the northern migration route with Parbati while she trained him in the art of mahout. The Discovery Channel made a documentary of the journey in 1993, and Shand authored a companion book, both with the goal to raise awareness and support for Asian elephants in India. I order the book and an old DVD of the documentary. Shand is dashing and free in his lungi washing his elephant. Every bit the explorer/writer as he rides astride a decorated elephant, wild sandy hair, pink scarf wrapped jauntily around his neck, army green T-shirt drenched with sweat. He laughs with both hands on his knees at something Parbati must have said. She sits on her elephant as if it is an extension of her body, or the other way around. Wearing a big camouflage jacket and a pair of jeans—male attire, taboo at the time for women in India. A cowboy hat of sorts is perched on her head and she holds a stick with two hands behind her shoulder blades. Smiling, but like the Mona Lisa, controlled, her posture erect and proud. In the book, Shand writes about Parbati with a sense of intimidation and slight mocking. She comes off as stern and impersonal, vague, and one-dimensional. There must be more to her than this? Now I imagine meeting and spending time with Parbati Barua; becoming a female Mark Shand, doing justice to her story by telling it from deep inside her perspective, bringing her history, personality, breadth of elephant wisdom, and current relevance to proper light.

It will be another six months before we know if we get the grant.

I text Jody: *I think we should try and go sooner, so we don't miss the story.*

Ya, is her response.

That is it for now. No discussion. As more time passes, my worries mount. What if Jody goes to India without me, or pitches to *National Geographic* and they send a more connected and famous writer? As my insecurities escalate, they render me tentative. So much time is passing with no set plans. While I wait for the initiative of others, too timid to take the next step, I do the things I am good at: researching and fretting.

4

We live our lives mostly concerned with what is right in front of us. There are so many orbits of simultaneous happenings across time, place, and cultures that our attention span can only seize on the soundbite, the small square of profound and exotic image. It is up to us to choose to learn more.

Asian elephants and Indian people have been living and working together, side by side and against one another, for thousands of years. I knew nothing of it. Now, snippets of it burst to life, through the depths of YouTube and into my office, halfway across the planet:

> *Mourners gather around a dead elephant in a ditch. Sprigs of jasmine and blooms of oleander and lotus have been gently placed in his/her eyes and along his/her feet, petals are scattered between sticks of lit incense placed in the cracked earth, thin trails of sacred smoke rise into the sky. A man in uniform, his face a smear of grief, tries to control the crowd. Human-made obstacles have killed this elephant, yet the mourners are crying and worshiping Ganesha. Ganesh, the elephant-headed son of Parviti and Shiva. As the Remover of Obstacles, he is among the most beloved of Hindu deities.*

An elephant calf, his tail on fire from a thrown firecracker, chases his mother across a crowded highway.

"Go, go!" says the boy who is filming with his phone, encouraging in Bengali as his friend approaches a wild elephant in a meadow. The boy walks two bare feet up the trunk before the elephant flings the boy across the field. He lands like a rumpled pile of bones. Weak moans can be heard in the background as the companion continues to film, and then the phone shakes to a drop.

At first, I need to dig for information—until I find *Asian Elephant Digest*. This miraculous gem of a newsletter compiles every relevant news story about Asian elephants. Twice a day, in my inbox, I can read a selection of carefully curated elephant news courtesy of *Save the Elephants News Service*. The headlines paint a landscape of the breadth and scope of regular events:

GOVERNMENT TO PROBE LATEST POISONED ELEPHANT DEATH IN LAHAD DATU

BS YEDIYURAPPA GOVERNMENT SEEKS TO CUT ELEPHANT CORRIDOR SHORT BY 100 SQUARE KM

WOMEN SITTING ON BIKE TRAMPLED TO DEATH BY WILD ELEPHANTS IN JHARKHAND'S LATEHAR

TWO JUMBOS DIE ON TOP OF EACH OTHER (SRI LANKA)

GUDALUR: MOTHER ELEPHANT GUARDING CALF'S CARCASS

SELLING OF ANIMAL PARTS ON FACEBOOK; TWO ARRESTED IN SEEDUWA

KARIMGANJ VILLAGERS LIVE IN ELEPHANT FEAR

An entire ecosystem cracks open. Yet the articles mostly contain a scant paragraph or two with reportorial facts that tell little more than the tantalizing headline. My contextual knowledge is missing—massive gaps of geography, culture, history, and science. As compelling as the news features are, they feel as cryptic as a physics equation, and my curiosity is kicked into overdrive.

These truncated news stories are perversely encouraging. Each time the news shows up in my inbox, I anxiously scan the India-specific articles, searching for our story topics, feeling a guilty relief when the source is seemingly obscure, and information limited. While animal lovers are pouring support and resources into protecting the African elephants in the war over ivory, wild elephants in India appear as just a tiny blip on the popular cause scene. Asian elephants are moving swiftly toward extinction at an exponentially higher rate than their African cousins, and for a multifaceted panoply of altogether different issues.

"It's too much to try and take on the entire human-elephant conflict in India," Jody has said. "There are way too many moving parts."

For this reason, we convince ourselves to stay focused on "Dying for Likes," a well-packaged, universal bridge kind of a story. Almost everyone identifies with the ridiculous measures people go to for a "like" on social media. A timely focus, as current news in the US media is suddenly filled with a random rash of people falling to their deaths, thousands of feet into the Grand Canyon, as they tried to get the ideal, one-of-a-kind, selfie.

Our strategy is to travel to Northeast India to get the untold story of wild elephants and selfie deaths and take a side trip to Assam to profile Parbati Barua.

Jody is home for a week at the end of February before launching out again, and we meet for dinner. I have mustered all my courage, even practiced what to say. The goal is to sound casual, cool, and unconcerned, but leave with concrete next steps. I am budgeting three weeks for India, more time than I have ever been away from my daughters. It may be a leap of faith, but I am committed. For Jody, single and childfree, with no regular job that requires showing up to a fixed physical location, three weeks is nothing. She is often gone for months at a time, and she decides when and where in the moment.

We catch each other up: travel, inspiring podcasts, and new work, avoiding the topic of exes. Halfway through my red blend and burrata, I make my move: "Um. What time frame do you think might work for us to go India? For the elephant project. Just to make sure we can sync our schedules."

She looks up from her salad. Calculating.

"Well, I was thinking of doing the Rickshaw Run this year. It's a tuk tuk race across India. I think it's the beginning of April for two weeks. Starts in Kerala and ends in Rajasthan. I've been wanting to do this thing forever." She says, "If I go, we could meet up after the race."

"A tuk tuk race?" This is a woman who, for all her adventures, is typically the one that falls out of moving vehicles and breaks bones; who gets dysentery and passes out on a city street; who disappears for days because she has a parasite causing her to vomit and have diarrhea in her shower, never thinking to call for help. A fourteen-day rickshaw run across India? I am certain that by the end Jody will be exhausted, sick, injured, or possibly dead, and I will be in India, alone.

"Yeah, it's epic. You do it with three people. The organizers teach you how to drive, then you go—no route, goal is just to get to the finish by the last day. If I go, I should be done by the fifteenth and take a rest day on the sixteenth. Maybe we could meet on the seventeenth somewhere?"

I lock in on "somewhere." My geography is pathetic. I know literally nothing about where we will go. Except for to Assam to find Parbati. There is a national park in Assam. If all else fails, I can always visit the park.

"Only problem," she continues, "is that my teammates both just canceled, so I need to find two people to do it with me. Want to do a rickshaw run across India?"

March 16, 2018. I do the calculations. If I am going to meet Jody on April 17, it will be necessary for me to get over jet lag. I cannot arrive thrashed. It takes thirty hours of travel and a lost day. I should stay in Delhi for a few days and acclimate. Even the thought of this makes my hair stand on end and stomach flip. Jody has put the call out for volunteers to do the Rickshaw Run on her Instagram feed. I watch the comments and see no takers. The race is now less than two weeks away. Still, there is no update. Should I book a ticket? Cool and casual isn't working. I text a long and desperate missive:

> *Hi there—any word back from your elephant friend? And are you able to make an intro moving forward—and also can we make a tentative plan for a meet up—a goal for what we want to get and a plan b—scout for social media story/create a related story somehow if the mahout falls out? I know it's not your style to plan and this is a bit unconventional—But, it's a great story and will be worth the prep going in. If you are losing momentum for it—let me know and we can cancel. Just don't go without me because I've already invested hours and hours of my time!*

Two hours pass. I must have said too much. Then comes her response:

> *Not yet but I should hear from him soon. Sure. I can meet next week if you're around. I can never promise that any of it won't fall through even if Avijan tells us we can meet her but there is a lot of stuff I do think we can cover on our proposal in that area. If we have to go to Plan B it will still be worth it. No, I don't want to cancel and won't go without you.*

It is enough for me to book a ticket to Delhi and back at least. In less than three weeks, I will be flying to India and I have no idea what I will even need. Is this an expedition? Will I be sleeping in the jungle with Parbati and her elephants?

From here, I kick into high gear. Jody hears back from Avijan and forwards his text:

Hey Jody. When will you plan to come here? I need your exact date. First of all Parbati Baruah is very rare in Bengal. So in that case you have to catch her in Assam. And for this you need an appointment. I will help you out regarding this matter. There is a small NGO known as HNAF (Himalayan Nature and Adventure Foundation) in Siliguri. They have continuous contact with Parbati Baruah. Mr. Animesh Bose is a resource person part of HNAF and a good naturalist. If you kindly visit HNAF first it would be very effective for your workflow.

Jody adds: *Keep in mind. Just because Avijan says he can try and set up a meeting, that doesn't really mean anything. It's India. We won't know until we are there.*

Anxiety mounts as the date for Jody's departure nears. She will be off the grid for an entire two weeks before I even arrive. How will I get ready? I send panicked texts.

Should I book a one-way to Siliguri or a round trip. How easy is it to book in country if I'm just booking one-way? Does the visa need all the air travel even if I'm not sure yet? Do you have a favorite and easy/nice hotel/Airbnb you like to stay in Delhi? I'm flying back to SUN on May 6th, do you think that is enough time?

In the silence that follows, the slightest beginning of understanding begins to form: I am on my own. If I want to do this, Jody is not going to be my tour guide or hold my hand. A partner is not a crutch.

While I am sitting in my office chair compiling stories and watching movies, reading books, and building my sense of the story, I am completely ignorant about how to move myself from the cerebral to the physical, the nuts and bolts of preparing for this journey. How to pack a proper bag, compile all that I might need, what to wear so I blend in (seriously?), how to get money, how to travel in country, where am I even going on the map.

Thinking about the girls, and how much I hate to lose any time with them, particularly now that our weeks are cut in half. What if something happens to them while I am so far away? I double check all the necessary emergency paperwork, triple check any school or health appointment dates. I confirm that the girls have backup contacts—David and my family to reach out to for any reason. They seem nonplussed about my impending departure, but my anxiety mounts even as I keep making the logistics a reality.

This is my moment. The beginning of the transition, when writing in other people's voices and imagining their stories is replaced with my own experience. The act of pursuing a story that has the power to make a difference in the world starts now. I need to prove that I am a worthy partner. I must somehow get competent. If I expect to earn the trust of a famous elephant whisperer who lived in the jungle with her herd of elephants, a woman with tigers as pets, who can climb an elephant's trunk without them flinging her off, I need to toughen up. I cannot show up and fail.

5

When I look at photos online, Siliguri seems random and decidedly not a popular Western tourist destination. I cannot fathom what to do if my meet up with Jody falls through. I do not know a soul in India. The internet is rife with warnings to solo women travelers: do not go out at night or drink alcohol in public. This could get you raped, mugged, or at least "Eve teased." Do I have what it takes to slap someone's hand away and yell in a crowded bus? Will I be in a crowded bus? What about a train? My parents warn me not to take a train as they have seen a special about trains in Mumbai and you can die trying to squeeze yourself onto one.

There is a young woman living in Goa, Rachel Jones, who writes a blog called *Hippie in Heels*. With archived posts covering every region in India, she gives detailed information on what to wear, what to pack, what you need, culture and safety tips. Essentially, how to be comfortable, stylish, and appropriate while traveling throughout India. Obsessed with her page, I collect flowing skirts and pants, loose blouses, imagining myself a beautiful bohemian. But, what of the jungle? With Parbati's elephants? I should be prepared just in case. Will a sleeping bag be necessary? What about those khaki polyester moisture-wicking shirts and shorts that male explorers wear in the movies while "in the field." Is this what I am doing? Going into the field?

"Siliguri is a shithole," says Thia, a friend and local photographer who frequently travels by herself throughout India. "I'd avoid that place if you can."

We are in Thia's apartment, and she is gifting me advice, valuable items, and stories. Filling my open arms with her favorite India-appropriate shirts, packing squares, and a special adapter/charger that fits computers, cameras, and phones. Thia and Jody were once roommates.

"She's meeting you *after* she drives across the entire country in a tuk tuk? Why don't I hook you up with my homestay lady in Gangtok? If you get stuck, go there and chill. It's gorgeous. She'll take care of you and you can write."

Thia connects us on Facebook, then shows me which apps to use for in-country travel. "Big bills are useless, no one has change, and ATMs rarely work."

She asks my shoe size and starts fumbling under her bed. "I wish I was going with you. It's magic over there. Be prepared to ride in a taxi with a chicken on your lap. Anything can happen."

As I am walking out the door, Thia resumes rummaging.

"Wait," she says, "don't forget these." She adds a thick *Lonely Planet Guide to Northern India* and her well-worn hiking boots. "Size nine, right? I wore them all through Sikkim during monsoon."

My bag may be heavy with supplies, but I depart with a new lightness, a profound sense of relief gifted by this supportive and generous friend.

Our guest bedroom is a staging area—stacks and piles dot the bed. A silk sheet insert for sketchy sleeping arrangements, water purifier straw, mosquito repellent bracelets, bug spray, sunscreen, enough shampoo and conditioner for three weeks, a Swiss Army knife, my silver Ganesh pendant (graduation present from a poet friend), and the medicine bag that takes up a quarter of my space, stuffed with Imodium, Tums, probiotics, activated charcoal, ibuprofen, Tylenol, and Bonine. The luggage options are strewn across the floor. Overnight backpack, day pack, and medium-weight waterproof duffel bag. The receipts from the pharmacy and clothing stores rival my plane ticket. New camera. A small camera, not my husband's Canon because I am the writer, not the photographer. I don't want to show up and look like I don't know my place.

"Do you think I'll need these running shoes or something sturdier?" I ask David, who has not been to India but has studied international law in Kenya and been on countless expeditions.

"Go with Thia's hiking boots. She gave them to you for a reason. You definitely don't want to step on a snake wearing something flimsy."

His advice is prudent, but I ignore it. None of the clothes I am packing will match with grungy hiking boots.

My daughters seem supportive but busy with the kaleidoscope of their teenage lives. They are not thinking about helping elephants, only that I won't be home for twenty days. Goldie, empathic with a high emotional intelligence, sees my stress level and promises to text encouraging quotes. Anhwei, already a budding outdoorswoman, offers advice to curb impractical packing choices. Raised to know few limits—gendered or physical—their daily lives are far more adventurous than mine has ever been.

From the time they were old enough to walk and hold a paddle, both girls were on skis and in kayaks. They are now downhill ski racers and class 4 whitewater paddlers. Both confident with their skills, they forge ahead without their mother's fearful baggage clinging to their subconscious. I learned long ago not to let my fear of speed, feeling out of control, and danger block their path to accomplishment.

Once, when Anhwei was ten years old, I was asked to write a story about paragliding from the top of the ski mountain (9,154 feet) to the town below. To my family's surprise, I said yes. Fly Sun Valley drove me up the switchback dirt road to the summit while, in the backseat, exhaust and nerves combined to make me feel queasy. The plan was to launch off Bald Mountain, in tandem with an experienced guide. Excited and proud, the girls would be meeting me in the field as I landed. As we were floating and circling, I began to feel queasy.

"Would you like to go up higher, do some tricks?" My pilot was eager to star in the story.

"No thank you," I said. "This is plenty." Air currents are apparently just like ocean waves and we were rolling up and over them.

"You're quiet," he said. "Are you scared?"

I was a barely tethered speck floating over an uninterrupted mountain range, but my only fear was the possibility of throwing up. "I feel a bit sick."

"Oh," he said. "Well, if you're going to vomit, let me know and I'll tip us over so you can do it over the side."

The thought of abruptly tipping to one side was enough to kick me into survival mode. That we landed and I had not vomited was quite an accomplishment. As my feet dragged across the ground, body attempting to stand upright, Anhwei sprinted over and threw her arms around me.

"How was it, Mommy?!" She was beaming.

"Hi, honey." I staggered a bit. "Whew! Wow. I am so sick." I steadied myself by putting my hands on my knees and head down. Her face transformed from expectant joy to a disappointed frown as she took several steps backward. My ill-timed response cost me the opportunity to recast her perception of me. Instead, confirming all Anhwei had been taught about me, and secretly hoped was wrong. I was timid and weak. Not the type of heroine she needed in a mother.

I've worked hard since to show a more adventurous side, pushing myself to face some discomfort to show that I can be fun too. Now on family trips, I play in the waves with the girls, bodyboarding, taking them parasailing over the ocean, even great white shark diving. Maybe these early memories will fade and be replaced by this more ideal role model: a caring and fearless, adventurous mom.

I am alone in the house on the morning of my journey. Goodbyes have been exchanged and the girls are off to school. David, in Philadelphia where he still has an office and a home, is on Skype with me as I make the final packing edits.

A text from the airline pops up on my phone. Due to unusually high winds, the flight out of our mountain town has been rerouted to the closest airport, two hours away. I have less than an hour to catch the bus that will take us there. I call David back, breathless. This isn't the calm, loving goodbye I had planned. My bag is too full, and I must take things out. I don't know yet which items can be scrapped. Some clothes and, reluctantly, the foldable electric kettle get tossed aside. Stuffing and stepping, the zipper falters. My carry-on pack is heavy and disorganized.

"I love you," I say, as if I am headed to war. As if I won't be able to talk to him throughout these next three weeks.

Hair wet from a hurried shower, I gather my bags and toss them into the car. Each movement feels like the last time. When I return, all will be changed. I will not be the person I am right now. A ridiculous thought. Nothing is stagnate. Every single particle on earth, and beyond, is in flux. We are not the same on a cellular level from one moment to the next.

The wind gusts across an open highway. In the rearview mirror, the mountain range shrinks. Tumbleweeds rip across the prairie. Our driver is reed-thin with sinewy limbs, her hands gripping the wheel in a desperate battle. My front-row seat is a poor choice. There are no seatbelts, and the windshield wraps around like a glass capsule for an optimal view. Several times, we veer recklessly into the oncoming lane, narrowly missing head-on collisions with transport trucks. Everyone has a tale of how dangerous the buses are in India, careening off cliffs as they over accelerate on a turn, trying to avoid cows, bikes, people, and traffic. I cannot determine if this experience is an omen or a metaphor; a joke from the gods or nothing at all. I do not yet realize that this ride is a lesson, maybe my first, that India will teach me in various forms over and over. A shattering of the illusion that we are ever in control.

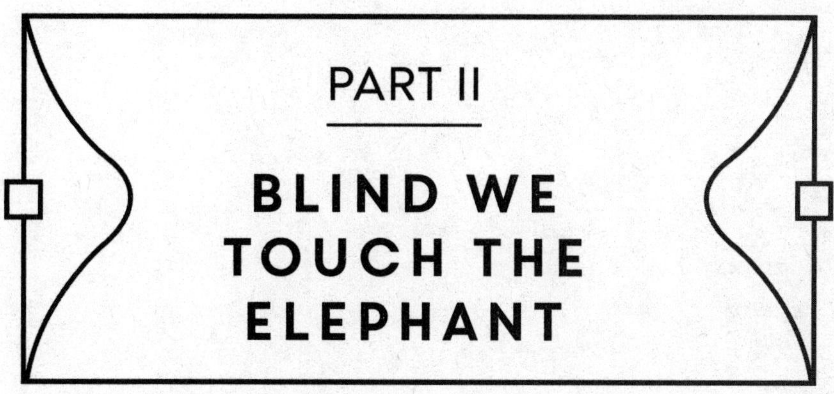

PART II

BLIND WE TOUCH THE ELEPHANT

Look up at the stars and not down at your feet. Try to make sense of what you see and wonder about what makes the universe exist. Be curious.

—Stephen Hawking

6

My plan to spend three days getting my bearings in Delhi, ahead of my meet up with Jody, has been a success. First, I made a soft landing at Haveli Haus Khas, a family-run hotel and the owner's ancestral home. Here, I battled jet lag in a quiet room with marble floors, embraced by comforting green walls and a large window facing out to a verdant park below. I lounged for hours, appreciating the art and culture books written by the proprietor, sipping masala tea and eating my first aloo paratha with homemade hot pickled mango in a courtyard thick with pots of flowers and jasmine vines. I eventually began navigating outside the courtyard walls—baby steps. Now I am back at the airport. The frenzied five-lane highway has been crossed, and an ice cream cone eaten alone in the parlor on the other side. New eyeglasses have been bargained for (albeit poorly) and purchased in the market, cross-city navigation on foot (with Google Maps discretely speaking through my earbuds) was mostly positive, with only a few hours of harrowing disorientation in a neighborhood labyrinth. And, so far, my stomach is behaving with a wide range of food, even the chicken and uncooked vegetables I had been warned about.

At the Delhi airport, Terminal 3 is familiar and reassuring with its modern elegance, high glass walls, orderly lines of people, and space to move freely. I have found my airline, checked my bags without issue, and am heading to the coffee stand to get an espresso when I see Jody approach the check-in line. She looks every bit the part of *National Geographic* photographer who's been in the field so long it is no longer the field but its own kind of home: colorless quick-dry pants, gray tank top, flip-flops, and a discreet scarf. She is surrounded by a black Patagonia duffle on wheels, large weatherproof messenger bag, camera backpack, and a large rolling black Pelican case containing lenses and cameras. My newly gained confidence wavers.

"Hi!" I say. "How was it? How do you feel?"

We hug. I am simultaneously relieved and terrified to see her.

"Incredible! Intense. I'm wiped out." She pushes her bags along the line. "How are you? You look good. How is it going?"

"Great." It's all I am willing to say. "I'm going to grab an espresso. Do you want anything?"

"Yeah," she says. "I'd love a masala chai. Thanks. I'm going to have a problem with my bag weight. I know they'll charge me for the carry-on. Maybe you can take one through for me."

"Sure, I'll be right back."

The exchange is easy, I feel grateful to be able to offer specific nourishment and help.

We sail through security.

"We should get cash," Jody says on the other side. We try three machines, finally finding one that works.

"It's not giving me more than fifty dollars," I say. I have tried a few times, our flight boards soon, and you never know what we will have access to where we are headed.

"We can try again in Siliguri," says Jody. "There are machines there."

We land and exit into a cacophony of humanity. The baggage area is smaller than the crowd who have descended on the luggage belt, blocking access, standing in tight groups. Most of the travelers are Indian families in multicolored saris, kurtas and leggings, fancy shoes, and many compact pieces of luggage, dangling extravagant purses from their arms. A small group of Western tourists are following their guide toward the exit. They are stocky and dressed for hiking. Two of the women have poles. There is an air of superiority that seems to cling to them; they are shouting questions and orders all at once in aggressive tones.

The airport is in Bagdogra, gateway to the Himalaya. Many backpackers come here and go straight to other destinations: Darjeeling is less than a three-hour drive. Darjeeling sounds romantic and historic—I wish we were going there instead. Exhaustion suddenly overwhelms me. I just want to go home, get into bed, and forget this entire thing.

"We need to get a prepaid cab," Jody says. We walk over to a small mob clustered around an office, where a small hole in Plexiglas is used to communicate, people pushing for their turn. On the other side of the office, outside the airport, is another Plexiglas hole—this one is full of taxi drivers clamoring and shouting. The shouting makes me think that the men are about to get into a physical fight, but instead, their fighting seems to crest and recede. Jody slides into the front of the throng of customers while I wait with the bags.

"Let's go!" says Jody, returning with the voucher. "Always get a prepaid taxi so you don't get taken advantage of."

A blast of hot sticky air, putrid with exhaust and body odor, assaults us as the doors open. I hadn't realized we were in air conditioning until standing outside.

The drive from the airport to Siliguri is everything I imagined India to be. With over a half million people, this area has developed over the last century from vast, thick forest to a British military post, then to a transport town with a railway to Darjeeling and Kolkata, and now a transportation hub linking the northeastern states to the rest of India. Known as the "chicken neck" for its sliver of land mass—less than thirteen miles in width, North Bengal and the Siliguri area are internationally bordered by Nepal, Bangladesh, Bhutan, and the special status state, Sikkim. Defined by the Mechi and Teesta Rivers, North Bengal has as its backdrop the Himalayan Mountain range. The base of this range, along the upper part of North Bengal and Assam (Parbati's ancestral home), is known as the Dooars (meaning "doors") for the eighteen identified passageways that lead from Bhutan to India and back.

These are facts I learn much later. For now, the Himalaya is covered completely in clouds and smog and I do not realize how close we are. I am engulfed by the riot of color, sound, smells, and movement.

We thread our way through highways, at one with the organized chaos. Slipping between spectacularly decorated busses and trucks, moving street art, motorcycles, and scooters in a constant zigzag, bright yellow electric tuk tuks, even some faded and worn cycling rickshaws, all speeding through or stopping at various hotels, stores, shopping areas. At the sides of the road, a blur of chai stands and outdoor markets, tables set out displaying various wares: helmets, knives, cookery, fruit. Electronics stores advertising phone cards and cell phones, billboards advertising new housing developments, high-end clothing stores, a sneaker company with a fit model working out on one half and relaxing on a couch on the other, with the tag line JUST DO IT. OR DON'T. Under the overpasses are scattered pockets of homes built from corrugated metal, bright-colored clothing strung across their windows and doorways. Women walk along slim dirt pathways with bags, carrying babies, young children scrambling to keep up or lagging as they pass old men sitting on overturned buckets reading newspapers.

Traffic chokes the entrance to the main part of the city of Siliguri, where we are stopped.

"Oh, the circus!" Jody says. Three paper flyers are stuck to an underpass cement cylinder. All are fluorescent green, yellow, and orange. One, a drawing of a woman in a majorette outfit twirling multiple hoops around her hands, legs, and neck, has letters written in Hindu. The middle poster has block letters that say in English, NOW SHOWING: KOHINOOR RUSSIAN CIRCUS DAILY 1-4-7 P.M. Flanking this is a drawing of a clown with green and black tufts of hair coming out from his otherwise bald head. The artist has rendered the eyes to shift so they are seeing you, almost winking with a menacing grin, as he holds a bundle of balloons in one hand and wraps his other around an unfortunate child clown who sits on his knee, arms reaching for the balloons. The Hindu writing below the image has the effect of dripping candle wax, increasing the macabre feel of it all.

"I need to find out where that is, I have always wanted to see a circus in India. They barely have them anymore. I am definitely going while we are here. Have you seen Mary Ellen Mark's Indian Circus? It is brilliant. I want to do a series like that. You probably can't even do it anymore; people would be upset. But still. I'm going."

"I'll go," I say, not wanting to be left out of anything. "That sounds fascinating."

But when I see that clown, all I can think of is how I will be stuck in an overwhelming crowd in some dirt lot far from anywhere while Jody is caught up in photographing side show artists in a back tent somewhere, lost for hours. Still, from the looks of outside, I don't want to be left here either.

I take another photo with my iPhone, and then video the traffic as it whirs by. There are no seatbelts—they don't work, only the strap is there, no place to plug it in. I've tried. Jody has not. I hang out the window to get better shots: Hindu deities lined up with incense on the stoops of what look like abandoned buildings, uniformed schoolgirls with arms linked, dodging lounging dogs along thin walkways, families stuffed into tuk tuks with sinewy drivers cycling at a steady pace, so close I could reach out the window and touch a shirt-sleeve; motorcycles driven by men with unstrapped bucket helmets and behind them, sitting sidesaddle, girlfriends with hair pulled back in braids, no helmet, in flowing saris, delicate feet dangling perilously near the exhaust pipes.

Sweat is dripping from every crevice of my body, creating armpit stains I have not seen since my hot summer trail-running years, my scarf still draped around my neck as I have been instructed to do at all costs. Next to me, Jody, in her gray tank top and technical pants, has leaned her head up against the open window frame, eyes closed, phone in pocket. At first, I marvel that she is missing this unfurled display of raw life—cows lying undisturbed in the middle of the roads, open trucks with men spilling out from the backsides, no one yelling, everyone beeping, not in anger but as a courtesy. Through the window intermittent blasts of hot air—an amalgam of smog, body odor, urine, chai, spices, cow dung, exhaust fumes, and an almost indiscernible aroma of tropical flowers and soil, even as you cannot see this.

Of course she isn't taking photos. To her, there is nothing unusual out her window. The past two weeks this woman has been driving an open tuk tuk across the entire continent. Nothing I am seeing with wild eyes is new for her. Would I take photos of the aspen and evergreen trees that line the highways of my hometown? I slink back into the seat and pretend that this is my normal too.

It is not possible to imagine that elephants, tigers, leopards, and even the extinct—in India—Asiatic cheetah once roamed where now there are only teeming streets. That one of the lushest sections of jungle, the age-old elephant corridor where herds grazed for great distances along the valleys of the Himalayan landscape known as the Terai, only barely exists in these fragmented remains, cement highways and buildings covering the once boggy soil. As we squeeze through narrow alleys thick with humanity and domesticated animals, I cannot imagine that we are mere miles from the nighttime path through which great herds of elephants still struggle to survive—crossing crowded roadways, sleeping in the scant patches of forest cover, moving from crops to crops, escorting each other gingerly (and often unsuccessfully) over active railroad tracks.

I am not thinking about any of this. While I expect to see wild elephants during our time here, it is Parbati Barua, the legendary "elephant whisperer," that presently occupies my mind. Mark Shand, in his opening of *The Elephant Queen*, tells how he traveled on his elephant across India always trying to meet her, but still she eluded him. She is famously difficult to find. A nervous Shand studying the art of elephant care (mahout) under Ms. Barua, at first light, is heading out on elephant-back to collect grass stalks for fodder, and she plies Parbati with a stream of questions. In the scene I craft, we walk together in silence as I observe everything. I will not make fun of her harsh assertiveness. Now that I have made it to India, it seems more possible that we will find her and she will agree to spend time with us in Assam, if not for a journey on elephant, at least to observe her in action with the animals she refers to as her children. The mystery of Parbati Barua is so compelling, even as she is supposed to be the side story, her history and guru wisdom have me gripped. Twenty full days stretch out in front of me, full of promise and opportunity.

This morning before I left for the airport, I woke to a text from Goldie. It was a photograph of me, David, and both girls, Goldie's arms outstretched front and center taking the selfie, a hint of mountain peak and an Alaskan lake behind us. She created a Polaroid-type border and a letter overlay that said YOU CAN VANQUISH YOUR FEARS BECAUSE YOUR FAMILY IS HERE FOR YOU. At the bottom, golden hearts surround a string of xoxoxo.

Now the warm-up is behind me, today begins the real journey.

In a few hours we will meet with Avijan, the wildlife photographer who first took Jody to the Nepal border to witness the wild elephant pooling. I don't know much more about him than this fact, his emails about a Parbati meet up, and his Instagram feed. Here, his images communicate a visual story about human-elephant interaction. The photographs are an astonishment: a tusker with one foot raised as he walks past a house at dawn; a herd crossing through a dry riverbank, dusky, undulating layers of gray-blue foothills in the background; a matriarch elephant's direct gaze as she guards the footpath while her herd crosses the tea garden behind. One of his images has gained international attention: *Night-time Highway*. At the forefront, in complete silhouette, is a mother elephant ushering her two calves across the road. Dark human forms outlined in the spaces between calf and mother are illuminated by headlights, creating gold and smoky sharp-shadowed contrasts. Avijan's photos are so different than the images I have seen of African elephants. His are the first intimate clue I have to the way people are struggling to coexist in a landscape that is now less lush and mountainous, more cultivated and popular. How will he lead us to Parbati? This is a mystery to me. Like a scavenger hunt, our next clue will come from him.

The Saluja Residency is on one of the busiest sections of Hill Cart Road, a market thoroughfare that was built in the early 1800s by the British to transport goods between here and Darjeeling. Barely able to make the slight turn into the alley that serves as the entrance, our hotel is sandwiched between slim cement shops and an abandoned apartment building. A guard stands at a thick iron gate, currently open. We step out of the taxi and into a spare waiting area with a simple reception desk that reminds me of motels in the 1960s. An officious clerk greets us, "Passports? Local phone numbers?" She seems to be in her twenties and does not look up to greet us. After checking in, our passports now behind the desk for an undisclosed amount of time, two young men compete to help us with our bags. The halls are narrow and seem to be white marble from floor to walls to stairs, but not the fancy kind of marble you imagine in temples and the Taj Mahal. We squeeze into the elevator, an old-fashioned one that does not have a solid door, only a metal gate to close and open manually. Stepping out and over the gap, we enter an open-walled hallway that looks across to an apparently abandoned apartment building with padlocked doors and dark cement stairwells. We walk past an open doorway. Inside a woman on her hands and knees wrings a dirt black rag into a bucket of water and thrusts it back into the bucket before swirling it around the floor.

"Why did you get two rooms?" Jody asked as we were checking in.

"Because they were so inexpensive, and I figured we could have some privacy. I've been getting up at 4:00 A.M. every day, writing and practicing yoga. I didn't want to wake you."

"Well, it's fine for tonight, but we should share from here out. India may seem cheap, but it adds up."

Now we agree to drop our stuff quickly and go down to the restaurant and eat. Behind the bed in my room is a square of light covered by a royal blue silk curtain. I pull it aside, exposing a barred window facing a cement wall. At least there is air conditioning. The bathroom, however, is not air-conditioned. Humidity mingles with a rising sewage smell from the shower drain. An enclosed fan whirrs thick black dust, an attempt at ventilation. Jody knocks on the door. We head downstairs to eat. The fact that this hotel has an on-site restaurant is why Jody chose it; the other eateries I have seen are open-air, belowground snack spots with running hot water unlikely. The space is dimly lit and decorated in a hybrid colonial style meets Indian sports bar. It is about 2:00 P.M. and other than two businessmen in the back corner, we are the only customers.

For the first time since I have been to India, I open a full menu of many of my favorites. Palak paneer and garlic naan, tandoori chicken. When the food arrives, it is spicy and perfect. I don't want it to end, there is so much desire to sit here and eat for the rest of the day and night, go nowhere, and talk to no one.

"What do you think we should do?" I say, kicking off our first strategy discussion since before the tuk tuk race.

"I don't know. I think we start by talking to Avijan and meeting the people at the nonprofit he thinks we should meet. In India, no one really plans anything—it just kind of happens when you are on the ground. You have to be flexible."

Avijan arrives as we are finishing our meal. Stocky and compact, perspiration dripping along his receding hairline. He wears stylish rectangle glasses, jeans, and a blue oxford shirt, sleeves rolled up and wet with sweat, and carries a backpack.

"Jody!" They greet one another, she with characteristic calm and cool, he with brimming excitement. He is full of enthusiasm for his work and for seeing Jody again. He has been rushing about and is late (a trait I will learn is part of his personality).

Jody works with *National Geographic*, and as a brand, it is the gold standard and a common language almost anywhere in the world. He is eager for her approval. We make introductions. Avijan has brought a colleague who is a snake handler. Another friend, a university professor, shows up—he is a map expert. He offers to us a map of the region so we can see the forest zones and elephant corridors. They all launch into a fevered conversation about the wildlife situation in this area. Avijan explains the nature of the elephant conflict in impassioned detail, but I can barely understand a word of it.

He pauses and asks us, "What is your plan?"

"We want to see the wild elephants at the border and document the conflict with the local community there. Also, we are hoping to meet Parbati so we can do a story about her," Jody says.

"I see. Well, the elephants have not arrived yet. It is not their time, I have been looking. So far only some lone bulls. Parbati Barua? Yes. She is very difficult to visit. Even I have never met her. But if you do this thing—go to the NGO and meet Animesh. He has been close to her for many years. First you need to learn about their work. He is the one you need to meet with."

I hear the part about the wild elephants but assume that Avijan means in a week or two. This is okay, we can pursue Parbati in the meantime.

"Sure," Jody says. "We definitely want to meet Animesh and see the work of the NGO."

"They are expecting us today. We are close, only a few blocks away." Avijan grabs his phone and makes a call. "They are ready for us."

We gather our things and set out. The sidewalk is crammed, requiring a brisk walk and tight squeezes. Storefronts spill out their wares, curbside food carts and chai stands crowd every other block, alongside dogs with flies swarming over their emaciated bodies, cows wandering into the road, beeping traffic. We cross the alleys and I almost get hit. Motorbikes, scooters, and bicycles stream from all directions. There is no organized process, even with traffic lights. You just need to become one with the flow and always look, don't hesitate. As Jody and Avijan talk nonstop, the map expert and I walk together, attempting conversation. It is problematic. I am not yet used to the accents and the cacophony that surrounds us makes my hearing even more muddled. I am so awkward, like the new kid at school, envying the ease of the others as they saunter along the sidewalks, comfortable in their clothing, their skin, their voices, their surroundings. I feel my age, my fear, and my insignificance. The exertion of trying to belong is overwhelming.

Himalaya Nature Adventure Foundation (HNAF) is down an alley lined with parked motorbikes; a store on the corner marks the spot with stacked tires. The entire organization is behind a single garage door, which is flung open. They are waiting for us in a semicircle of folding chairs surrounding Animesh, the director and founder who sits behind a light wooden desk, facing the room. A lanky man with a thick white beard, he wears a khaki safari vest over a white linen shirt, blue jeans, and sport sandals. He exudes style and calm, an air of wisdom, authentically casual. Posters of the Himalayan Mountain range, children at adventure camp, and slogans about not using plastic bags line the walls. Camping equipment spills out of the rafters and piles up in corners.

"Hello, Avijan." Animesh stands up and greets our group. On his right, in dress pants and a button-up business shirt, with a posture and air about him that communicates his authority, is the district forest officer, Mr. G. "Mr. G is in the area today. He wanted to meet you and hear about your situation." Introductions are made all around. "Sit, sit." Animesh waves his hand over to a few empty chairs and we each sit down. One of the women begins making tea. She smiles at us and sets to work at a banquet table along the wall with an electric kettle, various cups, and canisters of tea.

Avijan tells the group that we are hoping to document some of the human-elephant conflict in North Bengal, along the Nepal border and also to meet and spend time with Parbati Barua. He explains all this in Bengali and a lively exchange ensues.

"Jody, Kim, what is your plan?" Animesh asks, while tea is being handed out. I stifle a laugh. For months I have been asking for a plan and been told that is not possible. Yet, so far, we've been asked little else. Eventually I will learn the difference between being asked for a plan, stating one, and believing that whatever plan you end up with will turn out to resemble the plan you even remotely had. I think that what Jody has been trying to communicate is: don't count on any plan working out . . . ever, and anything is possible. But as it happens in that moment—we don't have a plan. At all.

"Well," Jody starts, "we are hoping to document the wild elephants as they migrate."

A heated and questioning conversation in Bengali takes place among Avijan, Animesh, and some others. Mr. G says nothing. Once he is asked a question and shakes his head.

Avijan turns to us. "It is too early for paddy season. The elephants are not yet here, but you can see them at the end of May and in June."

End of May. My flight returns first week of May, so I will not miss Goldie's thirteenth birthday on the ninth. Jody has the flexibility to stay.

I am crushed. How could we not have known this time frame ahead of time? We could have planned the trip for June.

"What about Parbati Barua? Are you able to help us meet her? We would like to spend some time learning from her." Jody wisely leaves out the part about hoping she will let us travel the ancient migration route on elephant-back with her. If we can meet her this week, I will still have two full weeks. We can fly to Assam, even do a brief elephant journey. We both believe this is possible.

"You must have Forest Department approval for any of these activities," Avijan says. "It will be easier. You must have the permissions." Everyone looks to Mr. G, who doesn't move. "Parbati Barua is very difficult to meet. But Animesh is her friend."

Animesh smiles and spreads his hands into the air. His fingers are slender and expansive. His eyes seem to dance and flash, they reveal his thoughts. Right now, his face is smiling, but his eyes look unyielding. "It is possible." He turns to Mr. G and they speak in Bengali to one another, then look to Avijan.

"He says," Avijan translates, "there is a workshop about human-elephant situation in Darjeeling. It begins on Friday. All the government and NGOs will be there. From everywhere in North Bengal, and many of the north-east states: Assam, Nagaland, Meghalaya. It is a very important meeting."

Jody and I exchange glances. Darjeeling?! Elephant workshop with everyone under one roof?! How did we get so lucky?

"Can we go?" I ask, the first time I have contributed to the conversation.

"It is up to the chief warden, Mr. Kant. Only he can make that decision," Animesh says. "It is good timing for you. This is only the second time we have all met in one place to discuss the elephant problem. For all of Northeast India. But it is for government and NGO only. Maybe you will get permissions." He tips his head left and then right, a common gesture that seems to mean yes and no at the same time.

They give us the phone number for the chief warden and reassert that we need to get Forest Department permission from him, for anything that we wish to do in the field. Animesh does not mention Parbati again.

Avijan has Parbati's cell phone number and has given it to Jody. He tells us she knows we are looking to meet her but also says we will have a better chance if Animesh paves the way. We leave HNAF with a plan: we will go to Darjeeling the next day and beg our way into the conference. How can they say no if we are already there?

By the time we return to the hotel, I am utterly spent and grateful for the solitary room to collect my thoughts. Such a mix of feelings: not seeing wild elephants is a massive disappointment and there is no easy lead to Parbati. But Darjeeling is an unexpected thrill and a way forward—firsthand stories from a wide array of experts all in one place. What kind of strange coincidence is this? We knew virtually nothing about timing or schedules or what is happening here when we planned our trip. I am missing the window for seeing elephants. Yet, this workshop makes me believe that we are in the right place at the right time.

The next morning, Jody texts from next door: *Something's wrong with my leg. I can't walk.* She is propped up on the bed when I arrive.

"I'm so out of shape because of the tuk tuk race. I was doing squat jumps last night and heard something pop. I went to bed thinking it would go away, but it feels worse. I called my cousin who is a nurse. She thinks I've pulled my quad muscle."

"I have some pain relievers." Desperately, I hope this is all she will need. This town is tight and mean, the sidewalks are menacing. I feel completely overwhelmed after yesterday's attempt to cross the street in search of a working ATM—a near-miss of getting hit by everything that was moving, trying to run across the mud-caked streets while keeping my feet away from random smears of feces. Wearing flip-flops, because that is literally the only footwear anyone has on their feet, plus Jody is wearing them and I want to look like I belong.

She sits up and moans in pain, "Can you go get me crutches, bandages, and ibuprofen? I think it's pulled or torn. I can't walk on it at all."

My face settles into mask mode, attempting to show calm and act as if this is a small ask, an easy task. Anyone can do it. *Anyone*, I think, *but me*. Crutches? Who sells crutches around here? "Yeah. Sure. Do you think anything is open right now?" This is a stall question and I know it. I quickly follow it up with, "I'll go see what I can do."

Out the door and into the streets, pretending to be someone else, someone who is brave. A woman who knows how to ask for things she needs in the most uncomfortable place she has ever been. I am masquerading as that person. And so, I go. The throngs of people and bustling activity of last night are an afterimage in the form of piles of garbage along the side of the road. Picked through by collectors, swept into piles by cleaners, and eaten by cows. Most of the buildings are shuttered and barred, closed. I find an open pharmacy and gather my courage. It works. Now I have anti-inflammatories, a good bandage, and directions for where to possibly get crutches. I walk and walk to the end of the sidewalk, to a dirt lot; no longer in an area that feels right.

Defeated, I turn around and begin the trek back. I have exhausted every pharmacy and possibility. Failing now, so early in our journey, feels like a terrible omen, as if I am confirming all that Jody may feel about me. Failure to secure crutches means I am not enough; I don't have what it takes to be like the people for whom I write. Why did I think I could be? Men on bicycles and a stray dog amble out from the alley to my right. On the corner is a pharmacy that must have opened since I last walked past. Propped up against the front window is a black cane. Scratches and lack of packaging tell me it is likely secondhand, but it is for sale. How it is here right now, where it wasn't just moments before, is beyond me. Either manifestation is real, or my Ganesh pendant is working. I am saved. My return is triumphant; Hercules accomplishing one of his twelve labors. For the first time since we embarked on this project together, I feel worthy.

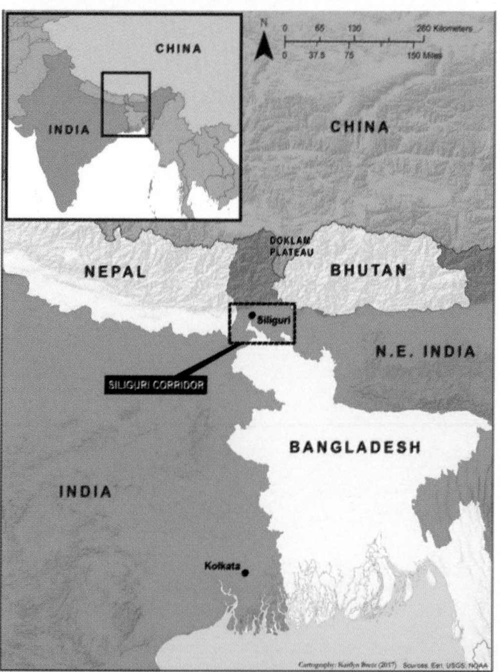

TOP: Families who live in tea garden villages clash with wild herds when natural elephant habitats are blocked. *Photo by Avijan Saha.* CENTER: Map of the Siliguri Corridor in North Bengal, India. *Map prepared by Kaitlyn Bretz and Philip McDaniel (UNC Libraries).* BOTTOM: Elephants in the mist. *Photo by Avijan Saha.*

TOP: Map and description of elephants. *Map by Human Elephant Voices.org.* CENTER: Old Map of North Bengal Forests, by D. K. Lahiri Choudhury, *from* A Trunk Full of Tales: Seventy Years with the Indian Elephant *(2006).* BOTTOM: A wild herd of Asian elephants moving along the Indo-Nepal border. Backdropped by the foothills of the eastern Himalaya. *Photo by Avijan Saha.*

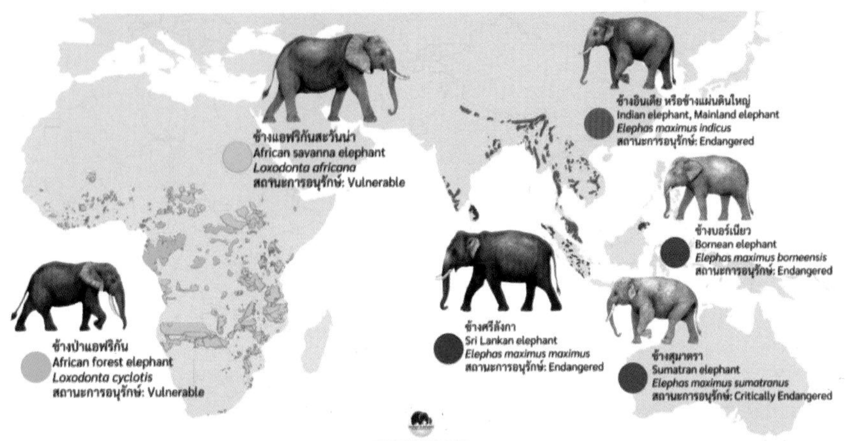

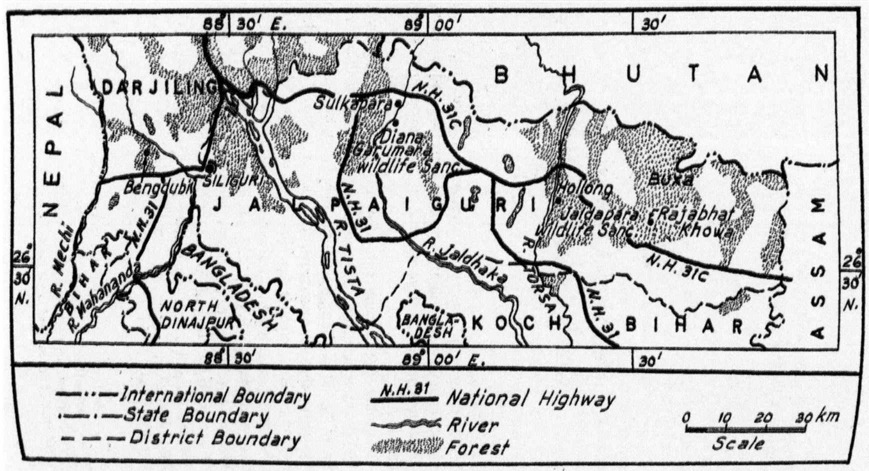

TOP: People often don't realize that Asian elephants are a different species, with different challenges, than their African elephant cousins. This chart from Wildlife SOS helps make the differences clear. *Map from wildlifesos.org.* CENTER: This highway crosses an ancient migration route in the forest. Now Forest Departments patrol at night to ensure safe crossing. *Photo by Avijan Saha.* BOTTOM: Elephants clustering under trees in tea garden. *Photo by Sourav Mandal.*

TOP: Dreaming and researching from the author's desk.
CENTER: Kim with her daughters.
BOTTOM: Portrait of Avijan Saha.
Photo by Kim Frank.

ABOVE: An elephant mother and her two calves cross the busy highway at night. *Photo by Avijan Saha.* BELOW: Jody photographing at Dhupjhora, Gorumara Elephant Camp.

TOP LEFT: Kim and Parbati Barua, November 2023. *Photo by Sourav Mandal.* TOP RIGHT: Parbati Barua, Queen of the Elephants. *Photo by Kim Frank.* CENTER: Kim and Jody with Parbati Barua, August 2018. BOTTOM: Parbati Barua watching over the mahouts, 2018. *Photo by Kim Frank.*

ABOVE: Kim with mahouts and elephants at Dhupjhora, Gorumara Elephant Camp. *Photo by Jody MacDonald.* BELOW: Mahout bathing a mother elephant while her calf milks, 2022. *Photo by David Concannon.*

ABOVE: Mahout Faridul cleaning Suriya's tumor. BELOW: Captive elephants on patrol for poachers with the Forest Department protecting endangered one-horned rhinos. *Photo by Kim Frank.*

TOP: Books in Lalji's study. *Photo by Kim Frank.* CENTER: Photograph of Barua women in album. *Photo by Kim Frank.* BOTTOM: Albums of photos taken by the Barua royal family photographer. *Photo by Kim Frank.*

ABOVE LEFT: Kim and David. ABOVE RIGHT: Kim and her girls, first Sundance trip. BELOW: Girls and Kim during their Sundance trip just after India.

TOP: Elephant herd at Nuxalbari_LB5. *Photo by Avijan Saha.* CENTER: Elephants cross the Nuxalbari Tea Estate road. *Photo by Kim Frank.* BOTTOM: Sonia has a tremendous responsibility and fights to keep trespassers off her property. *Photo by Kim Frank.*

TOP: Sonia Jabbar with her horses. She has established a riding school at Nuxalbari for local children. *Photo by Kim Frank.* CENTER: When the rice paddy fields begins to ripen, the scent brings in the elephants. *Photo by Avijan Saha.* BOTTOM: Farmers try to collect the ripened crops before the elephants arrive. *Photo by Avijan Saha.*

TOP: The tusker, Lama, seen in musth, eating rice paddy on the night Kim spent out with farmers. *Photo by Avijan Saha.* CENTER: Elephant charging local villager in Kolabari forest. *Photo by Avijan Saha.* BOTTOM: Home destroyed by an elephant, only the front door remains. *Photo by Kim Frank.*

OPPOSITE TOP: Kanchenjunga on a clear day in North Bengal. *Photo by Sourav Mandal.* OPPOSITE CENTER: Kim seeing Kanchenjunga up close for the first time, 2022. *Photo by Sourav Mandal.* OPPOSITE BOTTOM: S. P. Pandey from SPOAR and the West Bengal Forest Department raising awareness in elephant conflict area.

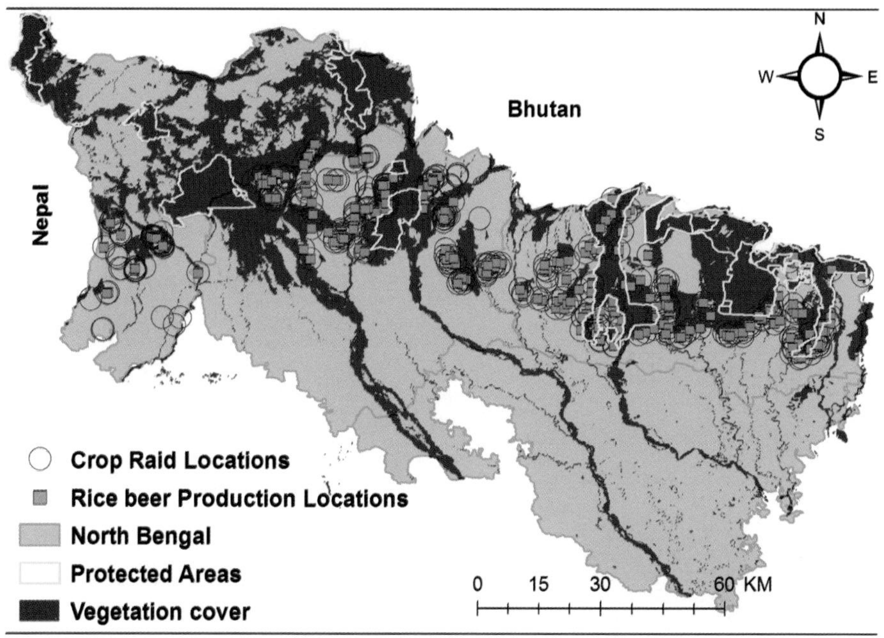

ABOVE: North Bengal map of conflict. *Map from "Elephants in the neighborhood: patterns of crop-raiding by Asian elephants within a fragmented landscape of Eastern India," 2020 by Naha, et. al. PeerJ. 8. 10.7717/peerl.9399.* BELOW: Kim with children from elephant conflict area villages. *Photo by Trevor Wallace.*

TOP: Elephants in a copse of Jarul trees with flowers in bloom. *Photo by Avijan Saha.* CENTER: The matriarch elephant from Kim's dream (photo seen months after Kim's dream). *Photo by Avijan Saha.* BOTTOM: After writing this book, Kim felt there was more story to tell. In the farmer's tent with Indian cinematographer, Sourav Mandal. *Photo by Jeremy LaZellea.*

7

We do not yet have permission to attend the "Right of Passage to Elephants to Mitigate Human-Elephant Conflict" intergovernmental and nongovernmental workshop, but we travel to Darjeeling anyway. A four-hour drive up a clogged and windy mountain road alongside a train track for a toy train, made small so it can handle the tight twists and turns. This train begins in Siliguri and travels to the upper tip of Darjeeling. Built by the British, it was formerly the main transport for tea, English expats on holiday, and other goods and services. Now on UNESCO's list of World Heritage sites, it runs mostly for tourists.

Urban Siliguri quickly yields to a seemingly endless landscape of bright green tea gardens with dramatic tree-lined entrances, interrupted only by the occasional fenced army camps. Sleeping cows litter the roads, and our driver honks the entire way. As we head into the mountains, the road becomes a tight series of twists and turns with no guardrails and sheer drop-offs. Trucks clog the width, and our van must skirt around them on the slimmest edge. Only when we are solidly on the road do I dare look out the window, over the edge. We both fight motion sickness and I battle the need to find a bathroom. There isn't one, and the traffic is backed up in both directions; peeing on the side of the cliff, in this crowd, is not an option I am yet ready to take. The views are breathtaking—layers of mist-covered trees with gnarled trunks growing at odd angles on such steep terrain. The valley deep green in the distance. Jody reintroduces me to Doritos, which immediately become the best thing I ever ate. I share my leftover M&Ms from the flight over, which becomes the best thing she ever ate. We are working synergistically in a way that feels intuitive and effortless, chatting most of the way with the ease of friendship. Who knows if we will meet any of our goals, but I am grateful to be actively moving toward one of them and eager to be en route to this legendary destination. In our imaginations, Darjeeling is mystical mountain town, where Mount Everest climbers used to meet and train in the time of Tenzing Norgay. And who hasn't sipped, at some point in our lives, the earthy mystery of Darjeeling tea? The hamlet promises history and magic, dramatic landscape, cultural heritage, and wonder. We will be one with the Himalaya, snow-packed peaks so sharp and close we may prick our fingers on them.

We arrive to a bitter damp cold, under a gray clouded misty sky, with no hope of seeing the mountain peaks that embrace us. Our homestay is an impossibly steep hike from the main streets where the conference is being held. There are no taxis or rickshaws, and walking is not an option. We've packed for blazing heat and humidity, not expecting near-snow conditions.

The homestay is a cement house run by two Nepalese brothers whose money ran out before they could complete the final wall that encloses the building. Their kindness and generosity make up for the missing physical warmth. We are hungry but feel incapable of heading back down for food. The brothers make us tea straightaway, and an omelet with onions and peppers. When the cup and dishes are set before us, steam wafts into the damp cold air, releasing a sweet savory mix of earthy green tea leaves with sugar and the familiar holiday smell of onions frying. My fingers are shriveled and numb from the chill. Wrapping them around my cup brings deep comfort. This is lunch and dinner. In all my packing, I did not anticipate cold weather anywhere. The warmest clothing I have are lightweight pants, a long-sleeved shirt, and a light sweatshirt. Jody has a thin down jacket. But none of this helps much in the face of a damp cold rain at forty-five degrees Fahrenheit.

Upstairs is a community space with big windows that look out onto mountains we can't see. Here, we can get spotty cell service and internet connectivity. It is the weekend and the government offices are closed, but after some sleuthing we find the direct cell number for the head of the West Bengal Forest Department. Surprisingly, he answers. "The permission is not mine to give," he says, even as we know that he is the top official. "You must ask the organizer, that is the right thing to do." We have this person's name, but no phone number; it sounds like he is already in town and will be at the hotel tomorrow.

Our bedroom has a dividing wall between the two beds, affording some privacy but allowing conversation. Mercifully, there are electric blankets. We eat the last of our chocolate and Doritos, put on as many layers of clothes as we can manage, crank the heat in our beds, and are grateful. We talk for a bit about Jody's new boyfriend and my long-distance challenges with David. We create a strategy for tomorrow. We have already arranged for a driver to take us to the hotel by 8:00 A.M., when we believe the meeting will likely start. Both of us are asleep within the hour.

The next morning, we dress in near silence, loath to leave the comfort of the warm bed. In search of hot water for instant coffee, I mistakenly stumble on what I think is the homestay kitchen but is in fact the family home. The brother's mother generously brings me boiled water anyway, but I am embarrassed by my mistake. Omelets with onion and pepper, toast with butter. Tea. A repeat of last night. I am grateful for any food. This feels like the part where we are on an expedition, experiencing some hardship and unpredictability. Though in reality we are in a highly visited tourist town. A driver comes and we embark.

The hotel where the conference is taking place had clearly once been an elegant place, a throwback to an earlier era of high-end clientele. It is shabby now, and cluttered with garish signs and banners, worn cloth on the furniture, restaurants that are closed. We are here in the off-season, May. By July, everything will likely be different. We ask to be connected to the organizer's room and try to call. No answer. We wait in the lobby, thinking that we might be too early and don't want to wake him. Military police come in and out. Worried that we might get kicked out, we ask the front desk clerk about the conference. It does not start until 4:00 P.M. The clerk tells us that we might have a better chance if we return at noon for registration. It is 9:00 A.M.

We begin the precipitous walk up the road. At this moment I do not know of the nickname "the Bright Spot" or that this city was territory owned by the once-independent Sikkim, or that its name was anglicized from the original "Dorje-ling" after a Buddhist monk who inhabited the highest monastery. I know little of its colonial history as a hill station for Britons and wealthy Indians from Kolkata to escape the heat of West Bengal. Or of the near-enslaved labor that had built the town and worked the boundless tea gardens. I have yet to see Satyajit Ray's iconic 1962 film, *Kanchenjunga*. Ray wrote the screenplay in just ten days from the terrace of the Windermere Hotel, once the swankiest address in town and still operating today as an example of the British Raj era. The film portrays the essence of Darjeeling as a misty health mecca, where one can get lost in romantic fantasy, face hard truths, or feel a true sense of self. Breathing the cold mountain air, taking languid walks along a promenade, hoping always to catch a fleeting glimpse of Kanchenjunga and even Mount Everest if one is lucky and the clouds clear.

With all that is happening, I have not done my homework. None of this romantic nostalgia, energetic healing, or sense of exclusive enclave is apparent. Trudging up the narrow street, passing cheap trinket shops and workers with piles of goods atop their heads, we only feel a bitter damp to our bones, giving rise to a growing sense of hopelessness.

The coffee shop has clearly been created for European backpackers. Coffee from Nepal, a hip menu with French pastries and sandwiches that seem impossible for this location. Lonely Planet guides to hiking the Himalaya and travel magazines are scattered among the urban modern–designed tables and chairs. Expertly pulled fresh espresso with rich creamy foam. The moment is precious and gone in a few sips. The hours stretch before us like a black hole with no grounding force.

Noon at last; we set off as if on a grand adventure. When we arrive there is a new, more knowledgeable desk clerk who tells us to return at 4:00 P.M.

Hopes dashed again, we begin the limp up the hill, back to the coffee shop. Along the way we stop in a Tibetan antiques shop as it opens. It is a small square of a place, a treasure box piled high with faded and torn vintage silk tapestries and monk's robes. In the corner there is a heavy crystal shaman stick with a magic ball on top and silk flags hanging from it. It compels me to reach for it. In my hand, its power is palpable. Once a shaman made magic with this object, healed others, said mantras that moved forces we cannot see. I cannot put it down, nor can I bring myself to buy it. Some things are not meant to be owned. This is such an object. Instead, I buy a small, jeweled elephant, and have it wrapped so it will stay concealed until after I see my first real elephant. In my hope of hopes it will be wild, but any would do. The idea that this trip, these precious three weeks of time away from my daughters, might yield nothing is beginning to loom as a dark specter, best left suppressed rather than evoked.

At last, it is 4:00 P.M., and we both wish we were heading back to our homestay with our heated blankets. At the hotel, we walk past the armed Forest Department police officers who guard the entrance and are directed up the stairs to the sixth floor where we wait by the registration area. A man approaches the area with confidence, and is greeted with deference, slight bows. We see his name tag when he passes, it is the chief warden Jody spoke to last night. Here is our chance.

"Mr. Kant," Jody says, and introduces herself. "We spoke on the phone last night, hoping to attend the workshop."

"Ah, excellent," he says, "you were approved to join us."

"Well," says Jody. "Not yet, we are still waiting for the organizer so we can ask him."

"Tell me again what you are working on?" he says.

We tell him that we are wanting to tell the stories about selfie culture and how it is hurting elephants in this area. "Is that a problem you have experienced?" we ask.

"Yes. It is a tremendous issue," he says. "Every day we are getting calls because people are trying to take selfies with wild elephants and are getting killed or injured. The people are angry with the Forest Department because they believe the wild elephants are our responsibility. People are taking big risks. Sometimes their photographs appear to tell one story that is not the full truth. The photographer that took the image of the baby elephant, for instance, where it looked like her tail was on fire. It went viral around the world. This man even won a wildlife award. But that elephant's tail was not actually on fire, the photo appeared that way because of the angle it was shot. People are getting injured now at a much higher rate because they are trying to get attention on social media. It is a big problem for us and for elephants."

While the chief warden is talking, a man approaches to say hello. "Jody, Kim," the chief warden says, "this is Mr. N, the organizer of this meeting. He is the person you need to talk to."

Jody delivers our rehearsed ask.

Mr. N shakes his head. "No, I am very sorry. This is a government only meeting for stakeholders. We cannot open it up to the public. Do you agree, chief warden?"

The chief warden says something to Mr. N in Bengali. Then in English, "If they are here to know about elephants in North India, this is a good meeting for them to learn. We do not have anything to hide."

Mr. N's brow furrows and he looks down, then peers around the room and the attendees arriving, greeting one another. The room is growing animated; my heart is pounding. No longer wishing I was in my room under a hot blanket, our conversation with the warden has made me desperate to stay.

"Of course, we do not have anything to hide," Mr. N says. "Please, be our guests. You are welcome to observe."

We take our seats, but not before Animesh from HNAF walks in with Mr. G. When he sees us, Animesh's eyes grow dramatically wide in surprise. A grin quickly follows, and he rushes over to greet us, grabbing our hands in a warm gesture of welcome. "You are here!" he says. His response feels like a sign that things are getting better. If we deepen our relationships, we will have better luck in being successful with this endeavor.

The workshop is called to order with a ceremony and blessing. Lights low, candles and incense lit, and mantra chanting for a productive work session. And then, it all unfolds before our eyes. Graphs of elephant corridors throughout the region, statistics and reports from NGOs, presentations from the head of the Department of Highways, the head of the Tea Garden Association, railway representatives, academic scientists, and Forest Department heads from several states in the Northern India region. I am beside myself with excitement and take notes furiously.

At the end of the evening's sessions, dinner is served. We are invited to stay. Treated like honored guests, the feeling of inclusion once again resonates. Almost every person takes a moment to introduce themselves to talk about elephants, their work, ask us questions. At the evening's end, one of the department heads orders the rangers out front to drive us back to our homestay. I close my eyes on the drive, imagining myself as a war reporter, a woman who would put herself at risk to document important news to show the Western world all they do not know. Of course, this is ridiculous. Jody is almost asleep. This ride does not strike her as unusual. "It is India," she would say. Anything and everything is possible.

The workshop continues all day the next day and as I take copious notes, Jody is becoming increasingly bored. This is not an ideal situation for a photographer—the lighting is terrible, and nothing is happening photographically. Yet, something is happening for me. As the speakers share statistics, solutions, and stories, I begin to grasp that there is a significant depth and scope to the human-elephant conflict issue.

I learn that the railways are killing elephants and though they are trying to figure out solutions, it isn't happening fast enough. Elephants are an issue in tea estates (but I'm not yet clear how, where, or why), and that the Forest Divisions throughout many locations are experiencing numbers of human casualties and elephant deaths. All the representatives are reporting out versus discussing and using terms such as *corridors* and *routes*. A university professor presents an interesting paper on shifting spiritual beliefs regarding elephants. He explains how young people are not as reverent regarding elephants as Ganesh reincarnated. There is one NGO, Wildlife Trust of India. Occasionally, one of their wildlife biologists will speak up and refute some of the positions of the government leaders. Then a lively discussion ensues. I document all of it—taking photos with my phone of every chart and graph, recording conversations, and writing notes until my hand cramps. I am captivated. A shift begins to occur. I feel myself slipping more deeply into the cause, the issues, the stories, and feeling connected to the people in this room who care enough to attempt to coordinate solutions. Yet most of it is academic, and I barely understand what is being said.

How can I just come here and tell one story about something that is so culturally embedded? About something that is so complex it must be deeply understood in context before it can be shared with the West. Who am I to tell a story about something I know so little about? An opening is happening inside, new space. A clearing of sorts. Humbled by my ignorance in thinking I could simply drop into one village where people are taking selfies of wild elephants and presume to know the truth. The selfie story may be a hook for a certain audience, but now I understand that if I try to tell it in one visit, with one experience, I will be doing the truth an injustice.

By the end of the day, I am satiated but still curious. And utterly spent.

Our last day in Darjeeling, Jody and I will return to Siliguri at noon. I wake at dawn and decide to explore in the hopes of seeing the mountains and finding a more peaceful, special place here. I am certain it exists. There must be something here that makes this town legendary, something that can defy the cheap hawking and shoddy tourist shops on the main streets. We are perched up high and have seen storms blow in, but still no sign of the Himalaya. I take my camera and slip out the unfinished section of the house, past the gate and into the morning. These moments of independence scare me. I am afraid of wild dogs biting, of men attacking, of getting lost. I try to push all these thoughts away, choosing a winding street above us.

Stray dogs curled up napping lie ahead and I breathe calm confidence. Monkeys are everywhere—they are jumping from trees. I have never seen one in the wild. Up the road then down the road, off into a side alley. It is warm for the first time since we arrived and there is sunshine. In the cloudless sky the jagged peaks of one mountain, bold and massive in scale, emerge from their hiding place. I do not know it is Kanchenjunga, the world's third highest mountain, whose sacred summit, at 28,169 feet, has been left untouched. "The Five Treasures of Snow," named for its five peaks, each with treasures: salt, gold, precious stones, sacred scriptures, and invincible armor. Where it is believed by the people who live at its base to be the birth of humankind, a man and a woman born from the snowy peak. I cannot know that two years from now, what I see on this first solo outing into the unknown—this famously elusive cloud-enshrouded mountain—will reveal itself to me only once again, also at dawn, on my most significant day in India. It resists being photographed and so I let myself feel it, the radiating presence. As quickly as it appears, it disappears behind a mask of mist, making me question if it was in fact what it appeared to be.

Jody and I still have no plan and no leads with almost two weeks stretching out before us. Yet this morning's walk has infused me with energy and hopeful outlook. Now I have a rich bank of new knowledge and contacts. Over two intense days, I have gathered so much new information—what would have been so difficult to research on my own, not knowing the stakeholders and through Western news sources. Now, missing the window for seeing wild elephants this trip doesn't seem so terrible. My mind is reorganizing. There is still the chance of spending time with Parbati Barua. After all we learned this weekend, she seems to be the person with origin knowledge if I want to explore elephants more deeply in India, the culture of human relationships with elephants here, and understand the nuances of the conflict. "Dying for Likes" seems now like a single facet in a kaleidoscope of threats stacking up against elephants.

8

Encouragement, Hope, Discouragement, Repeat is the name of the roller-coaster Jody and I are riding. Back in Siliguri with no plan, no connection to Parbati Barua, and no sign of wild elephant migration, we begin to sink. Moments after we check back into the Saluja Residency, this time with a larger shared room that feels luxurious after our rustic homestay, Animesh invites us to visit HNAF at 8:30 that evening. Jody is physically spent from her tuk tuk race and hamstring injury. I am exhausted as well, but do not have heroic excuses. Instead, I'm feeling my age, lack of exercise, and the effects of being wildly out of my element. After a comfort food lunch of French fries, tandoori chicken, and garlic naan, we nap. I immediately fall asleep, that exquisite heavy floating sleep that tempts you to stay. Climbing out of grogginess to the sound of an alarm. Sweet hot masala chai from room service helps wake us up.

At 8:00 P.M., we drag ourselves from our room, down the flights of stairs, and out into the mobbed nightlife of Siliguri. It seems odd to be meeting so late in the evening, did we get the time wrong? The sidewalks are not exactly handicapped friendly. Jody is limping with her cane, keeping up her spirits even as she is jostled at every step. We walk for what feels like the appropriate amount of time and begin to look for the alley to turn down.

"I think it's this one," Jody says, and we turn down a narrow alley tucked off the main street. As we get deeper down the road, shadowy figures stand clustered in pockets of doorways; the traffic does not come here, a lone motorcycle sputters through. My thoughts are of gangs and criminals and rapists. This is how it happens. My instincts sound off warning bells as we walk slowly past young men who stop talking to one another and stare. There is only darkness now.

"This doesn't look like I remember," I say. "Maybe we need to go back."

If we are attacked, Jody's disadvantaged state will make protecting ourselves even harder. I have only a heavy flashlight as a weapon, deep in the recesses of my bag.

"Let's just walk to the end to make sure," she says.

And I follow, like a horror movie scene where the people keep descending into the basement even as it is the obvious poor choice. We walk deeper into the alley until it opens into a parking lot with a few young men standing around cars and bikes. Stares. Now we must walk the gauntlet back. I feel a tinge of anger toward Jody, a confusing mix of envy for the ease with which she moves through the world unafraid, but also resentment, as I have always relied on my gut instinct to help me make safe choices and Jody's lack of concern is causing me to question my own judgement. Do I err too much on the side of safety, am I judging others unfairly by assuming I'm at risk here? And does any of it matter, since I clearly am unable to state my opinion? I am deferential to Jody because she is the expert here, and I am still marveling that she agreed to do this with me and am grateful to her. And yet I am taking the kind of risks I promised myself and my family I would not take. Yet here we are. Once successfully back on the main street, unharmed, sweat-soaked from nerves and heat, we forge on. Finally, we find the correct alley and reach HNAF, but the garage door is closed. We must have gotten the time wrong.

Defeated, we trudge the ten blocks back to the hotel and sit at the restaurant bar for a late dinner.

Jody gets a text just as we are about to order: *Jody it is Animesh. Where are you?*

The garage door was closed, but Animesh was inside.

We thought no one was there, she replies. *On our way!*

It is after 9:00 P.M., but we begin again. I feel sorry for Jody, who is in obvious pain, but I can't help her. She is persistent and does not complain. This time we don't get lost and the door is wide open. Inside is a row of chairs and many people. This is not a formal meeting; it is a social gathering. We have been included in the regular evening meet up of friends and HNAF volunteers of all ages. Almost every night this group gathers over tea and biscuits to talk about current events, art, entertainment, literature, and the goings on in their lives. From 8:30 until 10:30 P.M., when they each return home and eat dinner. We stay, talk, and socialize. Everyone here is so kind and welcoming. It is refreshing to attend a gathering where alcohol is not necessary to create vulnerability and the conversation is meaningful.

After about a half hour, Animesh, who has been intermittently texting and making some phone calls, hands me his phone.

"Parbati, Madam," he says.

I am confused but reach out. "Hello?" I say. The connection is crackly, and the voice on the other end begins speaking rapidly. I can only hear a word or two clearly in staccato sentences. I am desperate to understand her. Animesh is grinning and this must mean Parbati Barua is telling me that she will meet with us.

At the end, she says, "Okay? Okay?"

"Yes, Yes!" I say, "Thank you so much. Thank you."

I'm not certain to what I have agreed to.

Parbati says, "All right. See you then. Goodbye." Efficient and clearly used to delivering commands, Parbati's energy and tone gives hints to her personality.

"Thank you," I repeat. "See you."

Animesh takes the phone and continues talking with Parbati in rapid Bengali.

Jody's eyes are wide. "What did she say?!"

The terrible thing is, I have no idea. "I am not exactly sure," I admit, embarrassed at my inability to listen, and comprehend more easily . . . or at all. "She will see us. That's all I could understand. I think tomorrow."

Animesh completes the call and clasps his hands with a soft smile and bright laughing eyes that remind me of a guru. "Well then," he says, "Parbati Madame is my good friend. She is on holiday with her family close to here. She will meet you. No interview or photographs. This is just an introduction; she will meet you at Dhupjhora in Gorumara National Park. You can go there. Do you have a driver?"

No, of course we do not. Animesh arranges a car to pick us up at 8:00 A.M. the next morning. We will meet her at 11:00 A.M., more than a two-hour journey from here.

It is almost 11:00 P.M., and one by one the group has dispersed. The streets are quiet and nearly empty. Animesh asks two of his staff to ride us home on their motorbikes.

And now, I am riding on the back of a bike, with no helmet, hair wild behind me, night breeze balmy, the streets calm. My fingers in the driver's belt loops, as we ride along a sedate Hill Cart Road. Such freedom! I feel reckless and euphoric, as if in some type of protective bubble, liberated from layers of inhibitors. Perhaps it's the survival down the dark alley but more likely the giving over to visceral fact that I'm not in control. Once released, my fear temporarily dissolves.

Hope marks the morning, and we travel as if young children, in the backseat with no context for our surroundings, no sense of where we are going. For two winding hours, past lush jungle and over a historic bridge draped with prayer flags. Monkeys with grinning open mouths line the guardrails hoping for a snack from an unsuspecting backseat passenger when traffic inevitably backs up. Some smaller ones line up in groups plucking each other's fur, just like I have seen in nature documentaries. Below us, along a mostly dry riverbed, men collect rocks, families gather to eat a meal, squatting over a spread-out linen, and women wash baskets of clothing in the rivulets of running water. A message comes through on my phone, informing me the country I have now entered is not supported by the international day pass plan. I check our location on Google Maps and discover that we are skirting the border of Bhutan.

This is the Dooars, an enchanted land named for its doorways through the Himalaya linking Bhutan and India. Less populated than North Bengal, this area has several tribal communities that have peacefully coexisted with wild elephants for centuries. We have been told that in recent years developments and refugees from neighboring Bangladesh have created an influx of newcomers, eager to farm and not steeped with indigenous wisdom as to ways of living peacefully with elephants. The present conflicts have reached new heights, and the area's Forest Department is now among the busiest in the country during crop seasons.

The highway turns to rural road, which turns to village dirt lanes. We are lost. Our driver asks directions at every corner until we find our way. Jody is ready with the rehearsed speech. We have this one chance to convince Ms. Barua to let us tell her story, to share her elephant wisdom with us. No photographs or interview. Jody has brought her camera just in case something changes.

Along a gravel drive flanked with rows of bright green tea plants, we approach the entrance to the park. Six raised huts painted teal blue are perched above a grassy area. In the center a gazebo with a green metal roof, covered with a rounded built-in red cement bench, provides some shade from the blistering sun. The road continues into a thick forest fenced with thin wire. Across the way is a collection of soft yellow cement homes with corrugated red metal roofs and green shutters that form a U around a courtyard. Next to the houses, across a tree-lined path, is a tall open-air structure with dirt floor. The roof is metal and raised so high it looks like a covered horse's arena, but for giant animals. Dhupjhora is an elephant camp! Empty now, the arena shows signs that elephants were recently inside. A wiry young man wearing a plaid cotton lungi and a T-shirt is shoveling up leftover piles of grass in one of the areas near a post, then raking the dirt. The air is thick, smelling of fresh dung, a spent campfire, and the brackish musky scent of a low water river. Birds are still singing in the trees, layers of calls and response, with the buzzing of cicadas a constant background melody.

At our arrival, the manager approaches and greets us. "Madam is not yet here," he says. "Please sit." He gestures to the gazebo, where we sit along the rounded cement benches. Just moments from meeting a legend. The elusive Queen of the Elephants, Assamese princess, wild-elephant catcher, and sought-after healer. The woman with whom Mark Shand traveled across India on elephant-back. I think about his descriptions of her and try and prepare myself. I won't talk, only listen. She will likely rely on her instincts to determine if she will grant us a story. How I hold myself, my nonverbal communication, what I do and don't say, is vital—maybe even my thoughts. Will she be able to read my thoughts? I am certain I'll give myself away. This is a woman who hears, feels, and observes far more than the average human.

Under the gazebo, tension mounts. Two local women wearing red and orange floral saris and cropped blouses with sari draped so there are gaps to keep cool. They sit next to us, pointing and laughing when we attempt to make conversation. We wait and sweat; the chill of Darjeeling long forgotten. An hour passes when a car approaches from within the national forest. It is followed by another, and something about watching the two vehicles approach makes me think of a diplomatic envoy. The dust settles and the sedan doors of both cars begin to open. I recognize her immediately. The group contains one man and three women, among them Parbati, who is the slightest figure, diminutive in physical form only, a commanding force of regal energy, directing her family members toward the footpath that leads to the empty elephant stables, the *pilkana*. She is wearing a brown cotton sari with red accents and carries a slouchy, brightly embroidered grass-green fabric purse. She separates from the others and, in a combination of striding and floating, approaches us. Her expression is dour, a mask of disapproval. Slightly downturned mouth becomes a fixed frown, brown eyes set into a steeled look that does not quite look directly at us, but also seems to be staring through us and assessing everything. As she steps into the gazebo, the crimson bindi on her third eye catches the sunlight and glows as if a jewel.

"Hello, hello, Parbati Barua? I am Jody, this is Kim," Jody says as we both stand up.

I press my hands together at my heart and bow slightly with a namaste greeting even though I haven't the faintest idea if this is appropriate. Jody, more practical, does not seem as swept up in the awe-inspiring moment. She maintains her cool. "Thank you for taking the time to meet with us."

"Hello," Parbati says to us, then turns to the camp manager and women, all of whom have clustered around her in warm and deferential greeting. She speaks to them in Bengali for a moment, then turns to us.

"Tea? You'll have tea." It is not a question. "Sit, sit," she says to us and gestures with a graceful hand adorned with slim gold bracelets.

There is a sudden flurry among the women to make tea and appear busy. In the distance, Parbati's family is standing in a small group talking among themselves. They are waiting. Jody must see them too, for she starts our ask, rehearsed by now for hours over days. It comes out in an eloquent tumble.

"We are a photographer and writer and are doing a story about human-elephant conflict in this region. You are so well-respected for your elephant wisdom. We want to learn from you if possible, so we can understand . . ."

"Yes." Parbati interrupts the forthcoming specifics of our proposal.

"This is my vacation, not a working time for me. Mr. G and Animesh, they are my good friends, otherwise I would not have this meeting with you." She looks us over as if trying to sense our intent, and beneath that, our true nature. Before coming to India, I read that elephants, like horses and many other mammals, sense your energy, perhaps even your intent, to determine what and who you are. Mirrors to your soul, these animals reflect your inner emotions. Much like the way a stray dog tends to bite people who are feeling fear and hostility. I try to calm my nerves, to focus on how earnest we are, how we are the right women to tell her story. "They have told me everything about you and what you want," Parbati continues.

The tea arrives and Parbati gestures for us to be served first. The afternoon heat is getting trapped within the gazebo. We sip our tea and take a biscuit. The women and camp manager sit back down, surrounding us, fascinated by the exchange. We are not the attraction as much as Parbati. She is known and revered here. There is this sense of breathlessness, that moment of silence in which everything is still possible. The space between one sentence to the next, between the call and response, question and answer. We sit here, together, at least two of us perched at the edge of hope.

Desperation pushes me to blurt out, "Would you be willing to let us spend some time with you? So we can learn about your work with elephants and tell your story?"

Parbati looks out at her family members—a well-dressed man and two women, both in saris. They look rather formally dressed for a walk in the mud and dust. They have moved back to the car, digging through their belongings inside.

"Yes. But, not here like this. You must observe. Take time with me." She takes a sip of tea and stares past us. Memory or weariness from having been here before, maybe having said these things to countless reporters who begged for a story, then misunderstood her.

"These are not things I can tell you. You must see them yourself, observe me. Then, I would like to read what you write when you are finished. You must understand what is in my head, from my perspective. You must write from that place."

I nod my head and smile widely to show my affirmation. Just as I open my mouth for further assurance, she adds, "Your feelings are not my feelings."

"Of course. Absolutely."

Is this happening? Have I heard her correctly? The words are clear, but they are so much more than I imagined she would offer. What she is articulating *is* my vision for her story.

Jody and I look at each other and grin, stopping short of a high five; it's an effort to conceal our joy and amazement.

Family members have completed their task at the car and are hesitantly making their way to the gazebo. Regardless of gender and age, all of them seem hesitant to interrupt, deference that seems to be for Parbati rather than us. Parbati sends the employees off to make more tea.

"Come, take a seat."

We all adjust, making space for each other. Introductions are made.

"Did you see the elephants?" Parbati asks her group. "Bupesh says they were along this line, at the edge of the meadow, foraging. It is still too early for bathing. They are in the forest, I think."

"No elephants," the man says, "but it is a lovely forest."

Suspended in this space of languid conversation, my imagination twirls off to images of elephants and Parbati, riding through jungles together. Thank heavens I brought a waterproof backpack. She has said yes. Yes!

A fresh round of tea has arrived. We have conversation with Parbati's family. They are very friendly and make us feel immediately part of their intimate group. Once royalty, the Baruas have more than one famous family member. Parbati's uncle, Pramathesh Barua, is a filmmaker widely heralded as the father of Bollywood; her older sister, Pratima Barua Pandey, is a renowned folk singer; and her father, Prakritish Chandra Barua, was one of the most highly respected elephant men in the history of India. Will she take us to her ancestral home? To her father's study, where history in the form of books and maps, photographs and memorabilia, remain as if he were still alive? I imagine going through these items, touching this lost history with my own hands, while Parbati weaves story after story of sleeping on the grassy jungle floor, riding her beloved elephant through thick vines high above the threat of tigers and leopards.

Jody's voice cuts into my reverie. "So, um . . . Parbati," she says. "What would be a good time for you? We are in India for the next two weeks. We can come to Assam."

Assam is Parbati's home.

It is also a state bordered by Bangladesh and Bhutan. A gateway to special regions of Arunachal Pradesh, the matriarch state of Meghalaya, and the tribal kingdom of Nagaland. Home to an abundance of wildlife, among the highest populations of wild elephants, yet the Himalayan foothills have long been rife with insurgent activity, rebel groups fighting, and kidnappings. The unrest was the reason Parbati Barua and Mark

Shand ended their journey in North Bengal, rather than continue along the elephant route into Assam.

"Now? No, no. I am too busy." She barely pauses. "You must come back. In June or July is monsoon season, the parks are closed, and I have more free time. Or October, I am very busy with the elephant conflict. That is also a good time."

Come back in a month? Does she think we live here? All that it took for me to come, the sacrifices, cost, my family. A return so soon will be impossible for me.

"Is it still possible to trek across the migration route on elephant-back?" Jody asks Parbati. "Is that something we could do with you?"

Parbati looks out onto the forest, thinking for a moment. "Yes, I think it is still possible. Difficult, but still possible. Shall we take a walk to the river?"

We stand, but my body is empty of feeling, shallow, stuck, heavy and light at the same time. The elation we'd enjoyed just moments before has come crashing down. She said yes, but she also said no. Defeated, I walk with Parbati, my hands behind my back. Not asking any questions, we walk in silence. The dirt path is flanked by tall trees wrapped in hanging vines and surrounded by tall grasses. Birds call out across the canopy, the sound of hammering echoes in the distance. Past the empty pilkanas, toward a sweeping river with a rickety wood watchtower. On the other bank a woman washes a bright red shirt, and a young man in shorts, T-shirt wrapped around his head like a turban, prods a thin cow with a tall wooden staff. Next to me, Parbati is a wisp and simultaneously a rod, with an energy so strong it seeps into my pores. I am desperate to come up with profound words that will cause her to reconsider, to trust me, at least to find some value in my existence and mission. But nothing comes.

"Let us go. No elephants yet," Parbati says. And we all follow her command.

We are back at the band shell. The manager comes to greet us. We ask if it is possible for us to watch the elephants bathe. It is happening in a few minutes from now, according to Parbati. Parbati asks on our behalf. The manager shakes his head, the back and forth shake that in this case seems to mean "No, but I don't want to have to tell Parbati no." She turns to us. "I am sorry, only guests may go to the bathing. If you are staying here, you can watch and ride."

A man and woman walk out from one of the huts; they are greeted by a gangly man who is staggering a bit. He guides them down to the river to watch the bathing. We are so close, so close to seeing the elephants, but the manager is getting nervous now, worried we will make trouble.

"You can book online," Parbati says. "Okay, I am leaving now. You can arrange everything with Animesh. He will reach me when you come back, and we will spend time."

Out the car window, the stretches of tea gardens seem less vibrant, monkeys more aggressive than adorable, traffic incessant. Retreating into stillness, both of us. We had foolishly expected that, if Parbati said yes, she would allow us to follow her back to Assam where we would photograph and interview straightaway. Now, both "Dying for Likes" and Parbati Barua stories are either a dead end or require returning in a month. This means, I've flown across the world to simply gather information, as both experiencing wild elephants and learning from Parbati will not be possible this trip. While Jody is free to spend months on end in any given place, with no plan or structure, I do not have that life. My time and travel need to be chosen very carefully.

"What now?" I say.

"I don't know," Jody replies. "We come back. I can come back in June. I'll go to Bali and then just come back. I definitely want to get a filmmaker and travel on elephant for at least four months with Parbati."

This hangs in the air like a thick toxic gas, choking my breath. Jody can, of course, return anytime she wants. June, however, is only four weeks away. Four months? I never considered this. Of course, it would be impossible for me to go anywhere for that long.

"I don't think I can come back so soon. What about October? Not sure I could ever do four months."

"You wouldn't need to," Jody says. "You could just fly in and stay for a few days to get the story, then leave. I need to stay the whole time so I can deeply get the visual story. If June doesn't work for you, I'll just go, and you can come another time that does work."

It dawns on me that Jody and I have different expectations about what a partnership for this story means.

We are stalled now, in the thick clog of where the road turns right to Gangtok and Darjeeling or left to Siliguri. The roof of the world, the Himalaya—if we turned right and joined the fray, we could be in the legendary mountains. I feel a hollow pit in my stomach that isn't carsickness.

"Well, we can figure out the journey details" I say. "But I think it's important that our first time spent with Parbati is both of us, otherwise it will be hard to establish a relationship. We should do it together, then we can come out separately for different parts of it." I add this last part, even as I do not agree. We are a team, it doesn't make sense for me to get part of a story without visuals, and it doesn't make sense for Jody to get visuals while I miss the narrative.

The space between us in the backseat seems to grow. We slump beside our windows, frustrated and angry. Jody may be feeling the burden of a having a partner she no longer wants. I am feeling desperate that I am going to lose this opportunity. Sick with the knowledge that this trip was potentially a waste of time. Though, we still have permission from Parbati, a rare and incredible thing.

The next hour passes in silence, heads propped up, eyes closed.

"What should we do now? With the time we have left?" I ask.

The elephants are not migrating, we don't have Forest Department permission to document the captive elephants in the camp, and we learned overnight from Avijan that the Forest Department has shut down the selfie-taking and crowding along the border in anticipation of the June migration.

"I'm not sure. The elephant camp was cool. If we stayed there maybe, we could still get a story out of this. About mahouts and captive elephants."

With this, we start to perk up. A plan begins to develop. We will go back to Dhupjhora and observe, document the working relationship. We need Forest Department permissions, but we can write to them and hopefully get permissions while we are visiting the camp. Even without it, if we stay, we can photograph as tourists and collect content.

Back at the Saluja Residency, we search online for vacancies. There are none. We contact Animesh for help. He invites us back to HNAF in the evening.

When we arrive, the room is bustling with people and animated with conversation. Embraced into the fold, we are welcomed as if we are part of the group.

"There is no vacancy at any park," Animesh says. "This is high season. It is very busy, too difficult without securing a reservation week in advance."

"Why do you want to do a tourist park?" one of Animesh's friend's asks. "Aren't you trying to document wild elephants? And Parbati Barua? What good is a tourist area for you?"

"We want to understand the relationship between humans and elephants," Jody says. "If we start there it can help us understand the conflict better."

"Do you have the Forest permissions?" Animesh asks. His eyebrows have narrowed and the gregarious smile has faded.

"Not yet," I say. "But we are working on them." It's understandable that Animesh would be annoyed with us. He arranged the impossible, a meeting with Parbati, and now we are back. Other than a box of sweets from the bakery down the street, we have not exactly repaid the favor and already are asking for another one.

Some guys bring in a board and chips for the classic Indian tabletop game, carom. A wild frenzy of a game that requires flicking chips into nets. Shuffleboard, pinball machines, darts, I love these types of games and am eager to play immediately. "I'll play," I shout out, uncharacteristically. But no one hears me, so when Jody jumps up and joins the game, out of politeness I stay seated with our hosts. The players in the other room are all cheering and laughing. In our room, we have tea. A box of stale biscuits dumped onto a plate and passed around.

There is no plan, but we require a plan. There was no way to have had a reliable strategy ahead of time, but now we can't reach our goals without one. We knew what we wanted to achieve, but we could not have known how to accomplish it until we were here, meeting people, asking questions, doing exactly what we are doing. Shifting and adjusting, as things do and don't go our way. In the end, nothing, and yet everything, is by design. The plan reveals itself to us in the last moments, at very odd times.

Animesh sits behind his desk, mysteriously and discreetly on his cell phone, as more people arrive. In the other room, they gather around the carrom table. I reluctantly stay, talking to Mr. G about his photography and treks for butterflies. The conversation is stilted as I can barely hear or understand, and I keep saying, "What?" I pretend and shake my head and smile. Loud cheers keep coming from the other room—the game. Envy consumes me. What lesson is there in this for me? I am back in high school with a best friend who is cooler and more beautiful than I. It dawns on me that I am always trying to be that girl: making jokes that get laughs, life of the party, fun, and pretty. I've long tried to stuff down the part of me that is smart and introspective, hiding it because it made me invisible. Lost in my thoughts, stewing instead of joining in. Overthinking (which is my tendency). All is lost. We have almost two weeks and have hit a full roadblock. Nowhere to go. Animesh looks up from his phone.

"Two days?" he says to me. His voice is drowned out by the rowdy crowd in the other room. "Jaldapara for two nights, starting tomorrow. Yes or no?"

"Yes!" I say. Yes, to anything, because it is better than what we have right now. Yes, because I can decide something for the first time. Yes, because Animesh is trustworthy and whatever he has set up must be the right next step. Yes.

I go back to the party in the other room, and I learn how to play carom. It is fun and I am terrible at it. Finally, I score a point, downing one chip into the net. Calm and happy now. A proper party, and the people are lovely. The game ends and we eat. Tony, the volunteer who drove me home on his motorcycle, has brought a big bowl of lamb *makhani*. He cooked it himself and brought it in a large bowl balanced on his bike. Jody says no thank you, because the food is spicy and she has suffered in the past. But these are my new friends and they have made this special food. Because of their kindness and persistence, a story is now possible. I eat and eat. Later, in the street we say goodbye to Animesh, it is likely we will not see one another other again during this trip. We hold on to each other's arms for a long time as if sharing a special message, a message of care and support. The blockages have yielded. As if by magic. A new journey ahead of us, purposeful again.

9

We are creatures of habit. Even as the routines are new, we have settled into them like an old married couple. Jody calls her mom and dad almost nightly, keeps the TV on, and sleeps as late as she can. I try to find a quiet place to call David, and text with the girls. Journal writing the day's events is a habit I end up too tired to keep up and I fall asleep early (with earplugs), waking at 4:00 A.M. and smuggle my yoga mat and coffee maker into the stifling, muggy, un-air-conditioned bathroom. At 7:00 A.M., when breakfast is finally available, I wake Jody with the Clash's "Should I Stay or Should I Go?" because she likes the Clash and because I'm too timid to wake her with my voice.

We order the same room service everyday: cheese omelet, paratha, and masala tea. I am always disappointed when it's finished and I want more tea. Today, we pack all our things, having no idea when or if we will be back. The driver will be here at 9:30 and our plan for now is to go to the elephant camp park that Animesh set up for us, stay for two days, write a permission letter for forest access, and wait, hoping it will come straightaway so we can have daily access to study the mahouts and elephants being used for conservation work in the parks.

Filled with fresh hope and purpose, we pile into the car for the second day in a row. This time we anticipate the twisty-turny mountain roads but have no sense of how rustic our accommodations may be. We stop for fresh bananas, mangos, and oranges as if we are about to go into the jungle with no access to food. At first, we follow the same route moving from urban Siliguri to the verdant mountains and fields of the Dooars. The drive grows longer than yesterday's excursion. We are headed to Jaldapara, part of a national protected forest and open to tourists. This is all we know. The highway winds through towns where the walkways are dirt and open markets, sundry shops, and cell phone stores cram in together before disappearing into open road flanked by alternating forest and long stretches of tea garden. A few times we take a wrong turn through dirt road villages where women walk with packages and men ride bicycles wearing lungis (a cotton cloth that is tied at the waist, similar to a sarong) and short-sleeved shirts or bare-chested. Again, I am struck by the glorious colors that the women are wearing, as if daring one to suggest that their basic existence suggests poverty.

After stopping a few times to ask directions, we reach a dense town. Torn and faded billboards offering safari rides and promises of luxury hotels rise above rows of retail buildings, some abandoned and boarded, others with people inside. The streets are clogged with cars and trucks that mostly seem to be going somewhere else. The road is punctuated by empty lots, closed hotels featuring cracked windows, and a vacant playground where peeling painted tiger- and elephant-headed seesaws suggest a more festive time.

We turn into a dirt lane with open metal gates, a worn sign with the resort name. To our left is a path leading to the Forest Department office. Several jeeps are parked outside in various stages of roofs on and off, and clusters of tourists—families with children, couples, groups of businessmen—are waiting, buying tickets, or loading into the vehicles. The main building is the kind of rustic befitting an ecolodge. Brown clapboard siding. Corrugated tin roof. A low-slung open dining hall embraced by thin leafy trees. Faded and chipped cement stairs lead to the lobby with sign overhead that reads OFFICE OF THE ECO TOURISM AND RESEARCH RANGE OF JALDAPARA NATIONAL PARK. What it lacks in freshness and style it makes up for with the grounds. A cheerful courtyard garden in full bloom surrounded by bright white low-latticed fencing and freestanding cottages backed by a thick forest.

"Oh no," Jody says as we park in front of the lodge lobby. "This is a tourist trap. Ugh, not what I was hoping for. This sucks. It's not even inside the park."

Not sharing her dismay, I am comforted by the serene grounds. There is a swing hanging from a wooden arch at the far end of the courtyard. I have the sudden urge to run over to it like a little girl, to pump my feet under and up, under and up, stretching out my legs until they are framed only by the blue sky. A butterfly lands on a nearby flower. There are many flowers, multiple colors all in orderly rows in beds bordered with bits of brick.

"The garden is pretty," I say. "It's nice to see some grass and flowers. But, yeah, it's definitely not the eco-huts with the elephants right next door like yesterday."

"It's a bummer we can't stay there. We should try again and see if there is something for after here. This is awful."

The lobby is basic: colonial-style wicker chairs and a single green cushioned couch along the wood walls are sepia-colored photographs of wildlife and famous visitors. Predominantly featured, over one of the chairs, is a photograph that I recognize from Mark Shand's book. It is Parbati Barua's father, Lalji, sitting atop his favorite elephant. The photo is faded and grainy. But there is no mistaking its subjects: the leopard, wrapped in the tip of the elephant's trunk, getting flung across the forest. This story is legendary. How Lalji's elephant was so devoted that he rescued his owner from a leopard attack. There must be some meaning to this place if this photograph is here. It seems like another crumb dropped along our cloud-shrouded path, helping us to know that we are headed the right direction.

After filling out an overwhelming amount of paperwork and relinquishing our passports for an indeterminate period, we are given keys and informed of the limited times the kitchen is open for meals. The officious clerk explains that our fare includes a jeep and elephant safari, which we must schedule with him the day before. We walk to our cabin; the romantic grounds have lost some of their luster. We start to unpack; the tension between us growing.

"I'm not going on a jeep safari. You can go. It's too touristy," Jody says.

"I'll go. Might as well at least see what's out there," I say. I am in a remote part of India at a national park that people travel to for a special wildlife experience. Why not see it?

She sets the fruit we bought at the market on the counter below the television. "Guess we won't be needing these. It's hardly like we're out in the jungle. Want to go to lunch now?"

Storm clouds gather and the wind picks up. The safari starts in two hours. No one is in the dining room; food service is not for another fifteen minutes so we check our email and retreat into ourselves. Earlier Jody told me that I reminded her of a Canadian. It was not meant as a compliment. In short, the globally savvy adventurer is saddled with an annoyingly friendly, inexperienced dork. I suspect she has grown weary of me, and the lack of photographic opportunities on this trip, days ago. The menu is limited but we discover that we both love masala peanut *chaat* with roasted peanuts, chopped cucumbers, onion, cilantro, and lime juice. Paired with French fries and chai with espresso, our moods lift a bit.

Jody walks me to the ticket booth like a big sister following instructions from mom. Advertisements on the plywood walls show safari-goers standing up out from jeep roofs, yet the vehicles in the driveway right now are completely covered. I fill out more paperwork, they are stamped and stamped again. After the fanfare, the clerk hands me a ticket and yells out, "Okay, Number 10, you can wait over there." "Over there" is a group of mostly male tourists standing about laughing and joking with one another. There seem to be about nine of them, and I suspect that this means I am the tenth, destined to be crammed in a fully covered vehicle with little hope for the kind of adventurous outdoor safari experience promised in the colorful brochures. A few of the men look away from the crowd to stare at me with openly questioning expressions; others look right through me as if I am invisible. I am not invisible, but awkward in my stark differences. For one, I am a woman and not wearing a colorful dress, but army-green cargo pants, a gray T-shirt, and a royal blue rain jacket. The sky is a dense gunmetal gray, certain to rupture open any moment. At least I have prepared for rain and am grateful for having the right clothing for the situation.

Jody and I decide that when I return we will write the draft for Forest Department permission. Once we have that, we believe our access to all the important stories will crack wide open. We'll be able to go off for hours and behind the scenes, document on our own free time. We imagine that this signed form will mean our freedom from the scourge of being a tourist.

The safari will at least let me get a sense of the park. My jeep is indeed covered, but the canvas sides are all rolled up for full viewing opportunity. I am the only English speaker and the only woman in a jeep with five men and a teenage boy. We start out along the bumpy road. Inside, the men are boisterously talking to one another, voices and bodies taking over the crammed space, filling it with heat from their breath, sweat from their girth. The teenager has his first camera, and all are eager that he gets the best photos. When we stop to see an Indian gore munching a meal, the boy's father instructs him to step over me so he can get the shot. No one speaks to me or returns my smile.

As we drive, I hold my cheek to the open air. A soft rain soaks my skin and I let it gather then stream down along my neck. The damp grasses, leaves, and vines that cover the jungle floor just beyond our road emit a strong smell of dank musty comfort. The guide keeps telling the driver to stop, then says, "Look, peacocks! Look, barking deer! Look, bison!" None of it seems remarkable. The sky splits open into a downpour and rain runs in torrents down tributaries along the dusty road, turning it to a sleek sheen of mud. The forest layers glow vibrant green.

Outside, some young men and women are freely riding bikes up and down the jeep road. Who are they? Why do they get to roam while I am confined to this vehicle? We pass a Forest Department camp, a collection of rooms in a building, some small houses, in which families are gathering. This is what Jody and I have envisioned. Staying in a compound like this, with a community, documenting the mahouts as they train and care for the elephants here. This camp, Jaldapara, is one of the largest elephant training centers in this region of India. There are over 150 working elephants here. I strain to see the pilkanas, but they are far from view. The bustling activity and open grounds in the distance suggests this is the location. The smell of wet earth and dung clings to the air. It must be close. We are here in hopes to see the working elephant camp. Now at least I know where it is.

Our jeep pulls up alongside a wooden structure, an observation tower with stairs that wind around to the top deck, open for viewing and covered for rain protection. The rain has stopped, and a hot sun immediately sets to work. The guide opens the door and gives instructions in Bengali. Then, in English, he says, "Go up to the top. Do not stop and walk around. You can take photos from there." The men push ahead of me to pile out. The smashed grass makes a trail from parking area onto the first step of the tower. A large meadow surrounds us. Green grasses in a variety of species and height are interspersed with patches of open dirt. In the distance thick trees rise from the edge of this grassy area, promising biodiversity that seems to be missing here. Even though this is a natural area, it has a feel of an abandoned parking lot.

I don't even see the elephants at first. On the other side of the observation tower stands a circular hut consisting of a thatched grass roof shaped like a paper hat a child might make. This roof is held up by about twelve slim tree trunks stripped of bark and silver from the baking sun. Two elephants are standing on hard-packed earth, in the shade under the roof, piles of fresh cut grasses surround their feet.

They are much smaller than the elephants you see in the movies or in wildlife photography of African safaris. These are Asian elephants, and their size makes them seem less intimidating, more approachable. And cute! The female, like all Asian elephants, does not have tusks, but the male with her is very small and has two tusks that look as if they are just beginning to sprout. He seems to have more growing to do and I immediately experience the pair as mother and child. Their heads are shaped in two rounded humps coming together into a thin gully. Coarse hairs stand straight up from the tops of these humps, looking like a cartoon character with drawn pencil lines for hair. Mesmerizing.

"Keep going, please." My reverie is interrupted by the guide, who is disturbed that I have fallen back from the group. I begin to climb the stairs. No one seems to notice the elephants; they are using binoculars to stare off across the fields toward the jungle, in hopes something wild will suddenly burst out. Once I reach the top, no one pays attention to me again.

When no one is looking, I walk down the first level of stairs to get a closer look. My first elephants! Why would I stare off at a meadow? They each pick bunches of grass from the pile and stuff into their mouths. *Mark this moment. Here they are. Eating their meal—a mother and her child.* I tell my mind to slow down, feel and smell everything, to celebrate this event.

The sun is a temporary flash of warmth; in just these few minutes clouds have rolled back in and the air is thick with moisture. Thunder rumbles. It is loud and close. *How did that happen so fast?* Rain begins again. The mother and calf seem unfazed by the sudden storm and keep eating. The group is keeping their distance from me and I can't understand anything being said, so I wander off alone. Daring to move closer while no one is watching, still perched and under cover but now on the backside of the stairs. Thunder rolls through long and low as if unfurling before all of us. The mother stops eating. She stretches her back left leg far behind her body and extends her trunk toward her calf but does not reach. I zoom my camera in close. Then I see it. A chain is wrapped around the back ankle of both mother and calf, each tied to post on opposite ends of the hut. The mother and her child cannot touch each other in any possible way, not even with fully stretched trunks. While the calf seems to have more movement, with space between post and foot, his mother's rear ankle is so tightly connected to the post that she has no mobility at all, beyond her other legs and trunk. I wonder if she can even sit or lie down. A surge of adrenaline runs through me like electricity.

Of course, chains are used to keep elephants tethered while in the pilkana, but I always thought they had freedom of movement, like one would leash a dog, horse, or camel when temporarily leaving them unattended. I expected to see chains on captive elephants, as they are such massive animals, but not this. I put my camera down, feeling shame and nausea. It would be such an easy thing to post this to social media and speak to the unethical treatment of the animals, bemoaning the cruelty. Why wouldn't I do that? But that is not why I am here. I cannot simply float one piece of the puzzle out into the wide world before I understand more about the situation, more about the context. I don't even know enough to know what I am seeing.

The pair triggers thoughts of my daughters, a rush of images, of each of them separated from their birth mothers as infants, imagining, as I have countless times, those final moments of walking away, permanently parting—Anhwei at twelve days, Goldie at two months. Images of me leaving for graduate school classes with Goldie wrapped around my legs crying and begging me not to leave her, Anhwei stoically pretending it is okay. They are elephants, but their bond as mother and child seems to transcend the difference in our species and unite us. This physical separation in plain sight, much like motherhood post-divorce, our physical time together cleaved in half. What anxiety to each of us. Choking back tears, I climb back into the jeep. Loneliness wraps itself around me like a heavy coat in damp stifling heat. This claustrophobia. I miss my girls. The tourists are irritating, the rain depressing. The symbolic jeweled elephant bought in Darjeeling and left wrapped until the right moment will not be opened in celebration of my first sighting tonight.

Back in the room, Jody is watching *The Hangover Part III* on television.

"How was it?" she asks.

"Fine," I say.

"Did you get a nap?" I ask.

"Yeah," she replies.

"Want to get dinner?" she inquires.

"Sure," I say.

The service takes forever and is frustrating. We eat in silence. Tomorrow morning, we have tickets for an elephant safari. We can document, but even if we take a thousand photos and interview the guide, we will only be seeing one elephant ride from a tourist's perspective. Still, it is closer than anything else available to us without official Forest Department permission.

Settling into our beds, Jody says, "I really want to go out on patrol with the Forest Department. It is the only way I am going to be able to tell this story. I need to get in a jeep at night with the rangers. I am going to ask if I can go with them at night, so frustrating not to have permissions. I hope that Parbati lets me go on the elephant journey with her. If I can just spend some time alone with her, I know I could warm her up, it would be epic to be in the jungle with her."

As I listen, still heartsick from the afternoon, the last bits of my patience seeps out the screen window. "Why do you keep saying *I* with everything? What about *we*? How will I get a good story if only you are experiencing it?" My head is on the pillow as I talk to the ceiling, hoping I don't crack and get emotional.

"I am not saying you can't experience it, but it's not like you can go spend three months with Parbati, you have a family and kids. *National Geographic* usually just sends a writer out for a few days to cover the story, while the photographer stays for a long time."

"Well, I'm not *National Geographic*. That's not how I work. I came all the way here so I could experience as much as possible and write about it. We agreed to do this as a team."

"It's just that everything is so much easier and accessible when I am alone. Adding a person makes getting permissions harder. Usually I could just slip in, make friends, and go. But I can't even jump on the back of a motorcycle because you're here too. Honestly, I'm sorry, but I will pick up and go anywhere without you in a second if it means getting the shot."

I am not sure what to say to this. We talk a little further, backing away from the tension, having cleared the air with directness. Not that we have changed the dynamic or desires and expectations, but we have reset.

By 8:30 A.M. the next day, we may have missed the window for good light, but it turns out we also missed a tempestuous storm. Now the sky is spent, and while the sun is still behind clouds, there is no rain. We don't know what to expect; we get into a car with a driver and guide who takes us through the park entrance, along the same road from yesterday's safari to another ecolodge whose expansive lawn opens out to a viewing area. Here, we join fourteen other people in an open field with salt licks placed throughout. Moments pass and an elephant calf comes, along with his mother carrying a howdah (a seat or covered pavilion designed to carry passengers—or, in the past, hunting parties—atop an elephant or camel) with four chair structures facing out, back-to-back. Eventually there are four elephants and two calves. Sixteen tourists in total. The passengers sit with iPads and phones blocking their view, taking video and photos. I tell myself I am researching, maybe to write a story on elephant parks in India and the people who come ride the elephants, but can't seem to muster the enthusiasm. The mahouts aggressively whack the heads of the elephants as they steer them to the platform; the tourists pay no mind. For that matter, Jody and I do not refuse to ride, or even question the ethics of what we are about to do. I tell myself again that I am here to document and observe. Neutrality is paramount until I can fully understand. Yet the vision of tightly tethered mother and baby is etched into my memory, and no matter how intellectually I attempt to approach it, the only thing that remains is despair. We ride, take pictures, we see an endangered greater one-horned rhino. The experience is simultaneously peaceful and disturbing, exciting and shameful. When it's over, we spend the rest of our day writing and sending the formal requests that we were too exhausted and irritable to finish the night before. I skip the afternoon safari but sign up for the dawn elephant ride just to see if anything changes. Jody opts to sleep in.

Our last morning, my alarm goes off at 4:00 A.M. for the dawn elephant safari. I wake to a flurry of texts from David and FH. Goldie has just been evacuated from her school, which caught fire in one room. While everyone and the building are safe, she was not permitted to return to her locker where her precious panda stuffed animal "Pandy," a constant companion since toddlerhood, was tucked into her backpack. This is a child who suffers from significant separation anxiety, a result of her earliest years' separation from both her birth mother and foster mother within her first ten months of life. Goldie has had reoccurring nightmares of losing Pandy and her blanket in a fire. Now here we are. My daughter is traumatized and suffering, and I am so far away that I cannot hold, hug, or provide any comfort to her.

I get dressed quickly and go outside so I can text and call before the jeep comes. Across the world, in the opposite time zone, a tiny voice so very far away begins to sob, words unable to come out.

"Take deep breaths," I say, forcing back my own tears. "Pandy is okay, you are okay. I love you." The words feel useless and hollow, so I stop talking.

We breathe together, cry a little together.

"When can you get him again?" I ask.

Silence and sniffing then, "Tomorrow."

"Alright, that's good. Not long. Just know he is sleeping and safe and you can go to sleep and wake up and by tomorrow all this will be a bad memory. Pandy will be in your arms again in just a few hours."

"I know," she says, her voice evening out a bit.

"I will send you a photo of the baby elephant," I say as a distraction. And this sets off a fresh round of despair for me. What will I be sending to her? A baby elephant chained to a post who can't reach her mother?

"Okay," she says, and I can feel her trying to be strong for my sake.

Goodbye is tearful on both ends. I choke on guilt and grief. Goldie is in good hands, well cared for, but I feel like I've fallen down on the job. I should be home with her; I feel too far away.

This time approaching the park, our car is held up by a line of trucks. Behind the cabs, high corrugated metal sides with no roof so sticks of hay flew out the top when the wind picked up. As we approach, I am shocked to see elephants standing and peering out from the sides. The trucks, painted with swirls of color and reminders to honk please, are all pulled over on the edge of the road. Scores of men are rushing about and tending to the animals, leading them off the trucks into the meadow.

"What is happening?" I ask. Today's guide has been chosen for me—he speaks terrific English, and so far has been very informative.

"The elephants are coming to Jaldapara for training. This is a mahout training camp. They will learn to patrol the park and carry tourists. No photos, please. I don't think that is allowed."

There is a lot of shouting and directing; we wait for a while, then go. This morning's ride is not half as exciting as what was happening along the park entrance. But my guide on the drive is a treasure trove of knowledge. He explains the workings of the park, the 150 elephants and almost 300 mahouts who live and train here and then are sent out to other national parks.

"The babies, you see," he tells me, "they are only with their mothers for two years. During this time, they are permitted to stay with their mothers for eating and riding, but after two years they must be separated. Calves must be trained and will be unruly if they stay too long with their mother. You can always tell when it has happened. The mother wails in anguish, she stomps and screams for days and days. You can hear her all over the area. It is very sad."

I think of Goldie. Losing her birth mother, then foster mother, now facing her greatest fears without me. My guide falls silent and looks out the window, discreetly granting my tears some privacy.

We convene at the meeting spot and again the elephants arrive to take us on the morning walk. There are fewer tourists this morning. From my seat near the front, I watch mother and her calf walk along and periodically entwine their trunks, breaking off branches as they go, feeding themselves along our journey. Yesterday I'd felt relief at their companionship, that at least they enjoyed this freedom of movement, but now the guide's words rip through me like tiny knives, opening fresh wounds from this morning's phone call and deepening the pain.

It feels impossible to get a clear handle on the story and my enthusiasm for it is rapidly waning. If I am going to continue, I must check my own bias, both ways—this is not a romantic tale, glorifying a bygone era, and it isn't a scathing investigative journalism piece on animal abuse. Our vision from the beginning is to unearth the complexity of the story and tell it clear-eyed, all sides.

For now, it feels like the only way to get a real picture of how captive elephants fit into the overall human-elephant crisis here is to get behind the scenes. Until we get formal permissions, it will remain a mystery, just out of reach. Last night we finished our request and sent it to the chief warden of West Bengal. There seem to be no wild elephants around the area, but the captive elephant story seems compelling and a good Plan B. We still have over a week left in India; if we get the permissions in time, we can still get part of the story. We believe that with our permissions, we will have access to everything, such as staying in Forest Department lodging, camping in the park with mahouts, and spending our days documenting every aspect of the mahout-elephant relationship.

As we are packing our bags for a return to Siliguri, Animesh texts us that one night has opened at the eco-elephant camp where we met Parbati. We will go directly there. Giddy with possibility, we are infused with fresh energy. There will be no internet and limited cell service. There are three meals and no menu. We have new appreciation for our roadside bananas. This camp is at the edge of a different national park and has six working elephants and twelve mahouts. When we pull into the grounds, we feel an odd sense of homecoming, thrilled with our luck. Our lodging is basic—a square wooden bed in the center of a round room, windows with no screens and views of expansive green rows of tea gardens. That evening we learn not to turn the light on with windows open, inviting every flying moth and tiny insect from the region vying for a space on the single bulb—a hard lesson we don't need to learn twice. We arrive in time for the elephant bathing and are permitted to go into the river and help the mahouts wash the elephants.

Unlike the other camp, here we walk directly to the river and are greeted by six freely swimming elephants in various sizes rolling around in the shallow riverbank, hosing each other off with their trunks. The mahouts have paired up with their *patawalla* (assistant and mahout in training) to wash, scrub, and groom their elephant.

For the first time since we began this project a week ago, Jody can properly photograph. She is fearless and focused as she wades thigh-high into the river, toward the largest elephant while his mahouts painstakingly tend to him. Her camera of choice for this session is a beautifully designed, Leica, with the ability to perform below the water's surface. A gray-white sky is a blank canvas in the distance; along the horizon line thick forest provides a swath of emerald green. The meadow stretches to the riverbank, ending in clumps of grass interspersed with mounds of course sand. Leafy trees are like sculptures against the chalky sky. The river is so placid that the reflection is a distinct mirrored image, extraordinary in detail.

The tusker is named Suriya. He is the most massive elephant I have seen so far. His mahout, Faridul, is a slight young man whose limbs appear as long and thin as his torso, muscles sinewy and taut; his kneecaps, with every bone defined, jut out from under his rolled-up khaki pants. He is filing Suriya's nails with a forearm-length kukri sword, curved for hacking down grasses, flat-surfaced with ridging that apparently is the perfect tool for elephant manicures.

Jody leans down into the river, soaking her pants and tank top, ponytail tip creating the slightest circular ripple as she bends herself sideways. Then she waits until the water is so calm that it difficult to discern which way is up. Faridul and his patawalla are now standing on either side of Suriya. The patawalla, ankle-deep in the shallow part of the river, reaches with his left hand to touch the pink speckled tip of Suriya's curved and jagged-edged ear. Faridul, on Suriya's other side, has his back turned to us, palm outstretched as he catches the water droplets that drip from Suriya's flank. They slip through his thin fingers and continue to the river below. Human fingers to elephant ear, elephant skin pressed against human hand. Feet planted on the wet earth, surrounded by water, embraced by oxygen. The water is so still it reflects the entire scene, continuing the connection of man and elephant and nature and turning them into an organic circle, reflected in the water and part of the sky, milky white sky, earth in water, water in sky, all suspended and reflected as one.

Calling to their charges after bathing, each mahout climbs up along the rear back of his sitting elephant. When the mahout is properly situated, bareback, the elephant stands, and the pair gracefully saunter along the path toward their well-kempt pilkana. Here, the elephants will eat a feast of gathered and freshly cut banana tree stalks and carefully packed pods filled with nutritional supplements.

This feels like something softer, more compassionate, less brusque and disconnected. One of the mahouts has chalk and is drawing designs on his elephant's head—pink jewels, yellow swirls of labyrinths, and her name, Diana. He looks at her with an expression of fondness and love, she stands still, even tilting her head a bit so he can reach her.

At dusk, we sit at the watchtower, a smaller structure that has a single built-in bench and wooden gate that opens in for reaching the elephants. Across from the pilkana, Faridul is getting Suriya ready for a different departure. The division beat officer waits with his pre-independence rifle for the pair to complete preparations for night patrol. When they are ready, the officer gets behind Faridul. They remind me of warriors preparing for battle. The team is preparing for an overnight shift patrolling the core of the park, protecting the most precious resource, the endangered greater one-horned rhino. Earlier today, the beat officer who is about to head out for patrol told me a story about this elephant-mahout team.

"It was late at night and I received a call that there was a very large elephant herd in a nearby village. Maybe over one hundred elephants. The farmers and the other patrols were not having any success driving these elephants out. The entire crop fields were being destroyed, a year of work. Our last hope was this koonkie elephant, Suriya, to drive the herd back into the forest. Faridul and I went to the village. It is not far. We rode Suriya there."

Faridul is barefoot, all tendon and lean muscle in khaki shorts and a polo-style shirt, thick black hair balancing out his chiseled face. He leads Suriya along the path, past us, and into the forest. The short stocky beat officer sitting sidesaddle on the back. The low sun streams through the leaves, illuminating Suriya's flank as they saunter away from me. The words from the earlier story float through.

"When we arrived," the beat officer said. "There was a frightening-sized herd. I have never in my life seen so many wild elephants in one place.

Faridul instructed me to hold on. I admit, I was absolutely terrified. 'Do not be afraid,' he told me. 'I trust Suriya completely.' Then we charged into the herd, successfully corralling them back into the forest. They were both so calm and cool. I had never experienced anything like it."

The captive elephant-mahout relationship and how Forest Departments are utilizing elephants for conservation is unexpected and compelling. This is a new story, one that connects to Parbati Barua, who we will spend time with our next trip. No one spoke of special elephant-human teams who help with conflict mitigation when we were in Darjeeling. I'm so curious. Until now, I always thought of India's captive elephants as abused: forced to walk on hot pavement in crowded cities, chained to cement pillars in tiny temples, and carrying dozens of tourists on their backs. While all that exists, there is more to it. The human-elephant relationship has a long cultural and spiritual history, far more complex that we can learn in a day or two. We seem close to understanding a deeper story here. Only, we have only been here one day and will have to leave after tomorrow. We don't have official permissions yet to interview and photograph any more deeply than an ecocamp tourist. Hard to see beyond the veil.

However, we believe we are just hours away from getting permission from the Forest Department. So, the next morning, after breakfast and before checkout, we borrow bicycles and set out to find a place that we can stay, close to the camp. Maybe we can beg our way in to watch the bathing and interview some mahouts.

The surrounding village is like something from a tropical island. Huts on stilts, brightly colored shirts and sarongs flapping from lines stretched across garden plots, roosters in yards, baby goats with small strings roaming the roads. The first two places have promising signs, but dismal lodging. We ride up a drive to Riverwood Forest Resort. Our expectations are low, as "resort" seems unlikely in such a rustic area. We walk into the lobby, and it is surprisingly cool with fans. Beyond the glass office is a courtyard with shade trees, abundant flowers, and winding paths.

"Hello, may I offer you some fresh mango juice?" says the manager who comes out from his office. His features are rounded, soft, and friendliness emanates—it is more than obligatory hospitality—from his eyes. He is genuinely kind. "My name is Lama. Welcome to Riverwood."

The answer to mango juice is yes, and it arrives almost immediately, sweet and cold, an elixir. I will do anything to move in here right this moment. Knowing Jody's penchant for austerity, I am dismayed when she says, "Let's just ride around a bit more and see what is out there." Thankfully, the lure of mangoes and air conditioning proves too great, even for Jody, particularly as the price is very good in the offseason.

Here there is a Nepalese influence and we order *momos*, plump, homemade doughy dumplings stuffed with veggies, after we settle in. Through persistent and pleading phone calls and email messages all the way up the chain to the chief warden, we secure exactly one more morning to watch the elephant feeding and one more afternoon to watch the bathing. Then we must sit tight until we have any more permissions.

With Lama's assistance, I can ask the mahouts questions, and, because of our temporary permission, we are treated like a photographer/writer instead of tourists. The mahouts, who have been curious about us, welcome us into the pilkana. The one day granted is very helpful, but still the permissions do not come. Thankfully, Jody has sublime photographs of elephants and their mahouts. This snippet of time has only stoked my desire to know more, understanding that only the barest surface of this story has been scratched. Also, after watching the mahouts use their kukris for everything from chopping grasses and stalks to digging holes, carving designs, and grooming elephants, I am keen to bring home one of these historic small swords. Lama tells me they were designed by the Nepalese thousands of years ago. Not only do they function as a multiuse agricultural tool, they are also extremely effective instruments of war. He has offered to take me to a shop where they sell them.

Jody says, "Why get a new one? I'm sure you could buy one from the mahouts. They would probably appreciate the money. It would have a lot more character—they carve the sheaths."

"Really? That's such a great idea! Do you think they would do it?" Even as I want an actual mahout sword so badly, my body goes into fear mode, imagining how awkward and nervous I am to ask. We don't have permission to return to the camp today, I'm afraid of breaking the rules, intimidated to ask the question, and have literally no idea how to barter or what it should cost.

Lama offers to translate, and we set out for the camp, arriving through the entrance as if we belong there. We ask a mahout as he passes the courtyard. He tells us to wait here, he will spread the word and see. In a few moments, he returns with Faridul and three kukris. The one that Faridul is offering as intricate geometric carvings burnt up and down the entire sheath. The top end has a shoelace-thick string wrapped and secured for tying around his hips. Faridul's kukri is the only one being offered that has a full tang. It has been well-used, as there is a patina along the blade. Of course, I want that one. We agree on a price that makes us both grin broadly at one another.

By the end of our stay, we have the beginnings of a story, but far from a full one. When we return, there will be a plan, no chasing ghosts and begging for permissions. We will come back to India to spend time observing and learning from the icon, the legend, Parbati Barua. I am still not certain how I will approach my family about coming back here, and so soon. This was meant to be the one big expedition. But the past two days have given me new energy. I can see more of what is possible, the beauty and complexity. The lure of access to a legendary woman who has made a life in a man's world is so compelling to me, I momentarily forget about not witnessing the wild elephant conflict.

As we begin our journey back to Siliguri, Jody and I have come to terms with our disappointments and are emerging with a sense of accomplishment, weary from effort, but ultimately we feel we made the most of all opportunities.

The landscape from Dooars back to Siliguri now seems a familiar route, the flapping prayer flags and monkeys along the Coronation Bridge, rows of concession stands and soda sellers offering wares to the clogged at the intersection traffic. The endless green of tea gardens giving way to the beginning of a bustling town that is Siliguri. Windows open, breeze through our hair, there is a strange sense of homecoming, of completion, the certain knowledge that our mission has come to an end for now. A comfort in knowing there is promise of the next one. To the symphony of truck horns, motorcycle roars, music rising and falling from tuk tuks and cars, shouts from vendors, we find ourselves making the transition from professional work partners back into friends. Over our last bits of Dairy Milk Bubbly chocolate, we talk about our lives and loves, past and present.

"Did I ever told you about Chris?" Jody says.

"No, not much," I said, "Tell me."

"He was a unicorn. A beautiful and special soul that made everyone feel amazing to be around him. Chris was my brother's friend. I met him in Alaska, and we hit it off immediately. I had a good job, but it was in an office in a city. I was growing restless and depressed over being in a cubicle all day."

We are stopped at a light. Ahead of us is a bus, crammed so full of people that arms and heads are thrust out of windows at odd angles. On the roof among the piles of luggage are men crouched catching a ride. Earlier this week, during our downtime, Jody asked me if I had any interest in riding on top of a bus, hoping to try and hop one through part of India before the practice was banned. It is hard to imagine Jody contained in a cubicle.

While I am thinking about this, she continues, "Chris offered me a year, to come with him and live in his van, leave my job. Take my camera and we would live along the Pacific coast, surfing every day, paragliding. I would have the gift of time to figure out what I wanted to do. We would get married and travel, have children and travel the world with them."

Jody does not have children; she travels almost nonstop. My children are at home with a caregiver, waiting for me. But they are likely not waiting as much as living their lives. It is compelling to imagine a life where my daughters could travel with me. Jody, with her carefree adventurous spirit, could do it. I imagine her children, tangled hair, half-naked chasing after their wild mother along a Moroccan beach.

"I put in my notice to leave my job," Jody says.

I steel myself for what I know comes next.

"On my last morning, packing the remaining things on my desk, I got a phone call. Chris had been killed in a paragliding accident in Sun Valley."

Like a movie where you already know the ending, but still wish with all your might that this time it will end differently.

"What did you do?" I ask. This was the part of the story I didn't know.

"I went and did exactly what we'd planned. Only I did it by myself."

I want to cry and do, but these are not my tears to shed. It dawns on me that all this time I have been seeing Jody as a woman made of steel, who is happiest when living life on the razor's edge. This entire trip I have felt like the foolish and meek sidekick to her superhuman, savvy, and stoic self. But with context I see my friend more clearly. The decade spent on a sailboat, doing laps around the world while seasick, her failed marriage, her steadfast insistence on traveling alone, the risks she takes. This tough woman who calls her parents every night, who seeks a partner who is kind and generous, but can never quite get back what was taken from her. Straddling the fine line between adventure and isolation, daring and recklessness. I realize that this is vulnerability, that we are not fundamentally so different after all. That our differences are rooted in the way we respond to fear, how we face a challenge. Jody has taught me so much about myself this trip—through her actions, in the unsaid moments, observing how she handles herself. Because of her example, I have grown stronger and more confident. Most of all I've learned through Jody how to be flexible, to let change flow through me as it is impossible to maintain control.

After tonight, Jody will go on to Bali and I will head home from Delhi. Returning to Haveli Hauz Khas, my room and the courtyard are havens, yet this time I have courage to venture beyond. There is a new voice inside. A persistent whisper: *dive deep*. So much to tell, too much to understand all at once. The feeling of Himalayan mist on my cheek; the bristled wire hairs barely visible atop of an Asian elephant's head against my open palm; the ache in my thighs where I stretched to fit across the wide back of a painted pachyderm, rocking me through the dense brush. In my bag is the small, adorned elephant found in a shaman's shop, clods of mud-packed earth from the damp path to the Murti River, and Faridul's kukri in a carved wooden sheath. In my heart are new friends who hold the hope of an added voice to amplify their cries for peaceful coexistence. I feel like I'm departing during the beginning of a terrific series, episode one. Pieces of this place and unfolding story will come home within me but will be alien to my family. Still, I'm eager to return and discover more.

10

May 2018. Finally, home. Midmorning in Sun Valley, Idaho, finds me floating in a hammock under two thick pine trees that stretch up into a bluebird sky. The snow has melted from the yard, leaving mounds of vole trails along the dirt at the edge of the fence and clumps of leaves where daffodils will sprout. The mountain next to our house is a blanket of evergreens punctuated by leafless groves of bone-white aspens with snow still clinging to the rock faces. The sun is high enough to warm my skin. David brings out a chair so he can sit with me. He indulges my need to talk and talk, tell stories and relay minutia in endless detail. A good listener and best friend, he holds my hand as I give in to exhaustion, drifting in and out of sleep. There is no time for jet lag, though I am hit hard. Trying to climb out of the upside-downs and transform back into my role as mom and wife. The girls will be here after school today. Goldie's thirteenth birthday is in a few days and I am frantic to put on a good party. As a special treat, I am surprising the girls with a long weekend holiday to Sundance Resort, a place we loved when they were very young. It is a lavish indulgence, but worth it when I have been gone so long. I'm eager for mother-daughter time, to reconnect. In this way, I return home like a rocket plunging through the atmosphere.

When we depart for Sundance, the girls are excited but a bit wary. Anhwei has traveled to Utah several times over the ski season for races and she is hardly eager for the boring five-hour road trip. Still, we stop for snacks and have the enthusiasm of a small, determined team, setting out to accomplish a goal. The drive feels longer than we expected and the easy banter we have enjoyed gives way to complaining.

"My butt hurts," Goldie says from the backseat.

"Ugh, this town is dismal. How do people even live here?" says Anhwei, my copilot. We are crawling along Main Street with most visible signs of history erased. Stoplights every few blocks give ample opportunity to take in the scenery. Fast-food franchises are sandwiched in with mom-and-pop stores with names like Grannie's Diner. Elaborate spires of Mormon temples anchor both ends of the town. While the flat landscape is squared off with acres of agriculture, a looming mountain range provides a dramatic backdrop. From here, we begin our climb through the mountain pass, along a rushing creek, into a tight canyon where waterfalls stream from the rock faces. If we open the windows (and I do), you can smell fresh evergreens in the brisk damp air. Years ago, when the girls were very young, I took them to Sundance. When we reached the canyon, I would play special music—a dulcimer CD from an old friend who had died. This part of the drive was always a transition point, from the monotonous highways to a magical wonderland where all our problems would be temporarily suspended.

The girls no longer remember these trips beyond the photos that remain. They would not like the music, and I no longer have it. Instead, while we wind our way toward the tucked-in resort, I talk about elephants and India.

"You would not believe how tall they are. When I rode on top of her, I had to sit like I was on a horse, only their backs are much, much wider than a horse, it was like doing a split!"

Goldie barely nods; Anhwei says, "That's cool."

But I can tell she is only saying that to be polite and to show me she's listening, particularly in the face of Goldie's silence. This is often the way. I start to tell another story, but fall silent and think a bit before asking,

"Who is the Winter Soldier exactly?"

With that Anhwei perks up and opens up to tell me all about the characters in *The Avengers*. We saw the movie together, but I had struggled to keep up given my lack of Marvel character knowledge.

"The Winter Soldier is actually Bucky Barnes," says Anhwei. "He was Captain America's best friend in the 1940s during the war."

"How did they live so long?" I ask.

"Well, they did, and they didn't. Bucky fell off a train while he and Captain America were fighting HYDRA. Everyone thought he was dead, but actually Dr. Zola brainwashed him, gave him a bionic arm, and froze him in time until HYDRA could use him as The Winter Soldier—a bad guy assassin. Captain America was given superpowers by the government during the war. He's actually an artist, a quiet guy, but they injected him with stuff to make him able to fight. After the war, they froze him so they could use him later. He had a girlfriend. Peggy. It was sad at the end of that movie because she thought he died. Well, I mean he did die, but not really."

We are at the top of the pass, with views of the valleys, farmlands, and lake below. The depressing streets of an old town have been reduced to dots. Low clouds drift and hover along the ridges of the mountain faces. Almost there. It's rare for Anhwei to talk this much. I'm eager to listen and to try and follow all the storylines. She has become deeply attached to the Marvel characters; their perseverance and strength seem to be an inspiration.

"Captain America is supposed to kill the Winter Soldier for an assignment. But, when they meet, Captain America recognizes that the Winter Soldier is actually his friend Bucky. He is so loyal that he refuses to kill him. Instead, he tries to deprogram him and bring him back to his original self. It doesn't work at first. But Captain America doesn't give up. Eventually, though, he is able to do it. This is all in *Captain America: The Winter Soldier*."

Gone is the irritation, with fresh energy and enthusiasm as she continues, carefully unknotting each superhero's origin story and how they all met.

We are driving along the creek now; it is surging with spring runoff. Above us, a waterfall streams from an opening between the rocks.

"Look! Look at that waterfall!" I say. Goldie is asleep in the back. Anhwei misses it entirely.

At Sundance, the girls take advantage of the complimentary tea in the lobby as I check in.

Years ago, it was Sundance that inspired FH's and my cabin on the lake. We wanted to capture this active spirit that Robert Redford created to host filmmakers and screenwriters in a hotbed of creative force surrounded by nature's energy.

We sold that house last year. The costs were exorbitant to maintain. That little house was built on dreams I failed to achieve. But Sundance is still here. Still smelling like cedar and comfort, reminding me of something I wanted to give, feel I can still give, even amid that which is lost.

A decade ago, we walked these pathways, Goldie on my shoulders, Anhwei holding my hand, and FH taking pictures. The same photos that he sends now, flooding my phone with daily texts, images of our daughters as babies, of me with the girls when they were little and I stayed home full-time to care for them. Reminding me, and reminding him, of times we can never return to no matter how desperate the desire. He often sends them late at night and they are the first thing I wake up to. These photograph texts confuse me as I am unsure if he is sending them as poignant memories to cherish, or if he sends them out of anger, and because he is grieving for that time in our lives and he wants me to hurt too. I suspect the latter, even as I try to experience them as the former.

I try to remind myself that we are here right now. Me and my daughters. I have arranged for a pottery class and a hike to a waterfall with a picnic lunch. We have dinner reservations, with ice cream for dessert. I told them they can pick out something special in the gift shop. There has been a lot of travel for me these past few months. We all feel off-balance.

"Eww," Anhwei says from the deck outside. "There are dead bugs all over the top of the hot tub!" I come out. We were planning on slipping in before dinner. She is right. Several fat flies with glossy green eyes are floating and swirling. An intricate cobweb is draped between the steps and the lip of the tub. Flies and spiders. For all their toughness, both my daughters have a substantial fear of flies and spiders.

"Okay, hang on," I say, "I'll fix it. Go back inside both of you. I'll get you when it's ready."

My hand scoops the flies out of lukewarm water. The heat is not on. There is a layer of yellow pollen across the top. Finding the temperature gauge, I crank the heat. Time is running out. I swish the water around, hoping to dissolve the pollen but only succeed in marrying yellow to the gritty dirt that has settled to the bottom.

We are not precious. These girls camp in the woods, they paddle in snowy weather, swim in mountain lakes with all kinds of bugs and detritus floating around it. Inside our room, they are shivering in their suits, annoyed by the insects and having to wait. I am not sure why they are acting so irritated, spoiled even. I think of the flying bugs swarming the bulb in India, my gratitude for a toilet, how a glass of mango juice tasted like nectar of the gods after a steady diet of rice, lentils, and tea. The extravagance of the room suddenly feels out of proportion to the real world, or at least the world I was just inhabiting. It seems too that the luxury is lost on my daughters. They neither notice, nor appreciate it.

"Is everything okay now?" Goldie calls out.

Everything is not okay. I begin to realize this trip is a misguided endeavor to assuage guilt and make up for lost time.

Sundance is a misfire.

I am not pursuing this elephant project in India to be a good role model for my daughters. Even as I do hope they see me as courageous and independent, with the adventurous spirit that they value. In an ideal scenario, my actions will help them see that being a mother does not mean giving up your dreams and aspirations—it does not have to require lopping off whole parts of your drive and personality until you exist only in service to others. I want to show my daughters that following your passions, whether science or politics, baking, art, and/or parenthood, are what you must chase with all your heart. That by first being true to yourself is the only way to give fully to others. And living your soul's code is what makes the hard things in life feel bearable. I want to be able to show all this and also have them be clear that they are my most important priority. After Sundance, my steps toward this reality still feel so unsure.

At the beginning of their lives, my daughters both suffered traumatic experiences—abandonment by their birth parents. The stuff of fairy tales, provoking nightmares in children everywhere actually happened to these two girls. To prepare myself for the type of mother I thought they would need in the aftermath, I created my version of the perfect parent from a combination of my childhood desires and the impossible advice of popular parenting magazines. As a result, I set out to show my daughters that mothers are home when they get home at the end of the day; that their mother will always wake them up with kisses and joy in the morning, serve them hot chocolate and pack their favorite foods for lunch. That they can count on their mother to reliably drive them to school and always be on time at pickup. I vowed to myself that my daughters would return home to a calm, organized house brimming with snacks and dinner. My role is to help them with homework and be available to problem solve on an as-needed basis, give bubble baths and then read stories at bedtime. Consistency and care. Isn't that what I committed to? What I believe the job requires at its absolute best? As unrealistic as it sounds, I set myself up with this idealized version of the kind of mother I would be for them. Determined to make up for what they had lost, to assure them they would be safe from now on.

Since I've returned from India, full of new information and curiosity, I am eager to return, flush with excitement over the idea of making a difference out in the world again. Truthfully, I am struggling with the push and pull of my identity. Before I was a mom, I had an intense career, traveled constantly, and felt the fulfilment of doing something important that can create meaningful change. When I became a mom to Anhwei and Goldie, I jettisoned all of that to pour every ounce of myself into nurturing them. As I began to take baby steps out into the world again, it became confusing—how to strike the right balance.

Motherhood does not pace itself. We sacrifice our bodies, mind, and spirit until we run on empty, then below empty, seeking small spaces to fill up, just enough to keep going. Seemingly inexhaustible. One day, we wake up and it's over. That fast. Our children are launched out into the world, rarely requiring our services in quite the same way again. We peer into empty bedrooms, see ourselves in the mirror, and wonder where our lives went. All those classes, careers, and relationships we may have pushed down the road until our children were grown evaporate in the ether of loneliness and confusion. Our identities revoked overnight.

The weekend is not a total bust. There are moments. The hilarious movie we watch together, laughing uproariously while eating takeout ice cream; functional bowls we learn to make with clay on a potter's wheel that we can proudly bring home as a reminder, the hike to the waterfall where Goldie runs ahead like a gazelle and Anhwei and I talk along the trail. The hot tub eventually gets hot enough, but never loses its grittiness. Still, the girls dutifully get in it, faking enthusiasm to show me that they appreciated my efforts. Somehow, I get the feeling that all this is for me. What they seem to cherish is not the thick comforters in front of an open rock fireplace or lavish eggs Benedict for breakfast overlooking a flower garden, but my attention to them and what they love. They need me to see them, to listen to them, Avengers and all. I feel like I do this every day, even when I am traveling, but it seems I have more to do, even though I don't know how I can do better.

As we pack up and load the car, I go back into our room, looking for any remaining items. The fresh smell of cedar has combined with the smell of my rose-musk perfume, the girls' strawberry shampoo, and the dank bit of sweat we generated over the days. We remain as an after-image in this place of dreams, imprinted here, at least for now. Into the car for the trek home, we are well-fed and our bags a bit heavier than they were when we arrived. As we go back through the canyon, I point out the waterfall again. This time they both see it and call out, "Whoa!" "Cool, that thing is HUGE!" When we reach the highway, I ask Anhwei to tell me more about the Marvel characters. She tells me some, but it comes out as an effort. I let it go. Each returns to their own, reading, listening to music.

When the girls are back in school, I will return to India. I will be gone for almost three weeks again.

My parents and sister do not know that I am going back. I am afraid to tell them. Other than David, who understands enough to give me the benefit of the doubt, I have told very few people. When I have tried, my words get stuck, my mission suddenly sounding frivolous: "I am leaving my family and flying to India, without any sponsorship or payment, to spend time with an elusive elephant guru and former princess so I can understand the elephant conflict along the Himalaya, and hopefully to write a book about it." By the end of that run-on sentence, people's eyes glaze over, confused and lost about what exactly I am trying to do. They typically respond with a bland, "Oh, that's interesting. Who watches the girls while you are gone?" The implication is clear: I am a fifty-year-old mother of two, what gives me the right to embark on such a fantastic journey?

Already I am having to fight FH to allow me a week with the girls to balance some of my time missed. Even as the days on the calendar show me at quite a loss, the aftermath of divorce often finds the survivors basing each scheduling and financial decision on ill logic. He refers to all my trips as "vacations," regardless of whether I am traveling to build my career. When I am gone, FH sends me photos of himself and the girls cooking dinners, camping, kayaking, and videos of Anhwei practicing for ski team. When I ask for extra days, he will begrudgingly grant me one or two, but no more. It is a constant battle between us.

The erratic cadence of his communications is unceasing, creating tremendous emotional strain. Not just photos, but FH's communications arrive almost daily, many at wee hours of morning or dead of night, sometimes mountains of them, sometimes the rough ones are followed by days of silence until the pattern starts up again. Over the past four years and counting, the texts come in spaced minutes or hours apart, almost daily. The flurry of texts, ranging from new band recommendations to accusations that I ruined his career, are still unceasing.

A tremendous amount of my energy is allocated to managing these texts and my responses. I accept this constant barrage as the consequence of divorce with children. I live with the communications as atonement, in penance for having caused pain. Sometimes I fight back or I sympathize and feel bad; often I praise and encourage. I hide these exchanges and any of my struggle from the girls, hoping to maintain an illusion that they have stability, even with two homes. I don't yet see the ways I fall victim to his gaslighting, nor how my inability to set boundaries and fight back is putting my daughters at risk. For all my efforts to try and break the binds and free myself, FH still has the ultimate leverage and he wields it masterfully.

We are stuck in traffic as we head north from Salt Lake City after our Sundance trip. Tractor trailers, commuters, and pickup trucks all reduced to a crawl. There is no sense worrying about what is going to happen tomorrow when I have the girls with me, in this car, right now.

"Did you guys have fun?" I say.

"Yeah," they respond in unison.

I look in the rearview mirror at Goldie, in elaborate braids twirled around the sides of her head like Princess Leia in *Star Wars*. Pandy and her "Blankie" are next to her, she is engrossed in her iPad. I think about her greatest treasures locked in her locker overnight, while the school was evacuated because of a fire and I was in India, fast asleep.

"How are you?" I ask.

She looks up at me and catches my eyes in the mirror, mind processing what I am actually asking.

"Good," she says.

"What was the best part of the weekend for you?" I say, even as I know she wants to go back to her game. Even as I know this is for me and not for her. That I'm just trying to grasp something I can't hold, that will never be mine.

She indulges me. "I liked making the pottery. And it was cool watching the guys do the glassblowing." Like an amusement park puppet, she puts her head back down to signal that she is finished. Indulgence over.

"Anhwei," I say. And my oldest, dutiful daughter looks up. Sets her book down. Gives me all the attention I am asking for because she knows I need it and maybe because she knows she needs it too. "What was your favorite part?"

"The food," she says. "And the movie. That was really funny."

With that we launch into a recount of all the scenes in *Wedding Crashers* that made us laugh.

The movie is an old one, and probably inappropriate. Goldie zoned out for most of it. But Anhwei loved it and we are having fun talking about it now. Doubled over in laughter as we remember certain parts. In this way we make our way home, back to reality.

When we finally pull into the driveway of our house and go inside, I am struck by how the vitality I hoped to create at Sundance is here, right now. It is in our home, in the warmth of wood walls and smells of cedar and damp pine trees, of sandalwood candles and a crackling fire in the woodstove. In our living room are the cozy couch and armchair we used to curl up on for stories in our lake cabin and the coffee table that my father built from an Old West wagon wheel. In the corner, along a row of windows, is the partner desk. On top of it, two thick photography books with my writing and imprint credits inside: *Born to Ice* and *Amaze*. In a stack on the corner, several copies of *Sidetracked* magazine with my story about Alegra Ally's journey with the Nenets in Siberia. Outside, the sun is setting behind the layers of foothills. Upstairs, a pink alpine glow lights up the Sawtooth Range visible from the shared office that my father designed and built. I realize that over the past five years everything, and yet nothing, has changed. I am still a mother. These teenagers are still my daughters. Building a new career and going to India has not, and will not, change that. I am loved and supported in a healthy marriage, showing my children personal growth and loving relationships. Maybe I am doing okay. Maybe the girls are also doing okay.

PART III

SEARCHING FOR THE ELEPHANT QUEEN

I believe in everything until it's disproved. So I believe in fairies, the myths, dragons. It all exists, even if it's in your mind. Who's to say that dreams and nightmares aren't as real as the here and now?

—widely attributed to John Lennon

11

My childhood was spent living in a back-office apartment of my grandparents' motel in Ocean City, New Jersey. My parents managed the small ocean-side property and we lived there year-round, even as the offseason was gray and deserted, with most of the town shuttered. In the summer, the rooms were all booked with eager families who spent their days strolling the boardwalk, eating pizza and cotton candy, playing miniature golf together, getting their thrills on amusement park rides, and spending long days bodysurfing. I'd make friends with the kids who came to stay and we'd play Marco Polo in the swimming pool. Every Sunday they would pack up their car, loading pinwheels and hermit crabs, sunburnt with sand still stuck to their skin. The girls and I would say tearful goodbyes, our small hands waving until they disappeared down the street, over the bridge that was clogged with traffic, and back to the cities and suburbs. In those moments, I beamed with a sense of pride. As my friends pulled out of the lot, away from the ocean and the treats that lined the boardwalk, I remained. An enviable position. Of course, we did not shop for trinkets, go to the amusements, or have endless helpings of funnel cakes and soft-serve ice cream every day of the summer. Our parents worked long hours and we hung around within earshot, coloring and playing and waiting for something to happen. But we could hear roaring waves and seagulls, of roller coasters and happy screams, we knew it would take only a few steps for it to be ours. The pleasures of vacations seemed always within grasp. Knowing that on Sunday afternoon I could walk to the mostly empty beach and catch waves without bumping into anyone else and have an ice cream cone without waiting in line; just knowing I could do that set forth my fervent desire to live in a place that served as a sought-out destination for others.

Over the years, these wondrous dots on the map have contributed to lost jobs and broken hearts, been responsible for my choices in boyfriends and circuitous career paths. Concentrated centers of delicious food, interesting people who come in and out like the tide, and the extraordinary energy of wild nature. Life at the edges of wilderness, within the embrace of an open sky, along a shifting color palette of granite or water, under the spell of a riot of dazzling stars, at the mercy of violent storms, seismic disruptions, or elemental threats, reminds me every day of nature's bestowed gifts and ultimate power: fire, floods, avalanches, earthquakes, tsunamis. My attraction to these places is both moth to a flame and my Great Spirit.

North India along the Himalaya is such a landscape, and when Jody and I return to Dooars at the end of August 2018, we find it transformed by the monsoon. Wisps of clouds hang low and layered, rain arrives in relentless torrents. Riverbeds are no longer dried-out ditches where workers dig for stone, but now a rushing brown current spilling out over embankments. The dampness saturates our breath and smooths our high-altitude-sapped skin with moisture. The heat is relentless. I thought rain would mean cool. But the downpours come and go without a change in temperature. Steam rising from asphalt as motorcyclists shake off the drops and continue onward. Sun bearing down as if angry with the storms that threaten her reign. Monsoon is a season here—vaguely between spring and fall.

All the national forests are closed to tourists during monsoon season. But we are equipped with our special Forest Department permission letter that finally came through a month after our return last May. Parbati has, through her mysterious powers, arranged to meet us at Dhupjhora, the elephant camp at the edge of Gorumara National Park where we met her for the first time. We will be staying with her at the ecocamp, but only the Forest Department staff, mahouts and elephants, and Parbati Barua, who will arrive later today, will be here. She has gifted us ten days to interview, observe, and photograph her as she conducts a training for mahouts and works with the elephants here. I'm giddy with excitement and feeling far more confident in the comfort of returning to known places.

After meeting up in Siliguri, Jody and I have spent the last two days at Riverwood Forest Resort to see Lama and avail ourselves of air conditioning, good food, and the internet, so we are refreshed and ready for our journey with Parbati. "Come by anytime you need to," Lama says. We have booked a few nights after our time with Parbati ends, and already I'm looking forward to returning.

Each of the raised camp huts are under construction, except for ours. Perhaps even ours, as they are moving piles of fresh plywood away from the stairs as Bupesh, the manager, sees us arrive. High-pitched chainsaws, thunking hammers, running diesel motors, and shouts above the cacophony invade the formerly tranquil setting. "Hello! Hello!" Bupesh seems happy to see us, a much different situation than last time when we were a source of pesky trouble for him. Now we are welcomed as special guests and led to our room. "Parbati is not here yet," he says. "Maybe, a few more hours."

"Okay," Jody says, "We'll go watch the bathing while we wait."

Bupesh's face turns sour. "The park is closed right now. I need permission from my supervisor," he says.

Jody holds up the paper with the chief warden's signature on it. "We already have permission. This is the permissions from the boss of all bosses."

He smiles and shakes his head left then right, the no/yes, yes/no.

"We are all good," Jody says, walking away. "We are going down to watch the bathing after we unpack." It is not a question.

"The Division Forest Department officer will need to give the permissions," he repeats.

Smiling and nodding, Jody holds up the paper again, pointing to the words. "Thank you," she says, "we can go." And we set about our business.

Up the ladder-like stairs to our new home, as soon as we throw our bags on the bed, the wind kicks up, knocking the shutters and whipping the bordering forest trees into a blustered frenzy. The dark clouds that have been amassing on the horizon for hours descend on our small meadow and open into a torrential rainfall. The tea garden out the back window is empty, not even a cow or rooster to be found. We consider closing the shutters but decide otherwise and go back to unpacking. In mere minutes, the rain abates, turning into a light drizzle, then a soft mist. A peek of sun, no rainbow. I look out to check, hoping for one. Instead, more clouds are approaching. So fast you can see them move. “More is coming,” I say, searching for my new wind-filtering, fold-up umbrella.

Jody has already packed her camera into a waterproof backpack and is wearing a rain jacket with flip-flops, not sneakers, no umbrella. She is always ready first. “I’m going to head down and see if I can catch the mahouts bathing the elephants before Parbati gets here.”

“Okay, I’ll see you down there.” After she leaves, I eat a quick snack, sneak some chocolate, and throw another date bar in my bag. Food is always on my mind, particularly when access to it seems uncertain.

The black clouds are rapidly approaching, the air is an eerie calm. Even the construction noise is gone, having cleared out with downpour. There is a brief window and I take it. I remember the way to the river, but as I set out, the guide for the ecocamp (who should be off duty because the camp is technically closed) sees me and insists on leading. He is clearly intoxicated, weaving along the path, trying to get in front of me. Doesn’t he know we have permission from the Forest Department? We believe this gives us the ability to walk around anywhere we want, unescorted.

But we are too confident in what we think is our official pass to all the forest. Along the riverbed, not yet visible, I imagine Jody (who is dressed for the job) freely setting up her equipment and getting uninterrupted shots. In the interest of showing Parbati and the mahouts respect, I have chosen to wear a skirt. It is ankle-length, the thickness of a light sweatshirt, the color of muddy tie-dye. Perhaps it is not a skirt at all, but pants, for there are two holes, one for each foot, and full fabric connecting those holes along the skirt's bottom. Picture a contemporary hippie twist on an Ali Baba pant. You must be able to envision this skirt for what comes next.

Reluctantly walking behind the guide, feeling certain I know the way, we arrive at the small stream crossing that, this past May, required only a couple hops on rocks to cross. Now it is unrecognizable. No longer a stream, but a small river coursing at a quick clip. I pull up my "skirt" to cross. At its deepest point, the water is just below my knees and while I have fabric bunched into my hands as high as my waist along my sides, the garment apparently doesn't work that way. The bottom of my skirt/pants—the entire length of fabric between ankle holes has not, in fact, bunched up. Unaffected by my efforts at adjustment, the material drags fully in the water, becoming heavier and heavier. Reaching the bank, river and mahout watchtower in view, the guide is now hurrying me as the sky unleashes bullets of rain, mocking my futile attempt to wring out the skirt and continue. Like a toddler's poopy diaper, the entire ensemble sags behind me along the mud, defying any attempts to pull it up.

The mahouts are gathered within the top of the watchtower, a rickety wooden structure that looks as though it was built decades ago, but in fact is new. The river, so bucolic four months ago, is now a torrent, swift water rushing straight up along the meadow, whitecaps frothing at the top with the added wind of an impending storm. No sign of elephants and the rain is coming down in sheets. Pretending I do not have a long, wet train of fabric in my wake, I hoist my extra burden up the splintered steps. Shouts ring out above me as the mahouts are deep into a card game. Once inside, I am greeted with mostly smiles of welcome recognition and what could be eye rolls from a few gruff oldies, purposely ignoring a woman in tight male quarters. If they notice my sodden skirt, they do not register a response. Of course, Jody is dressed for the rain, not a 1960s music festival. Faridul, Suriya's mahout who sold me one of his kukris, is sitting on a narrow bench with another mahout, facing the river watching for their elephants. They slide over to make room for me. Thankfully, being tie-dye, the wet skirt hides the fact that I can wring it out and most of the heavy wet is around my ankles (I squeeze a little at a time while no one is paying attention). On the ground, packed in a circle, is a group of six men throwing cards into a center pile, taunting each other, and laughing. Several more are standing over them, engaged in the banter. Overall there are about fifteen of us perched on four thin stilts, in a wobbling structure that has tacked-up tarps along two sides of the roof to protect against the sideways-driving wind and pelting gusts of rainfall.

Someone yells out. Upriver across the bank, two of the elephants have appeared with their patawallas crouched low on all fours balancing on the backs. They choose a spot in the river with a slightly more gradual bank entry and begin to cross. At the highest point, the elephants are swimming, fully submerged, with only a small slippery square for the men to balance on. If they slip off, they will be carried swiftly downstream in the raging current. The elephants do not seem affected by the precarious nature of those supposedly in command, shouting out instructions over the torrent. The elephants roll on their sides, seemingly enjoying the extra water massage. One patawalla takes the opportunity to quickly scrub the side of his elephant before she emerges, and together they make their way up to our side of the bank.

There is still a job to be done, though. Elephants need to be regularly bathed, a daily checking of trunks, tusks, and nails. It is both bonding and preventative care, regardless of the weather. A lightning bolt in the distance kicks everyone into action. The watchtower shakes with the movement of men rushing to their posts. A few more elephants arrive and a swift, but thorough, cleaning ensues, in the slimmest eddy of calm water. A clap of thunder cranks the dial on the sense of urgency—shouts increase, movements are fast and efficient. Jody is quick to follow. Despite the lightning, she is in the water, taking photos. The energy is nothing like the tranquil mirrored images from last trip. Everything is surging, voices stern and focused, no playtime, this is about safely getting back to cover. Still, they scrub, quickly and efficiently, but no duty is shirked.

The mahouts have quickly climbed onto the backs of their elephants and are standing tall, balanced with grace, as the elephants retreat to shelter through the tree-covered path up to the covered pilkanas. Here, the mahouts will feed the elephants before taking a break to have supper with their families.

"What is that thing?" Jody asks, pointing to my wet dragging skirt/pants as we follow the last mahout pair up the trail.

"It's a clothing faux pas," I say. "A malfunction." I do not say this is my misfired attempt at a culturally appropriate fashion choice, or that I'm trying to fit in, because I obviously don't. "Look," I do say, because poking fun at myself seems to be called for. I grab the still wet material at both sides of the pants and try again to pull up the middle as we wade through the stream turned river, both of us laughing.

The day before, while we were staying at Riverwood preparing for this week, I found an article online, written fifteen years ago in the *Telegraph* (India) featuring Parbati Barua and talking about her rise and fall from fame:

> However, life's camera rolls on with Parbati Barua in the spotlight, and the phandi continues to do what comes to her naturally: care and share her world with elephants. Ask her about her family and she politely tells you, "Ask only about me and my elephant family." Her first marriage in 1978 to a banker ended in divorce in 1988. Then she married S. S. Bist, the director of Project Elephant. Today, however, Barua is unlikely to meet with an entanglement. "The very sight of a man makes me sick," she once famously said during a press conference in Guwahati though she now claims she was misquoted.

I am struck by how many news stories about Parbati say the exact thing—that she is slight and frail-seeming, but mighty, a nymph in stature and elusiveness, yet fierce. Timid voice and iron will. But for anyone spending more than five minutes with her, these are the obvious, and I want something deeper. There are stories inside this woman, important stories of a history, people, and activities that no longer exist. Stories of royalty, of great camps, tales of legends and truths intertwined. In her lifetime, Parbati has been the daughter of a prince, whose titles and wealth were stripped away when India gained independence from Great Britain. Remarkably, that prince was also a famed *phandi* (elephant catcher), respected throughout the region, and Parbati's guru whom she followed into the jungle where they lived within the rhythm and cadence of nature.

It is said that Parbati has taught her elephants to understand more than a hundred commands, that she has memorized an entire apothecary of wild medicines by studying what elephants eat to cure their ailments. I want to learn the root of human-elephant relationship from her wisdom, to record her stories in her voice. This is what I am committed to. I want to show how she is special, a lone woman leading a charge for elephant conservation in a country still dominated by men, where women do not wear army jackets and lasso wild elephants, do not teach other males how to sharpen their kukris for optimal elephant nail filing, or correct high-ranking Forest Department officials for patrolling elephants in less-than-optimal conditions.

Most of all, I have come to believe that if I want to tell the complex story of the human-elephant conflict in India, I first need to deeply understand the roots of relationship between the two species. Parbati is one of the few living humans who has both experienced the traditional ways and has an active role with the current situation. In my mind, she is the key to understanding the entire scope of elephant history, culture, connections, and conflict.

I am seeking a guru—a guide to the past, present, and future of the Asian elephant.

There is more to the relationship between elephants and people than the consistent stereotype of tortured temple elephants. I believe if I can impart the full complex and cultural truth to a Western audience, more support will come to helping conserve Asian elephants here.

The Queen of the Elephants is waiting for us when we return from the pilkana. Watching us from the bandstand area, sitting along the bench, tapping her foot. Most likely she is dubious of our scurrying about like wet monkeys, trying to get photos at every chance. Making the most of our permissions. When we see her sitting at the table under the enclosure of an open-air dining area, we walk more swiftly, taking a shortcut over the wet grass instead of using the path like children late for school. "You must not walk across the grass with exposed feet," she says, in greeting. "There are leeches. They will suck your blood." She manages a thin smile. "Welcome, she says, "we will have tea." Dripping from our rain jackets, we don't dare stop at our hut to change.

"Parbati, it is so good to see you," Jody says, "Thank you again for taking this time with us." None of us really knows what to say; there is an awkward silence. We are looking to her and she seems to be looking to us for direction.

We walk together to the open-air dining area, grateful for the distraction of sipping hot liquid and chewing on dry biscuits. We sit in uneasy silence as Parbati checks her phone, rapidly texting. Bupesh, the manager, comes over to ask some questions. He and Parbati talk for a bit, and I get a sense she is keeping the conversation going longer than necessary so she does not have to talk to us. They stop for a moment, and she turns in our direction.

"Well," says Parbati. "I will have my time now. We will meet for dinner in a couple hours. Then I will have my time again. Nighttime will be my time each day. In the morning we will start our program."

She gathers her things and walks to her hut, making a phone call as she goes. We can hear her talking rapidly on the phone in Bengali, but have no idea what she is saying.

I wake to a downpour. Rain beating on the roof, rhythmic as a tribal call. A sensuous rain. I think back to the early years with David, when he still lived in his suburban home two thousand miles away from my home with the girls, and our time together was always fleeting and urgent. Unlike in the arid mountain climate of my town, in springtime on the East Coast, a steady downpour for much of the day is common. When I visited, waking up tucked in David's bed to a rain-soaked morning felt like pure freedom. The large second-story room, with hardwood floors and windows that looked out onto an unruly green lawn and a tangle of woods, dense with moss and ferns, seemed transformed into a treehouse. Here, I was no longer anchored to my small town, my problems, the needs of children, a relentless ex-husband, the distractions of housework or deadlines. This was a bed that seemed to float above all that was required of me, where I could lose myself . . . where I could become myself.

But now I am not in that peaceful spot, in a house David no longer owns. I am lying awake at dawn alongside Jody, who is still fast asleep. Our bed is not a billowing cloud of down feathers, but the thinnest padding over a hardwood platform. A tumultuous storm is not unfurling through open windows. Our screenless windows are firmly shuttered to keep out pests, the wood rattling against the frames.

Dawn passes, hidden behind storm clouds. A lone rooster manages to crow from a yard of mahout homes across the lawn. No birdsong. Jody wakes and we dress in silence, sleepy and alone with our thoughts about what the day might bring. Parbati is meeting us for tea to go over the plan. I am careful with our screen door, shutting it without a sound, but firmly, to keep the wind from knocking it about. Outside, layers of mist hover above the rows of tea gardens. The rain is softening. A light is on in Parbati's hut next door, but there is no sign of movement.

The dining area is octagonal and has an enclosed kitchen as well as a half-open walled eating area covered by a tall overhanging roof. There are long tables for sharing meals, benches and chairs, a rustic and simple setup. Jody and I choose a table and sit down, talking in a whisper, anticipating what might come next. Water drains from the roof corners. We have no idea what we will do with these ten days, but we are eager for all of it. The elephant whisperer will reveal her secrets.

A few moments pass. The door at the top of Parbati's hut opens with a creak and she steps out. She is wearing a long cotton dressing gown, not yet dressed for the day. Approaching seventy years old, her hair, still black, has no sign of gray. It is pulled back into an artful bun, held together with a tiny stick and dangling ornament. She lifts her nightdress as she walks down the stairs, making her way toward us. The first rooster crows, the last note suspended in the air, drifting across the courtyard lawn out from the mahout homes and over the green grass toward the tea garden beyond.

"Good morning," Parbati says. "Did you sleep well?"

We exchange normal pleasantries, eyes averted out of shyness. A woman in a bright orange floral sari, forehead wide and smile wider even at this early hour, brings out a tray with insulated teapots, cups, and a plate of biscuits. We are grateful for the diversion.

Parbati speaks to the server in a quick clipped voice as she reaches for the pot, pouring the hot amber liquid into each cup. A few tea leaves swirl at the bottom. I think about people who read them and what these might say.

"What is your plan?" she says after the first few silent sips.

Of course, this question again. I stifle a laugh.

Jody takes the lead. "Our plan is whatever you are doing. We want to observe you and document your work."

Parbati's face is elfin, wildly expressive—with deep creases along her forehead, likely from the brow-furrowing she is doing right now. Her expression shifts rapidly from concern and confusion to what seems to me a false smile, the kind of look you would give a small child when they have made an error, but you are trying to be patient, benevolent.

"I am here for you," she says. "Whatever you want or need from me, that is what we will do. This is your time."

Our time? Jody and I exchange glances. Surely we are here in this camp, at her choosing when it is closed, because Parbati has been hired to train the mahouts. What could we possibly document unless she is actively working with the elephants?

"We just want to understand about your knowledge of elephants and photograph you while you work with the mahouts." Jody essentially repeats her first statement. Slowly it dawns on us that we may have had a communication misfire. Which, of course, would not be a huge surprise, considering we have only spoken to Parbati for less than twenty minutes during her family vacation, several months ago, and have conducted all of our arrangements since through an intermediary who speaks less English than Parbati. We do not have a translator, and while we are fully clear about what we want this time to look like, it seems there may be a disconnect between what we want and what might be possible.

"I do not have work with the elephants and mahouts here." Her voice breaks into my thoughts. "I have solely dedicated my time to you."

It is as if I can see inside both Jody's and my head at once. In hers, the rapidly shrinking loss of images: Parbati teaching mahouts better ways of washing elephants, preparing the elephants for patrol, handling all the materials and tools, feeding them, showing mahouts traditional methods of grass cutting out in the meadow, maybe even a mock demonstration of *mela shekar* (the capturing of wild elephants with a lasso). In the absence of actual work and activities, we are certain to end up with potentially uninspiring handful of staged photos of Parbati participating in daily mahout tasks in a forced and unnatural way. Simultaneously, I am witnessing multiple observation-based storytelling opportunities go up in the ether. My hope to learn from Parbati as her wisdom organically unfolds begins to dissolve. Instead, this time will be reduced to series of formal interview sessions—something I likely could have done on a phone call. The disappointment for each of us is hard to recover from as our expectations rapidly deflate.

We have to adjust, because already Parbati is telling us what we need to do before we can start. Including informing an entire local chain of command of our permissions (i.e., getting multiple permission to enact our permissions). Parbati requests a list of questions that I wish to ask her and a photo shot list from Jody. When the formalities are out of the way, then she will begin our "program." The program, which will remain a mystery until she reveals it, moment by moment. In a series of surprises.

For now, Parbati leaves us to it. "I am going for my bath," she says. And with all the grace of a woman raised to be regal, she rises, calls for the staff person with directions to bring a hot bucket of water to her room, and bids us goodbye. "Finish your tasks. I will meet you here at nine o'clock. For breakfast and we will talk."

We have an hour to get our wits about us. Assess the situation. First, we borrow bicycles from the jute weavers who have just arrived for the day. We ride them across the tea garden trail and through the main road, dodging the stray dog, baby goats tied to trailing lines, and the random chicken, until we reach the entrance for Riverwood. There, we wait for Lama to arrive, while we furiously type up emails to the Forest Department local chain of command. I begin a list of questions, knowing that I will have many more as we go. This is not at all how I expected to converse with Parbati; my hope was that it would all be natural and organic. Not a stiff interview with questions assembled before I even know all that I can ask. Will she answer anything beyond these?

Jody is at an utter loss. "How am I going to give her a photo shot list?! I don't work like that. Who even knows what we'll be doing?"

We return to camp at precisely 9:00 A.M., questions and photo shot list in hand, emails sent to all the supervisors of the supervisors. Parbati is waiting at the table. She is dressed in a crimson red tunic with bright green leggings. Around her neck is a white scarf with red embroidery, not what we were picturing for a day of elephant work.

"Did you get everything taken care of?" she asks.

"Yes," Jody replies.

"Here is the list of my questions," I say. She reads through them.

"Okay," she says. She pulls a resume out from her purse and hands it to me. "This is my CV, so you know what I do."

There is something absurd about this. I read through the résumé, as if I am conducting a job interview for someone I have already hired—or, more accurately, for someone I begged to hire me.

Parbati presents each of us with a traditional Assamese scarf, white with red embroidery. I am grateful for the gift I brought. A vintage authentic Western-style shirt, brown plaid with oyster-shell buttons because I had read that Parbati loves American Western films and Charlton Heston is her hero. When I hand it to her, she unwraps it, smiles slightly, and smooths down the collar, which has bent slightly during the trip. I am immediately angry at myself for not ironing, fixing the wrinkle. I worry she does not like it. Still, we did not show up empty-handed.

"This morning," she says, "we will walk, and you can ask some of the questions. Then we will rest. We will do elephant bathing after lunch. After that, my time is my own."

The day passes like sets of waves. We walk along a dirt jeep road skirting the park and Parbati says very little. I record on my phone, but there are long periods of silence with short answers to our questions. At one point, she stops moving and holds her finger up to stop us. "Do you hear it?" she says. We do not. "Listen. There is a wasp's nest. We must go." Pausing, we look up into the tree canopy and sure enough, high in the branches hangs a bulbous nest swarming with wasps. We still cannot hear it and, if not pointed out, we would have never seen the threat tucked into the leaves, high above our heads.

"Elephants do not like wasp's nests. They will stop and not go any further." She turns around and begins walking back to the watchtower.

We climb the painted green stairs and sit on the uncomfortable benches. The insistent whir of the chainsaws in the opening to the forest behind us—trucks and men hard at work—is a distraction, creating a layer of anxiety and tension to our attempts at easy conversation. Each question I ask, Parbati answers with clipped, vague responses.

"Some of these mahouts are not from a mahout family," she tells us. "Badel's father tried his level best to give both his sons the training they needed to be the best mahout. But that boy, he is a good boy, but has no urge to learn the art. Only to ride the elephant and give it fodder, not to understand the elephants. He is not satisfied with his job. And, when satisfaction is not there, it cannot be good. Look at Jody. She loves photographing; she is dedicated to photographing. Then, the photographs are good. Everything is a hard job. The mahouts' daily work is hard. We must think for the animal and not just ourselves. Some mahouts, they do not think, 'It is my duty to go for patrol.' The dedication is not there. They are always talking about themselves, not the elephants. They should not complain but do their work with dedication."

At her description of Jody's work, I feel a sinking. *She doesn't like me*, I think. *She sees Jody running around shooting but I am not doing anything except recording her and asking stilted questions.*

We try and ask more questions about mahouts, but she is resistant to say any more. The conversation stops and the construction noise takes over. I am struggling to think what to say, how to get something going in a comfortable flow. In my imagination before we arrived, I pictured that we would be laughing and sharing stories. This is not happening.

Jody says, "I liked what you said yesterday about how you like to do difficult things."

"That's Jody's mantra," I say, trying out laughing.

Neither of them laughs with me.

"If you do hard things, you get to know yourself better," Parbati says. "A smooth life is not good. In Indian society, the ladies should produce children, do the cooking and the housework. That is not a life—that is stereotype life. Life should be an adventure. There are so many kinds of adventure. I chose this life, this adventure. Capturing elephants is a very risky job, you may die." She chuckles, "You may come back, you may not come back. So many adventures. I like it."

"I do too," Jody replies.

Again, the sinking feeling. Aren't I that woman with the stereotypical life? Who has children, cooks, and minds the household? It dawns on me that Parbati and Jody share this decision to not be a traditional woman with a domestic life. I did make that choice. Now I am a mom who cares for her children but also wants to be out in the world sharing stories beyond her local community. Does one have to make a choice? The two women in front of me did.

And what of adventure? In this era, people who work with animals are supposed to be doing it for conservation purposes—even photographers, writers, and painters are expected to be contributing to social change. Is there still a home for those who love adventure for adventure's sake or beautiful art that doesn't contribute to something altruistic or meaningful beyond its existence?

The clues to Parbati's past come only in small clips. I imagined colorful stories about her family, the jungle, and hunts, about elephant catching. Yet she says little about this. I ask about caring for elephants, hoping to elevate her energy.

"When bathing, elephants like to be fully wet, then you can brush and scrub. They like to be massaged everywhere."

She stares off beyond my face, as if seeing her own elephants rolling in the river, sprays of water from their trunks. When the reverie has ended, she looks straight ahead, toward the camp entrance. She rests her hands on bony knees whose shapes protrude through leggings, reminding me of a praying mantis. Parbati starts tapping her foot, as if listening to music that only she can hear.

"Time marches on, memory stays," Parbati says. "Let's go."

What I know so far is that the Baruas are descendants from the original raja bestowed by the Mughal emperor in the 1600s. Parbati's father and the Barua family spent the summer months in a mansion that sits high on a hill overlooking the river and the family's property, protected from the monsoon floods. While Parbati was raised in this house, Lalji (as he was known by the elephant men who revered him) was an avid hunter who preferred to spend the entire dry season in the jungle hunting wild game and refining the art of catching elephants.

These are not facts I learn from Parbati, but from research done on my downtime. And there seems to be plenty of downtime. Our first day has been stressful. Parbati, like India in general, defies all expectations. She tells us bits of things. But she is not here to work or train. She tells us when we can talk to her and when she needs rest. If we take photos or inquire about the mahouts, she tries to distract us. When we talk her stories are truncated, a sentence or two. She has been on the phone much of today with Animesh, our mutual friend from HNAF in Siliguri. Unbeknownst to us, she is begging him to come and rescue her, to provide a deflection.

She does not understand what we want and does not know what to do with us. We learn this from Animesh much later, but for now we just feel her agitation and constant phone calls. And how can we blame her? How will she trust us?

By dinnertime, we are all exhausted. We eat mostly in silence. At the end, Parbati says, "Meet me for tea tomorrow morning here at 5:00 A.M. We will go with the elephants through the forest tomorrow."

After dinner, Jody and I walk to Riverwood, use the internet, and call our loved ones. There isn't any privacy to tell David what is happening or how I feel beyond the basics, and the girls don't like to talk on the phone. I take a video of myself telling them to have a wonderful day, but I look old and haggard, almost sick. To combat this, I try again, this time smiling a lot, so the fatigue doesn't show as much. When we are done, it is dark, and we walk back together but separate, as if there is a wall between us. We are alone in our thoughts; in this way we give ourselves space. When Jody is in a mood, I feel anxious, as if I have done something wrong. The night feels lonely and confusing. We have come all this way, but this is not what we expected. The rain is losing its adventurous charm.

12

After traveling together in quarters more intimate than comfortable, Jody and I have developed our own routines, which, in near silence, we embark on for our second day with Parbati. Tap water splashed on sleep-encrusted eyes, bottled water to brush our teeth. The rustle of sliding cameras into waterproof backpacks, the zip of rain jackets. Our movements have a synergy, there is ease, and this morning, a shared sense of excitement. Today we will accompany Parbati, on elephant, into a part of the forest we have not seen before.

From the dining area, we wait for Parbati and for tea. Rain again. It falls in sheets, spilling from the roof and through the half-open cement walls, streaming onto the floor near our feet. We do not hear Parbati open the door or walk down the stairs. She appears as if an apparition. A chartreuse bandanna wrapped around her upper forehead, just above a bright red bindi. Still the gold hoop earrings. This morning she wears the oversized camouflage army jacket, baggy cuffed-up jeans, and rubber flip-flops, a look I recognize from the book cover about her journey with Mark Shand. Jody and I exchange a knowing glance and hidden smiles. Finally, we think, we are getting to see the real Parbati Barua, the one we came all the way back to India to meet.

"It is raining," she says as a greeting. Wrapping thin fingers around a steaming cup of tea, she stares up at the clouds then out to the pilkana where the mahouts are already shoveling and raking the stalls. "We will still go, I think."

She finishes her tea and pours another. We don't dare break the cadence of the natural sounds—rain dropping, distant rooster crowing, the rise and fall of our breath in sync. Parbati drains her cup, then stands up. We gather our things and follow her, a commander with her soldiers.

The moment we step out from under our shelter the rain eases and an orange-pink dawn begins to break above the emerald tea garden horizon. We walk toward the watchtower where we sat for interviews. At the top, a wide gate swings inward to facilitate easy loading.

It is here that those of us without special skills and existing relationships with working elephants will climb aboard, from this place of ease rather than climbing up a trunk or commanding the elephant to sit so we can scamper up her back. The officers also embark in this manner, from the tool hut across from the pilkana—they have already left for morning patrol an hour before dawn, rain or shine. There are duties to perform. There are no tourists in this camp, and while the elephants regularly take rotations during tourist season between rides and patrols, this morning's elephant journey has been arranged by Parbati. Two elephants emerge from the tree-lined path. First is Kaberi, with her white and pink-chalked Hindu designs drawn on the triangle swath of forehead above her trunk by her mahout, Dinabandu, who had once flown with an elephant to Japan to teach the art of mahout to the handlers at the Tokyo Zoo. Behind Kaberi is Diana, also carefully painted, her name on her side, entwined with yellow chalk daisies. Her mahout, Badel, is the son of a mahout whom Parbati trained years ago.

Jody reaches for her camera; rapid clicks of the shutter join the gentle calls of direction from the mahouts as they approach the tower gate.

"Barefoot is the best way to ride an elephant," our guru says. So, I leave my flip-flops behind and let the warm, rough sandpaper folds of Diana's neck and sides envelop my feet. I massage her as a thank you and wonder if she can feel it, hoping she does. Parbati explains that we are specks of weight for her, that there are strict rules based on best practices for weight and care of working elephants. "They do not work in the heat of the day, only for up to four hours in the morning or evening. Afternoons they spend foraging for food and socializing in the forest, then baths. They eat all day and night."

Have you ever ridden a horse across a western landscape, rocky beach, or undulating countryside? When perched on the broad back of a large elephant who is languidly plucking branches and leaves as she moves through the dense vegetation, a few things happen.

One, you understand how and why elephants are the best transportation through this landscape, how with their superior stealth movement and massive advantage of height your safety and forward momentum is essentially assured. No jeep could possibly penetrate this tangled mess of vines and grasses to silently surprise a rhino poacher. A human who attempts to cross this pathless forest on foot is certain prey for all the wildlife he startles as he attempts to make his way. It is no wonder that, for thousands of years, elephants have been to the jungles of India what camels are to the desert and horses are for much of the world: ideal transportation and protection. In countless cases, elephants have effortlessly assisted flood-trapped humans across raging rivers, saving lives.

Two, you feel completely transported to another time. The metronomic rhythm of her walk beneath you as you tuck your hands under the soft-plied ropes, looking out toward the faintest outline of the Himalaya. A time of kings and maharajas, before British colonialism violated the ancient laws of conservation protecting elephants from being killed. A time when elephants were partners in wars, were wholly worshiped as deities, and thrived in wild places that were left undeveloped in delicate balance of coexistence with the forest people they lived and worked alongside.

Three, you can't help but think about the politics and conservation outcry against riding elephants. It remains a complexity. On one hand, the perfect world is for elephants to be free in the wild. But, when there is no forest and an overflow of abandoned and orphaned elephants, where do they go? To a sanctuary where they do not need to be tied with chains or hit with sticks or ever be ridden by anyone again? While a sanctuary is ideal, how does one fund the ongoing maintenance of such a place? There are some impressive models around the world, such as Lek Chailert's Elephant Nature Park in Thailand, but they rely on a strong social media presence and significant international support to fund the round-the-clock care that captive elephants require, whether they work or roam within bounds. This care is very expensive and the elephants' caregivers must have consistent, reliable funding mechanisms to support all involved.

In India, there is a centuries-old relationship with people and elephants. This relationship is fraught with a history of abuse and cruelty. It is also a relationship renowned for its deep bonds and care.

It's important to clarify, Elephants cannot be domesticated. Domesticity involves selective breeding over multiple generations. All captive elephants are a tamed version of wild elephants. Historically in many regions, Asian elephants, once captured, are placed and tied into a small enclosure where they are subjected to stress and deprivation designed to break their wild spirit and create obedience.

Best practices evolve over time. Now there are organizations, such as Elephant Aid International and Elephation, that work with mahouts throughout Asia to train and maintain relationships with elephants that are compassionate—free of dominance, punishment, and infliction of pain. With a consistent food source, ample space to roam and bathe, and best practice guidelines for care, captive elephants under these circumstances seem at least a better option than euthanizing.

There are no perfect answers, and certainly I am not seeking to romanticize elephant captivity. I personally believe that tourist riding should be banned. With the right infrastructure and support, tourists can have meaningful observation experiences with elephants. Then, revenue to support these elephants can be generated, while giving them space to be more free. I wonder what it would take to make these changes here.

"Hold on!" our mahout breaks me out of thought. Jody is turned around, facing Diana's rear end, hands not in ropes, so she can take better photos. My job is to warn her when the uphills and downhills are steep enough for her to need to hold on. Badel would prefer Jody hold on the entire time; he is unhappy at the risk she is taking. Parbati, however, couldn't care less. She is stretched across Hillary, not holding on at all, but absorbing all the jungle has to offer. Raindrops on fat leaves, branches cracking underfoot, the periodic soft calls of the mahouts—*Meil, Meil*—small streams pouring over rocks. Plodding feet, slow and deliberate. Parbati appears like a movie star stretched out dramatically for a photo shoot. And perhaps this is the case; while she has been very reticent with personal stories, she also contradicts this with bouts of barely hidden vanity. I cannot help thinking that she is posing at times. And why wouldn't she be, this heroine of our story, the subject of our cameras. She often seems conflicted, flattered one moment and retreating the next.

"Steep downhill," I say, as we head toward a riverbank. I can't see the path.

"How steep?" Jody replies. We are practically on the lip.

"Steep! Hang on!" I say as we begin to go vertical.

Jody laughs as she almost slides off Diana's back. I contort behind to grab her waist, an act that is more show than effective. We climb into a river rushing with rapids, the current pressing up against the elephants' flanks, reaching our feet. Our elephants forge effortlessly across; the river's mighty force is no match for their girth. In the middle of the crossing, the elephants could be swimming—it feels as if we are floating—yet they still maintain a steady line.

I think of my daughters, who paddle rapids in slim boats with fierce determination and a transcendent confidence that has always been a source of fear and wonder to me. I am kayaking an elephant. Connected to my girls in the spirit of adventure that I've always been on the outside of. But, even as the consequences of falling into this river would be dire, I feel neither brave, nor afraid. Suspended in the curious space between truth and mystery.

We lift out as steeply as we came in, and without any drama set off into a part of the jungle we have never seen before. Alternating between a slim winding path and thick undergrowth, the continuous tree canopy shelters us from the rainfall, which has begun again.

Eyes closed. Breathe in and breathe out. I conjure Parbati at fourteen years old, exactly the age between each of my daughters now, Goldie thirteen and Anhwei fifteen. Trying to picture them perched on the back of this small, swift koonkie elephant, lasso in hand, scouting, swinging, rising up, then deftly capturing a young wild elephant, proudly taking her into camp. *Mela shekar*: the ancient, and now forbidden, art of capturing wild elephants with a lasso. A technique that only phandis could employ. This sprite of a woman lounging on the padded *chatti* (traditional cushion for riding elephants) at utter ease, lost in thought. Almost a year has passed since I first read about Parbati Barua, and somehow I have made it to this moment.

After almost an hour, we come to a clearing. Here, in what seems the deepest part of the forest, is another pilkana with elephants and mahouts returning from morning duties, carrying grasses and banana stalks for breakfast.

"Where are we?" Jody inquires as we approach the lodge. It is painted the dark green of old hunting camps that wish to be camouflaged. A structure from another era, colonial in style, with paned glass windows that overlook sweeping vistas. Inside, the walls are ochre, with rooms tucked away from the main hall a plastered Calke green.

"This is a forest lodge. It is a very peaceful place to stay," Parbati says.

We walk through the rooms in a building over one hundred years old, down a narrow hall lined with wildlife photography and paintings, which opens up to a great room. Wicker chairs and loveseats with faded toile cushions look out on a large, covered porch with arched overhangs. The kind on which you can imagine taking English-style tea in the afternoons, over discussions of the wild and romantic landscape of the Dooars compared to last year's Kenya safari. In fact, the veranda, with its smattering of rocking chairs and tables, faces a manicured lawn perched high above a valley of variegated greens, from the lush grassy ground cover to the wispy foliage of trees flanking the Murti River where it snakes along the valley. Parbati pauses under an arch, above a set of stairs overlooking the vast forest. She seems like a soldier surveying a battlefield with her camouflage jacket, hands on hips, legs spread in a triangle, bandanna tied around her head. Inapproachable. She takes in the scenery. Her body language dissuades approach, reverent as if in prayer or meditation. I stand back several paces, feeling her energy radiate outward, creating a force field between us made up of sadness, exhaustion, love, and peace.

We've been out for over three hours, returning to the elephant camp by 9:30 A.M. Breakfast is ready, and I am ravenous, as if I have not eaten for days, as if I have time traveled (it feels like we have). The breakfast is simple, an omelet with onion and spices, dahl and rice. Another bout of rain.

"Would you like to see some things?" Parbati asks. "I brought some old photographs and books that we can look at. I will tell you about them."

From her single piece of luggage, a hardcase suitcase from the 1960s, Parbati withdraws a small stack of books and photographs. She pulls out a slim, square, photography book that looks like it is for children. The text is in French.

"This woman, Gabrielle Bertrand," she says, "was a French photographer and explorer. She spent a month living with us at our elephant capturing camp. Her book shows all of the work we do, the capturing, the training, everything."

"This is me," Parbati says, pointing to a young child sitting on her father's lap as he goes over the next day's hunting plan. "I am four." I sit with her as she turns the pages and describes what is happening on each one. She pauses at a photo of an elephant tied by his feet to a post, both front and hind legs. A roaring campfire is in front of him and the mahout in charge of training is waving a stick of fire in front of the elephant's face. Jody and I exchange horrified glances. Jody puts her camera down. This is Kraal training, or "The Crush" as it is widely referred to and condemned for its inhumane treatment of elephants. I am stunned to see it presented this way, as a statement of fact, with little emotion. I don't know what to do. So, I listen.

"Elephants are afraid of fire. Very afraid," Parbati says. "But, if you have a working elephant with you, you will be camping and cooking, so they have to learn how to be near it so they do not run away or trample the campsite. This might be difficult for you to see. But this process happens very quickly. The elephant learns quickly. When this part is over, we sing to the elephant and bring him sweets. Once he has learned this way, our bonding can begin."

As Parbati goes through each page, a strange feeling passes over me. As if I have pulled away from the scene and am hovering overhead, seeing all of three of us from a completely different perspective. From this vantage point, I see a woman struggling to bridge the vast gap of culture, language, and the shifting of opinions. The images in this book reflect Parbati's home, her family, her entire life experience with elephants. Her attachment to this landscape, and the animals within it, are infused into her essence. She could easily transition into the jungle and survive with less than the materials she has in this room. Only when I float above her can I see her this way. Frustrated and misunderstood.

And me, from a distance? I look earnest but ineffective. How can I truly understand? Everything I see raises more questions, inspires me to want to learn more, get deeper into all of it. And Jody, standing above us on Parbati's clean bed with her bare feet so she can get the best shots of what is being shared? It feels absurd. We both know that these images are compelling, but a far cry from documenting Parbati in the field, with her elephants.

We eat dinner early. At home, David will just be waking up on his birthday, alone. I promised him that I would wake him with a call. I set out in the dark, with my flashlight. We have done this walk to Riverwood and internet access before. It is simple and seemingly harmless. But tonight, I set out only a few steps before I hear a door open. Parbati's door.

"Kim!" she says. "Where are you going?"

"Oh, hi, Parbati," I say. "I'm headed to Riverwood so I can call my husband for his birthday."

"Is it an emergency?" she asks.

Hmmm. This is an interesting question. It feels like an emergency because I made a promise, because he has been so supportive and encouraging, because he has lived a life where few people have ever celebrated his birth, because I want him to know how much I value and love him.

"I guess not," I say. "But I told him I would call."

These connections to my family ground me, they are also a switch I cannot simply turn off and on. When I am home with my children and husband, I am still a writer, thinking about and working on projects, creativity marinating and simmering in the background. When I am working, far from home, I am still a mother and wife. When I am alone, looking at photos of my family gives me courage and energy. They are always in my thoughts, wondering what their days will be like, worrying about them and wanting them to know that I am here, thinking of them. Yesterday, I created an excuse of needing a printout so I could run back, find a quiet corner, and make a video message for the girls' first day of school then have a brief call with David. A birthday is a big thing not to be home for.

"You cannot go," Parbati says. "It is too dangerous. There are leopards in the bushes of the tea garden, they could attack you. And men have been drinking in the town. It is not safe. If it is an emergency, I will go with you. Otherwise. You must stay here."

"Thank you." I hear the words come out of my mouth, even as I feel desperately sad and claustrophobic. How will he know that I tried? What if he is waiting for me? My husband understands being away like this far more than I ever will. He has decades of experience. But still, it is his birthday and I promised. Dejected, I head back to my room, falling asleep with images of attacking leopards, gangs of drunk men, and David in the distance, alone at a table with a single candle and uneaten birthday cake.

I wake and walk to Riverwood after post-dawn tea. There is an hour before we start our day with Parbati; each morning she has a hot bucket of water brought to her hut and she practices yoga and then bathes. As soon as I get into range, the texts begin coming through. It is evening at home. David is worried because he has not heard from me. Goldie has emailed me a questionnaire about family history for a school assignment. She wonders if

I can answer the questions by tomorrow. Her texts say: *Hello.* Then, *What day r u coming home?* And a third, when I didn't answer because my cell phone was not activated, *What day are we with you?* I respond to her first, explaining what happened and why I have been out of contact, committing to the questionnaire, then making a quick video for her and sending it. Something is not right, but she will not communicate more on text or talk on the phone.

When I call David, the number rings and rings. It is likely he has gone out to dinner, not wanting to be home alone on his birthday. I leave a long message. With forty-five minutes to spare, I start filling out Goldie's assignment on family. These assignments are always a trigger; Goldie doesn't know who her biological family is, and we will never know the traits of her great-grandparents or aunts and uncles. So, we do the work as if my genetics somehow transfer to her. In an odd way, it does. We see so many commonalities that seem to indicate that nature and nurture can blur the lines. A Facetime call from David comes through. I answer. The line disconnects. I call back. I see him for a second, a big grin. I love his smile, green eyes squinting just like my blue ones do. He calls back, no video. "Hi! Probably better to just use the phone. Everything okay?"

"Yes! Happy birthday. I'm so, so sorry." I explain what happened.

"No worries, I totally get it. And, honestly, I'd rather you not get accosted by leopards or men."

His voice grounds me. Deep and secure. His surety always gives me a boost of confidence. "How is she?" he asks.

"Tough," I say. Outside in the garden, a holy man in a white shirt and white linen sarong is chanting mantras, a stream of incense trails behind him. "I miss you. I miss the girls. I am really struggling to make a story out of this. She won't say much. I can't believe I missed the girls' first day of school for this. I'm sorry."

Now I'm crying.

"They are fine," he says. "I am fine. We all love and support you. This is how these things go; you will find the story. Just a few more days. Stay in it, hang in there."

We talk for a little bit longer, then hang up and I text Anhwei: *I love you. Have a terrific day at school. Good luck at volleyball try-outs today.* She responds with *Love U 2* and a heart face with a blown kiss.

The holy man has entered the office and is standing in front of me. He gestures for me to open my hands, then places a small clump of what seems to be fennel seeds gently on my palms. He continues his chant. I do not know the meaning, but calm washes over me. I need to start trusting the process. Stop blocking my own way. I came this far for a reason. Knots are not always tied with a single string.

In the afternoon, I notice that the tusker, Suriya, is not at the river bathing with the other elephants. When we arrive back in camp, Faridul is boiling a large pot of water, mixing in herbs. Suriya is waiting for him next to the row of houses, alongside the well. With the help of his patawalla, Faridul brings the pot to his elephant and makes a poultice from a mixture out of his pocket and packs it into a section of cloth. Suriya stands still while Faridul presses a hand to his girth, then bends to one knee beneath him. For the first time since my arrival, I see the massive lump on Suriya's front leg. Faridul, with tenderness that I can feel from a distance, applies the compresses to Suriya's leg. In turn, the elephant is patient, even kneeling on command, allowing Faridul to get deeper into the wound.

Traditional mahouts used to follow their sick or injured elephants into the jungle, because the elephant seeks the medicine they need within their habitat to heal what ails them. The mahout would then observe the natural healing and document the medicinal source, contributing to an Indigenous knowledge of medicine that is still used today.

Suriya's boil looks like a tumor, but no one is certain. A veterinarian is coming out next week.

I wait until the job is complete and Faridul is free for a few moments before approaching. Lama is here for a couple hours to help me translate.

Faridul is thirty-two years old. He has a wife, a daughter, and infant son. He has been paired to Suriya for fourteen years. Mahout wisdom purports that an elephant picks up the temperament of his mahout, and vice versa.

That, over time, the two mirror one another. Faridul and Suriya are living examples of this ancient adage.

"Can you tell me about your relationship with Suriya?"

Faridul is still holding the cloth, and water droplets make splashes in the newly formed puddle below. One hand rests on Suriya, keeping him calm.

"When Suriya is happy, I am happy," he says. "When he is angry, I feel anger too. If he is unwell, it makes me the same."

"Faridul," I say. "If you had so much money that you would never have to work another day in your life, would you still be a mahout?"

He looks down at Suriya's lump, distractedly caressing the taut skin, and softly nods his head with a shy smile. "Yes, of course," he says. "I will be with Suriya for my entire life."

Yet, when I asked if he plans to teach his son the art of mahout, his face clouds over and he looks out over the row of houses, the children gathering to twirl and chase one another across the grass, then back at me.

"No," he says. "It is too difficult a life. I do not wish that for my children."

I reflect on Faridul's words for a long, long time. His is not an isolated answer. The art of mahout is dying. The traditions developed and practiced over centuries reside in the minds and hands of men like Faridul, men who likely will not be replaced. His one elephant will be cared for during his lifetime, but what about the growing number of elephants that need care tomorrow? With resources and habitats shrinking, the single, best alternative for elephants in India is dwindling too.

13

The temperatures have soared. The heat is oppressive, and the electricity keeps going out, which means the only source of moving air, the ceiling fan, no longer works. A storm is coming. My only comfort is that Jody is as miserable as I am. For all her acts of adventure and extreme travel, the fact that she is also exhausted and immovable lends validation to my own torpor. It feels as though our bodies have a layer of lead weighing us down as we walk through air that seems so thick, we expect to see it.

We lie down on the wood bed, close our eyes, and try to sleep. The fan comes back on, and for the five minutes it whirrs we feel like the luckiest people on the planet, then it goes off again. In the silence of another power outage, distant thunder. A blessed storm is coming. Wide awake now, we wait for the storm. It does not disappoint. Driving rain, booming thunder, cracks of lightning. When it leaves, the temperature is survivable again. We meet Parbati outside.

We walk along a tea garden road, passing signs that read ELEPHANT CROSSING. I ask Parbati. "This is a migratory path," she says. "For thousands of years, elephants have passed through here. But now these landscapes have so many tea gardens. The elephants don't have a choice but to come through here to get to what remains of the forest. It can be a problem."

"A problem?" I say. We learned about this in Darjeeling during the Tea Garden Association report. But like most government meetings, the representatives reported the successes and minimized the problems. Beyond the sign are bright emerald tea bushes stretching out to a far-off cluster of trees. A thin dirt path winds through, hardly wide enough for an elephant, I mistakenly think.

"Tea estate owners do not like elephants in their gardens. Many try to dig ditches or put electric lines to keep elephants out." Parbati's pace picks up as we approach a dilapidated two-story building that appears to be dormitory housing. "Owners sometimes hire me to help them keep the elephants out or help when a problem elephant comes. I would chase it away with my elephants. Years ago, I used to live in a cottage on a tea garden property to protect from wild elephants."

For the life of me I cannot imagine a single wild elephant simply showing up among the tea pluckers that are scattered throughout the field.

The fiery sky at sunset makes our hut on stilts seem elegant. Mismatched metal pieces for a roof, faded teal paint peeling from bamboo siding. We are surrounded on three sides by dense old-growth forest that drips thick twining vines down through the open spaces. Dinner will be a mystery. I am not sure how there is the means or capacity to feed us, we seem very isolated. Still, Parbati is in control. She asked if we like fish. That pond out front concerns me, but this is part of the deal. We are not here on a luxury, chartered safari, but on an expedition, a quest. I want to show Parbati that I could live in the jungle, eating anything that was put in front of me, having the toughness to live under the most simple and challenging conditions.

After dinner (fish) we fight to fall asleep in the stifling heat, under the fan, which is our only hope for any temperature drop. Hidden surprises are everywhere—low-hanging wasp's nests, stinging ants, venomous spiders at the bottom of bathing buckets, and clusters of moths drawn to any light, swooping in like an Alfred Hitchcock film through screenless windows. We wake to a power outage—the fan is dead. It is so still you must stay calm to breathe, as if we are in an oxygen-deprivation chamber. We drift off again, listening to the claws of rats as they scurry in the walls behind our heads as we attempt sleep on a single wood bed. Jody wakes to the bristled fur of a thick rat making its way across her cheek in the middle of the night.

"What is that?!" Jody leaps out of bed with a scream. "It's a rat! It's a fucking rat!! It just ran over my cheek."

We both howl and scramble to our feet, searching the floor. The power is out; we cannot turn on the light. No one comes, not that we are seeking help. We understand there is not really any help to be had, nothing can be done. I have a flashlight, slim with two powerful beams. After sweeping the room with light and not finding any rats, we try to go back to sleep. In the silence, we can hear more rats scurrying through the ceiling boards and rafters, scratching and crawling in the walls by our heads.

"I'm never going to sleep," Jody says. "That was horrible."

"Maybe light would scare them away," I say. "Let's try to jury-rig my flashlight so it shines into that hole up there. I bet that's where they are coming from."

We spend the next several minutes pushing our bed away from the walls, into the center of the room, and building a stand for the flashlight, estimating it has at least a couple more hours of continuous battery life left. Hoping the power comes back on, so we can make it until morning. I position the light to shine into the hole, our only hope for deterring another rat. Exhausted and utterly spooked, we fitfully sleep to the sound of scratching for the remainder of the night. At dawn, the power returns and we are up for the day.

At breakfast, Parbati appears calm and seemingly unaware of what transpired last night.

"Did you hear us screaming last night?" Jody says.

She laughs. "Yes," she says. "Our friends the rats have visited you?"

"One ran over Jody's face while she was sleeping!" I think this should qualify for Parbati to be at least slightly impressed.

"Oh yes, I heard you. Rats?" She shakes her head, laughing. "I leave tea biscuits for them in my room. They run across my body and I just let them. Rats will be rats. Jungle people are used to such things."

I am obviously not a jungle person.

This is our last day with Parbati. We sit on the slim back deck no breeze, sip tea, and look out at the stretch of jungle beyond. I can easily imagine a wild elephant approaching us. It feels as if Parbati's very energy could summon one.

"Here is a story," Parbati says. It is raining again. We sit on plastic chairs along a wall that blocks any hope of a breeze, not daring to move. The heat is as impenetrable as the jungle that spreads out before us. Parbati, in a grass-green tunic and athletic sweats, rainbow flip-flops, and chipped red nail polish, takes up half of the chair space; she may be floating.

"Young people today," she begins, "have too many distractions. When I lived in the jungle with my family and our elephants, catching and training in the wild, we had nothing to do except bond with each other. The elephants have a special place in our lives. We talked about them and we sang to them. There are so many songs in our folklore. All are about nature. There are love songs, and songs about how we inter-fit. The elephant herd is about being female. No king, only a queen. The male is the guard, but the female is in command. She tells the others where to go and when to go. In our folklore there is one story:

> *The first wife of a Brahman was abandoned by her husband and cast out. Every day she went to the jungle to pick flowers and fetch water from the river. There, unable to contain her grief, she wept many tears. Downstream, one day, the king of elephants was drinking water with his herd. The water was salty. The king asked his herd to look upstream and find the cause.*

Parbati pauses and considers. "At that time, everyone could talk—even the birds." She continues:

> *The full herd came to the wife and asked why she was making the river so salty. She said, "I am so sorry" and explained her plight. The king of the elephants said, "Come with me." So, he took this lady in his trunk and traveled to his home at the base of the Himalaya. He told the other elephants to bring seven pails of water from seven streams. The king poured these over the wife's head, and then placed her on his throne. He told the elephants, "From today, there is only queen and you must obey her."*

With enlivened eyes and amplified voice, Parbati expands with fresh energy that is palpable and contagious.

"When I was young and traveling with my father on elephant-catching journeys, we would go deep into the jungle into this part of Assam." She runs a thin finger along a map in an old book she has brought out with her, following the border of Bhutan and the Himalaya mountain range. "You cannot travel through this area anymore. It is very disturbed with extremist groups now. It has become dangerous. But at that time . . ."

She stops. "This one is a true story," she says. "Not folklore."

"In this area there are many, many elephants. There is a lady in the jungle. I have met her two times. All the elephant people know her: elephant owners have heard of her, old phandis and mahout families have met her several times. We call her Goddess of the Forest. She is a human being, but she never talks. You cannot get too close to her. We pray to her for permission to capture elephants in her part of the jungle. She will show you a finger. If one, then you can take one elephant. Two fingers mean two elephants. Sometimes she will throw her hands down like this." Parbati flings her hands out in front of her lap. "That means 'no catching.'"

"This lady always has a laughing face. When I have seen her, she wears a beautiful sari and is alone.

"Maybe she is like Mowgli in *The Jungle Book*—an abandoned child, adopted by the elephants. When we track there, if we see an elephant footprint alongside a human one, we know we are among her herd. Sometimes she will shout '*uh oh ho*' and just where she is sitting, on all sides, wild elephants will come and surround her. None will harm us. But if you say the wrong things to her . . . then that fellow will be killed. He will be thrown by her elephant. We have seen that also. Her elephants protect her. It has been a long time since we have entered that part of the jungle. As elephant catching is no longer going on, we don't travel anymore. But that was our path, years ago, and twice I met her. She allowed us to capture six elephants."

Parbati lifts one arm high over her head and the other curves at the elbow, low by her waist, stretched out to the railing. "Among her herd," she says, "one bull has tusks like this. One is up and one is down. The Goddess of the Forest sits on his lower tusk like a swing."

She takes a sip of tea.

Jody is leaning so far at the edge of her seat the plastic begins to warp.

Images dance and blend in my mind: elephant queen placed on the throne by trunk, the silent goddess of the forest swinging on a tusk, young Parbati with her lasso overhead as she rides and captures.

She searches our eyes, trying to gauge the effect of her stories. Here we are, the three of us, women who have traveled far more than miles to get to this moment. We are joined by suspended disbelief, rapt with attention, fully embraced by jungle, consumed and committed to every word.

Parbati stares out on the dense leaves and vines. "People will not believe these things," she says. "This is not folklore. This is truth. This is magic."

And we believe. Imagination and actuality. Here, only by blending myth, legend, history, and science, can you understand the truth.

Shifting from past and present, I realize this is only the smallest surface scratch. Jody is still hopeful about taking an elephant journey along the ancient migration routes. But I am starting to understand that this might not be possible. Still, at the very least we want to see Parbati's home, with her elephants. As India evolves its conservation efforts and simultaneously continues to decimate elephant corridors, the future for elephants here seems grim. Yet Parbati keeps the faith. "It is what I know to do," she says. "It is my life."

"In the days when we lived with our elephants in the forest," she explains, "time passed slowly. No television or computer. No mobile phone. At that time, people dedicated themselves to their job. There was nothing to see.

They gossiped about their work only. Now that is missing. Now, mahouts with knowledge and skill do not want to share their wisdom. They think that if they know something they will have a better chance at a promotion over someone else. They think that only they should know the art. It is short-term thinking. This is the difference between government mahouts and family mahouts."

Riding an elephant through a camp forest with Parbati in the rain is special, but I don't think it is the story. I want to know more about the Barua family and their relationship to elephants. To experience as much of her past and present as possible. Mark Shand visited Parbati's ancestral home in Assam, where the family spent their summers. Her father's study was still uninterrupted twenty-five years ago. What does it look like now? Is it still intact, full of elephant wisdom?

If Parbati is willing to take us to her home, it could help unlock the secrets to elephants and their thousands-year-old relationship with humans that we are not fully finding here. Parbati reminds me of the Goddess of the Forest who swings from elephant tusks. I want to go deep into that jungle, following my curiosity, and search for this treasure. To sit in Lalji's study and read his journals and books, uninterrupted; to rock on the breezy veranda and be utterly transported to another era.

We still have not seen wild elephants, as we have missed the migration windows. I still do not know what the conflict actually looks like. Parbati remains a mystery. Only glimmers of openings, of stories, then she closes up again. She is an amalgam of contradictions, but perhaps her stories are parables, metaphors, ways to communicate something else entirely. With more questions raised than answered, I am compelled to keep seeking, to follow any crumb she throws for us. Maybe this is how we build enough trust to travel with her on elephant, across the migration route to see how the landscape has changed after two decades. I sense that Jody is losing enthusiasm for our subject, particularly as the elephant journey seems unlikely. Will my family support my return? This is definitely no longer a quest for a single story anymore. I think back to Jody saying that the human-elephant conflict in India is too complex to tell in one article. She is right.

14

I do not have a soft landing when I return home. Delirious with jet lag and sick with a severe cold, I launch into trying to make up for lost time. There are volleyball games to attend, lunches to make, and bedtime tuck-ins. The holiday season looms.

One night Goldie goes into her room, clearly upset. When I check on her, she hands me a note. "I'm sorry," she says, "this is how I feel." The paper is folded into tiny triangles. Inside, a knife to my heart: *I feel like Anhwei and I are your bottom priorities beneath your work, David, yoga, and the dogs. We need you as a responsible, hard-working mother and I personally feel like this: your kids and family need you throughout every single day of our/your life.* This letter is confirmation of my deepest fears. Gathering my courage and emotions, I knock on her door, then enter her room to talk about it. She is pretending to be asleep, but I know she is awake. "I read every word," I say. "You were courageous to tell me how you feel. I will work harder to show you that you and Anhwei are the most important priorities of my life."

No one knows about this letter. I tuck it into the back of my bedside drawer and lie awake half the night in distress, hoping I don't die and people find this proof that I am a neglectful mother.

The note tips me into a tailspin, confirming my growing fears: that I am falling short of the bar I set for myself as a parent. The next day, I wake the girls and make them breakfast—Anhwei a smoothie, Goldie some sausages with syrup—and make lunches while they are eating, as I do every time they are with me and have been doing since they began school. We have two dogs, Oscar and Lucky, and both also clamor for attention first thing—wanting a treat, to be let out, fed, and already asking for walks. David is across the country for work. This is my routine. Anhwei drives off to school after I help her load the car with their overnight bags as they will be at FH's for the next three days. I beseech Goldie to hurry so we don't miss the bus; we drive six miles into town for her bus stop. When I return, the dogs are exuberant. I take them out then clean the kitchen.

There was no time this morning to make peace or work things out with Goldie. She was kind in the car, and I could tell she was feeling a bit sorry, but we don't discuss the note because the drive is short and it will be a few days before we are together again. I try to keep things sunny; show her all is well.

An antique steamer trunk sits in the corner of our living room, holding all my memories: decades of photographs, letters, notes, and journals since I was a young teenager. I'm drawn to it, wondering if it has any answers, a sign, something to help guide me. The lid creaks as I open it and when I remove the thick quilt that Anhwei's birth mother sewed for her, some photos slip out onto the floor. Photos of Anhwei from the orphanage, a chubby, wild-haired baby, smiling as she touches her pinkie to a colorful stacking toy; ten months later, a shaved-headed baby touching nothing, eyes vacant as if someone has turned off a switch. The adoption agency gave us those images. The first was our referral photo and we did not realize it had been taken months before. The second was a surprise updated photo, sent via fax from China to the agency. When I saw it, my stomach turned. My daughter, who I had yet to touch, seemed to be disappearing from the inside out. We could not get to her fast enough.

I reach in and grab a handful of whatever comes up. A stack of wedding photos spills out of a ripped envelope. A lifetime of planning and playing fantasy weddings, seven years of hoping that this was the one.

More follow. Me, holding up a toddler-size sundress, bright blue with red flowers and Chinese lettering to a crowd of loving friends at our baby shower. The girls when they were little muffins, dressed in frilly skirts and polka-dot tights, shiny dress shoes, FH with a hand around my waist and one set lightly on Anhwei's hair. A family trip with grandparents to a luxurious hotel, where the girls ran around the hallways and stared with amazement at the layers of tiny sandwiches, tea cakes, and crumpets during high tea.

The trunk is now empty. I am sitting, unmoving, surrounded by piles of photographs, journals, and mementos of another life. Another life that is somehow still this life. Outside the sun sets, then darkness falls. No one is home. No one is coming home tonight. I cannot stand up to turn on any lights. I bury my face in the blanket Anhwei's birth mother wrapped her in before placing her in a market stall, never to see her again. After fourteen years, it still holds its musty-earthy scent, red silk with golden lilies cover, sewn with basic stitches, over a large piece of rough wool blanket. Glossy photos stick to my bare legs as I curl myself into a fetal position, clutching the blanket to my heart, eyes wide open, staring into my loss.

In the morning, I face the heavy load of memories from last night. So much of what lies inside the trunk is painful, memories I do not need taking up space in our living room. Not ready to throw it all away, I stuff it all in the garbage bag and move it into a dark closet, out of sight. Clearing our family space of the relics from my past is a first step. The photos of the girls go into a cardboard box, the quilt wrapped around them. I place them gently back into the trunk and close the lid.

I need help.

Trying to build a career and become my full self with confidence in the context of less time with my daughters is a massive adjustment. Physically it works, but emotionally I'm grieving the loss of the other half of my life as a mother, and I constantly fear that the change has caused my daughters great suffering too.

I am also stuck in the past. Often kept there intentionally by FH, who sends a sporadic but steady stream of photos and videos of the girls and me from the years before we separated. It has been over five years since I left the marriage, but I did not leave my children. I am an easy target, steeped in unresolved grief and guilt rooted in the divorce, and he constantly reinforces this so I can't move on. The past and the present comingle to such a degree that I cannot move forward; the detritus clings to me, wrapping around me like fine threads that create strong tangles, restricting movement.

I need to close the open wounds, to heal. Those close to me can see what I have been blind to. I am firmly stuck in the past and fear the future, all while my present offers me an abundance of exactly what I have been working toward for over a decade. I cannot fully embrace it.

There are no easy answers. Does being a mother mean you must set yourself on a shelf until your children have flown the nest? When does sacrificing your dreams for your children's sake make sense? At the intersection of guilt and selfishness, there is a signpost with no arrow pointing to the right path.

I embark on a healing journey. One I build myself, with partners. Studying some relevant books, trying out new tools, discussing all of it with David, who acts as a sounding board and gives terrific advice. For years now, I have been moving at top speed, hurling toward new goals, staying upbeat for my family, focusing on helping the girls through this significant life transition, pouring attention into creating a healthy love relationship, and absorbing the gamut of FH's emotions. I have never, not even the first few months in these past five years, taken the time to mourn the failure of my marriage. I have not clearly seen that expanding a bold career means making room for, and accepting, that identity again. After eleven years as a stay-at-home mom, as the girls are growing more independent, I am still clinging to my identity of "the supermom," even as I can no longer perform at that level. Maybe it is not as critical to the girls' well-being as I once believed—perhaps it never was. If I cannot accept myself as multifaceted, how can I expect my daughters to accept me?

It takes months of arduous work to accept that what happened in my past is over, practice staying in the present, and create the energetic space to shape my future without the shackles and weight from what happened before today. The texts from FH do not cease, but I try new techniques that help me not react in the same useless ways and practice not internalizing them. Allowing me to stay in the present and heal.

A butterfly is a caterpillar who ingests herself to re-create her new form. Her essence still exists, but she does not carry her chrysalis as she flies.

By March, I feel new clarity. I understand, for the first time, that when it comes to travel and cultivating my vocation, no other voices matter except my daughters and my husband. David's support is solid, but I have yet to have a heart-to-heart with my girls. Several weeks ago, Goldie apologized for her letter, saying it was written in a fit of unfair anger and that she is embarrassed by it. Still, I believe she meant what she said and tell her that she should never feel badly to speak her mind.

The girls are fourteen and sixteen years old now, certainly old enough to weigh in, consider, and articulate their needs. If I am going to return to India and take this project to the next level, especially if I still do not know what that level is, theirs are the only voices in the chorus that matter when it comes to whether I am giving them what they need.

We three are gathered in my room. Atop a waist-high wrought-iron bed, each of the four legs on risers, requiring a hop and climb up onto the mattress. This way, we have a view out over the hills and can watch the moon rise and the stars spread out through the windows. When they were babies, they slept with me, and I with them. Tucked into the hollows of warmth, knees behind kneecaps, little stick legs tucked in among my fleshy thighs. They would splay out in sleep, a fist on my head, a foot against my stomach. To have them here now, almost as long as I am, feels like embarking on a voyage. Like *Bedknobs and Broomsticks*, only sailing back in time.

I am not sure where to start.

"You are the most important beings in my life. It may not always seem that way, but I promise that you are. I am trying to grow a career; I want to be a writer who tells important stories that impact how people live their lives. This town is very small, and it is hard for me to make my voice heard if I do not travel and try to connect with others around the world. I have a chance to reach this dream. But none of it matters to me if I don't have your support. If I am not meeting your needs as your mother, then I need you to tell me so I can fix it."

Goldie is relaxed and listening intently. Anhwei is not a fan of emotional conversations of any sort and I feel her stiffen, retreating.

"Your voices are the only ones that matter to me," I say. "You are old enough to be in touch with your feelings and completely honest with me."

A silence settles. I think that Goldie will talk first. Anhwei surprises. "Mom," she says. "I thought you knew that we support you. We are proud of you."

Tears well up. I try and hide them.

"Thank you," I say. "That means so much." I hope my people-pleaser child is not simply telling me what she knows I want to hear.

"I support you too," Goldie says. "But there are times I really need you."

"That's helpful and fair," I say. "Are you able to let me know ahead of time when it's important that I don't miss something? I mean, there is the obvious, but sometimes I don't know what might be super important to you."

"Yes," she says. "Like, I want you to be at my eighth grade moving-up ceremony."

"I would never miss that," I say.

This is not what she needs to hear. So, I adjust. "You let me know, and I will be there. One hundred percent."

Her eyebrows furrow, as if she is thinking of more. "First day of school this year, because I'm going to high school," she says. "Probably my birthday. I think those are the most important. It's getting easier, my separation anxiety seems to be more manageable than it used to be."

"That is good to hear. And, no problem—I will not miss either of those," I say.

Something cracks open in my consciousness. They are not babies or even little girls anymore; they are teenagers with their own activities and lives. Helping with homework, driving to and from school, organizing playdates, making breakfasts, bagged lunches almost daily from preschool through high school, planning favorite dinners, attending sporting events, and celebrating all rites of passage—these are steel threads of my daughters' health and stability that I have woven for their entire young lives. Still, I continue to try and weave it, to show them they are loved, that I am here for them. Maybe it is me who has been grasping too tightly.

Constantly feeling out of balance, I consider the concept of dynamic balance. A veering toward tipping over but weighted just enough to keep balance in motion. Instead of fearing that all is not equal, I begin to recognize that life and relationships blossom in chunks of time and experiences. If viewed from a microscope, the day-to-day may appear wildly out of control. But, when I look from the bird's-eye view over a span of my adult life, there is beautiful equilibrium.

So far, these India trips have been self-funded, an investment. I feel deeply grateful that I have had the resources to go. But, without some publication interest and financial support, the prospect of a return trip is looking bleak. I am trying to keep my spirits high, trying to stay encouraged. Now comes the hard work of writing proposals, pitches, seeking funding, seeking publication. In the weeks after my return, a story about the elephant conflict is accepted for publication by the *Explorers Journal.* I partner with Avijan because his photographs of wild elephants intersecting with humans are exceptional. My credentials for the Explorers Club membership have been slowly building. I am accepted as a Fellow, an accomplishment I have earned by the skin of my teeth, but now can grow into and engage more deeply with all the resources available within.

Jody and I labor over the pitches for *National Geographic.* At first, the response is hopeful. We hold our breath, cross our fingers. They turn us down, for now. Telling us that the story is compelling, but they need more images of a softer Parbati, a more magical setting. They are not going to pay us to return to get those images, but the magazine holds out the incentive of taking the story if we can obtain them.

April arrives like a bullet train, and I realize there is only one window of time in which I could return to India without disrupting everyone's schedule: mid-May. Less than thirty days away. I am in a complete quandary. When I send messages to my Indian contacts, to build some type of a schedule, the responses are as casual and noncommittal, as if I live down the street. Again, I am reminded of Jody's wisdom. You need a plan, but you cannot possibly plan. Avijan is eager for me to return, he has a new story about leopards and a forgotten tea garden full of inhabitants that he wants me to see. Animesh is out in the field. For days, he is silent. When he returns, he gives me Parbati's phone number and tells me to call her.

We have a brief but thrilling conversation on the phone. I do not understand much except that she is open to spending time with us in Assam, at her ancestral home where her father's study is still untouched since he died. This is a dream come true for me. Parbati gives me the number for her niece-in-law. I am to contact her now for all the arrangements. I call Jody.

"She is letting us come to Gauripur, to spend time in her father's study," I say.

"Will she let us see her elephants at her house?" Jody asks.

"No, I don't think so. She was evasive," I say. "But still. This is incredible. Can you go?"

"I think I have to be in LA in the middle of that week," she says. "I don't think I can go in May."

I am crushed. It is my only window and Parbati is available. May gives us a shot also at seeing the elephant conflict, as it is the start of spring paddy season. I cannot fathom going without Jody. I also cannot bear to give up this opportunity.

"What do you think about me going on my own? Just to keep up the momentum. It has been so long since we have seen her, I don't want to lose the story. It's been almost nine months." I hear the words spill out of my mouth and marvel that I am saying them.

Silence on Jody's end. My stomach is in knots. "Yeah. Yeah, that works for me. It's probably a good idea to keep the momentum going."

When we hang up, I grab my desk with both hands to keep from falling backward, and the room seems to spin. Who am I to think I can do this alone? Who will take the photographs? I can barely function in India with Jody at my side, how will I ever have the tenacity and independence to do this on my own? And Assam? Didn't Parbati say it was too unsettled with rebel forces for traveling? David is unreachable. I start googling: *Terrorism in Assam*, *Rebel Groups in Assam*, *Kidnapping in Assam*; what I find is terrifying. Then I fall down a rabbit hole, reading all the gory news accounts about foreign journalists recently taken hostage across the globe.

By the time David gets home, I am equal parts too afraid and wildly eager to return. But Parbati's window of time to spend with me begins right away. I had almost given up hope that anything would happen for May, and now I am full steam ahead. There are exactly ten days before I have to be there.

"Do you think I can do this?" I say.

"Of course," he says. "You can take my Canon."

"I don't have any idea how to use it," I say. "Plus, what if I get raped or kidnapped?"

"I will teach you how to use the camera. You have an incredible eye, it will be fine," he says. David, who is no stranger to traveling in high-conflict areas, begins to order some unobtrusive weapons that I can use to protect myself. "If you have the right tools, you will feel safer," he says. "Just make sure you are always with someone you know." He pauses and looks directly at me. "You can do this. You should do this."

There are no words, then or now, to describe the feeling of knowing your loved one, who does not want you to leave, does not trust where you are going, does not quite even understand why you are so obsessed, still flings open a door and encourages you to take the risk and walk through. I can see to the other side just enough. Once again, David is holding out his hand, the branch to balance on while I cross the rushing water.

"Are you sure?" I ask.

"I am certain." He gives me a wink. A wink that I can still see in my mind's eye. This single gesture that tells me I will not be alone, even if I am thousands of miles away on my own. A wink that says "you've got this."

With permissions granted, blessing bestowed, and solutions offered, I begin again to plan my return to Northeast India. In less than forty-eight hours, I somehow manage to have each day of my trip completely accounted for. Ending in Siliguri to meet up with Avijan. He has three days and will take me out into the field, where my hope is that I will finally see the wild elephants and the conflict.

Going solo is a challenge beyond anything I could ever imagine. For the first time, I viscerally understand those words I wrote for Paul Nicklen: "Fear and fascination are often two sides of the same mind, and in an internal standoff, one will ultimately prevail. Even as fear fights a robust battle within me, fascination almost always tends to win." When I wrote these words earlier in Paul's voice, I was channeling his grit and courage, his story. Never did I identify with them myself. Yet, here I am, poised at the edge of the cliff, my personal edge, almost paralyzed with fear, and in my internal standoff, fascination is prevailing.

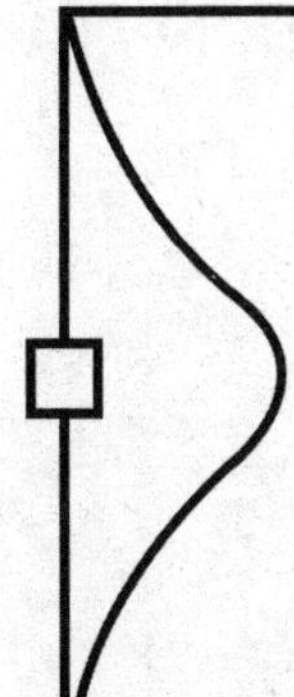

PART IV

STUCK IN THE LABYRINTH

You don't change the course of history by turning the faces of portraits to the wall.

—Jawaharlal Nehru, "Tryst With Destiny" Speech, 1947

15

I return to India on their Election Day; the atmosphere is tense. My hosts at Haveli Hauz Khas in Delhi are happy to see me, but anxious and distracted. We spend the evening discussing Indian politics and listening to the radio as the results begin to be tallied. Freedom of speech, freedom of religion, and tolerance between Hindus and Muslims are all concerns. When the other tourists have left the dining area, I stay for more chai and we talk about the similarities between our countries, how world leaders seem to be increasingly gaining popularity for their antagonistic points of view, and how fearful we feel for the future, particularly after so many of us have worked for decades toward peaceful coexistence in the form of equal rights, compassion, and social justice. Now it feels that with a simple pull of a thread, so many years of work can be unraveled, with fear, greed, and hate filling the hole that remains. Violence and discrimination seem justified in the name of progress to make a country "great again."

I do not yet fully understand the past and current situations regarding the religious relationships in this region, refugee situation along the borders, the drive to develop the swaths of natural forests and destroy conservation easements, displacing the Indigenous people who reside there. I am just beginning to see how the political climate deeply affects the elephant crisis. Beyond the historic caste system biases, the current government has been criticized of encouraging a rise in Hindu nationalism; with each trip, I sense an atmospheric increase in tension, fear, and anger. My colleagues tell me that immigrants, who are increasingly illegally living on the Indian side, are granted voting rights so local leaders are catering to them. These immigrants arrive with a different view of elephants than their Indian counterparts. They do not see elephants as a god, but as a pest.

In Jody's absence, all decisions are my own. I reach out to the Wildlife Trust of India (WTI), one of the largest conservation organizations in the country and a grantee of Elephant Family, the Asian elephant charity organization founded by Mark Shand. A few of their wildlife biologists attended the elephant conflict workshop in Darjeeling. Their compelling presentation and meeting contributions left a deep impression on me. WTI founder, Vivek Menon, was out in the field during my time in Delhi, but the woman who runs the Elephant Corridor Project, Upasana Ganguly, invited me to visit WTI headquarters and, at the last moment, asked me to present the work that Jody and I are undertaking.

Despite extreme jet lag, and a complete lack of preparation, I am thrilled to meet the group that is working across India to secure right of passage for wild elephants. Into the thick of Delhi, an hour's drive, the WTI is a tall, narrow office tucked off a main street. Upasana greets me and we walk to a conference room where several staff, scientists, wildlife biologists, and field workers were gathering. They make a place for me at the front and connect computer to a big screen. As I stand in front of them, I realize that have no business presenting anything about Asian elephants to this crowd. "I am here because I want to understand what is happening here with elephants and people," I say. "I'm interested in helping raise awareness in the western parts of the world about the plight of elephants in India through storytelling. People do not know what is happening here and I want to help change that, so there is more support for groups like yours." I show them the article I wrote with Avijan for the *Explorers Journal* and the story about mahouts and elephants that Jody have been working on. They ask me some questions, but I don't have many answers. They should have been giving me the presentation. After about ten minutes, I say, "I want to learn from you. What are you seeing in the field? And what is WTI doing currently to help?" I sit down and close my laptop.

The individuals in the group begin sharing. They introduce me to the 101 Corridors Campaign that they are conducting within key elephant pass through areas throughout India.

Upasana has organized multiple on-the-ground partner organizations to help educate villagers about living with elephants safely. With the help of Elephant Family, two villages within direct elephant path were relocated after years of conflict had continuously destroyed their property, crops, and cost lives. In most situations, however, volunteers work with tea gardens and farmers to create a safer passage for elephants and employ nonviolent strategies for keeping crops intact and to give both elephants and people a better chance at peacefully coexisting. One hundred and one corridor areas have been identified, with Green Corridor Champions volunteering throughout the area. The aim is to use a grassroots approach that will create a smoother movement.

Elephants do not simply migrate in a particular line across India but are in constant motion because of their size and food needs. Once, when there were plentiful jungles where all wildlife could roam freely, elephants would begin at the base of the Himalaya coming through Bhutan and make their way toward Nepal. Their migration was seasonal to escape excessive heat and seek higher ground during monsoon season. In the modern age, however, abundant forests have ceased to exist in uninterrupted swaths. Railways, highways, tea gardens, and population centers create tremendous barriers. In addition, the food supply has been largely pulled out of the forest by humans seeking food for themselves and to sell. What was once an area sustainably harvested by Indigenous communities, sharing with animals, and ensuring that there would always be enough supply of trees, bananas, fruits, nuts for the subsequent seasons, has been gutted of all food by people coming in from outside for profit. Not an unusual story, as it is the central story of our planet. Now, elephants must make different choices for where they will get their food and how they will travel to get there. They have begun a new migration, one to coincide with seasonal crops of rice and maize. At one time, elephants only infrequently ate crops, with some villages across northern India sharing their bounty with wandering elephants. But, in this war over dwindling resources, the paddy and maize, along with the fruit trees that villagers grow in their yards, have become a primary food source for both solitary bulls and large matriarchal herds.

Now I understand why we always seem to miss the elephants—they come when crops are ready and one never knows exactly where and when that will be. The most likely windows are roughly September through October and again from end of May through June. After all this time, neither Jody nor I grasped an understanding of this, and we missed them by mere weeks each time we were here before. In hindsight, I understand that Parbati is likely quite busy during conflict season, so she would prefer to schedule her meetings with us when things are quiet. We created our own barrier!

The team at the WTI leads a walking education and awareness-raising campaign along blocked migration routes, teaching children in these areas to love elephants again through Hathi Sathi (Elephant Friend) programs, working with a wide group of stakeholders to save lives.

"What will you do while you are here?" one of the field scientists asks.

When I hear myself describing my upcoming visit to Parbati's ancestral home and hoping to document her work with mahouts, to learn more about the relationship between captive elephants and people, I suddenly feel ridiculous. I am wholly missing the crux here.

His response is gentle, "Ms. Barua has tremendous elephant wisdom, and her father was revered for being the most knowledgeable elephant man. But sometimes her point of view is a bit, ah . . . how should I say it? Outdated. We have better, more evolved, methods now."

I had become so focused on chasing Parbati, hoping to learn from her wisdom, and documenting the relationship between mahouts and captive elephants as the root to understanding the human-elephant conflict that I had forgotten that we had originally shifted our focus to her only by chance, because we were not able to see wild elephants and the conflicted interaction with humans in action. Upasana and her team reinspires and refocuses me; I could go on one of the walks through the corridor and visit some of these affected villages. Why wouldn't I do something that shows me the problem firsthand, something meaningful? Isn't this what my core vision has been all along? Instead, I have been so concerned with exploring the past that maybe I am stuck there with this project, much like I was unable to move on from my own past.

"I am planning a few days with Avijan," I say, freshly grateful for the opportunity. Avijan is well-known among WTI staff as a Green Corridor Champion, and they utilize many of his images for their publications. People are nodding and smiling. "I am hoping to see elephants in the wild and some of the conflict. And he wants to show me some villages that have issues with leopards."

This sets off an enthusiastic conversation about leopards and tea gardens, but I am still focused on elephants and blindly compartmentalizing the issue by animal, not grasping that a solution for one animal will mostly often benefit the entire ecosystem. Later, I set up a tentative plan with Avijan. Our time in the field is brief before I return to the U.S.

Saying goodbye to the WTI team, I see new possibilities for how to get back on track. Back in my room, I write down new goals. One, *National Geographic* has expressed potential interest in the story if we can capture some "softer images" of Parbati. I have been studying the camera and hope that Parbati will be more open in her ancestral home. The challenge compels me. Two, I am convinced that Lalji Barua's study contains all the elephant wisdom in books and journals that is lost to future generations. Third, Parbati represents a bridge between past and present, both culturally and in conservation. If I can learn that link, then I will understand the current elephant conflict in the correct context. That she is a rare woman in a man's world, and I have a chance to tell her story, keeps me going. Finally, I still think that Parbati could be a vehicle to organize an elephant journey through the conflict zones, a sequel to the BBC documentary she and Shand did twenty-five years ago.

A greater one-horned rhino statue greets me as I enter the baggage area of the Guwahati airport. Life-sized gods and goddesses stand in a diorama amid welcome banners. Light floods through tall glass windows and bounces off the shiny green leaves of plants in the open foyer. The airport feels like a vacation destination airport, and in a way it is. Guwahati is the gateway to one of the largest national parks in India.

And there she is, just outside the waiting area door, wearing a white cotton sari embroidered with swirling periwinkle flowers over a bold royal blue blouse. Parbati's expression is soft and lights up into a rare, welcoming smile of someone greeting a long-lost dear friend. To my utter surprise, she hugs me. "Welcome to Assam," she says. "Welcome to my home." Her demeanor could not be more altered since the last time I saw her. This is encouraging.

Parbati beckons me to follow her across the road to where the nondescript, but familiar to me, sedan is parked. We load all my gear and I climb in the back seat next to her and behind her driver. Between us is the grass-green embroidered flower bag that never leaves her side: I know not to touch it or move it out of the way.

We have almost a five-hour drive ahead of us. Parbati's driver is deft and needs to be. Post-election Assam is in a fervor—the rural population here appears to be extremely emotional about the election results. Our car is forced to stop completely as a large group of people march ahead, blocking the road with music and banners, in red and yellow hats. They are chanting, cheering in shouts and slogans that I cannot understand. I do not know if they are protesting or celebrating. Our car is engulfed, parting people as they march through.

She has chosen the back road, the old road, rather than the newer four-lane highway. We pass through village after village, town after town, peppered with industrious individuals in bright swaths of color—cooking, polishing, fishing, chopping, weaving, talking, playing, and running, riding their bicycles. Astonishing, the way life goes on during monsoon season. Rickety bamboo bridges only two feet wide placed over water bogs, leading to huts. Marketplaces whose paths are thick with mud, yet throngs of shoppers sludge their way wearing flip-flops or simply barefoot, sloshing through puddles.

As we make our way through the drenched landscape, Parbati points out collections of cement houses with corrugated tin roofs, faded colors, all tucked into thick groves of trees.

"Many elephants used to live here. Private elephants. But there is no longer room to keep an elephant and people are losing interest in it. No more buying or selling of elephants is permitted. In Assam, you can still own them. All these used to be mahout communities, but now they are gone, and the legacy no longer continues."

I have learned to not watch the road, as the oncoming traffic is terrifying, and at some point you must grow inoculated to it—honking trucks and busses hurl toward us as we squirrel our way into slight holes to pass trucks, cars, and motorbikes on our side of the road. If there are lanes, they are irrelevant. Exhaustion and motion sickness overwhelm, and I keep falling asleep then wake with a start, acutely aware that I am squandering precious time. At one point I drift off and feel Parbati's slight hand tap my arm.

"Kim, Kim . . . wake up. This is the Brahmaputra River, at its widest point. This is the life blood of Assam."

With a jolt, acutely aware that I am behaving poorly, I clamor to the window. "Oh. It's stunning," I say. "Thank you for waking me, that would have been terrible to miss."

The Brahmaputra is the highest river in the world, flowing from Tibet (where it is known as the Yarlung Tsangpo River) and crossing India and Bangladesh. Awake in time to cross the bridge, the sight of the river causes a great welling of emotion in me. Not because it is so beautiful, but because of its symbolism, this history. This flowing body of water has born witness to wars and boundary shifts; the snow and ice from the Himalaya melt into this life-giving force, part of which evaporates into the air, helping to create rain in these valleys and snow in the mountains. A cycle that has continued since the dawn of time. Yet in this moment of our crossing, plans for a mega dam are in the works by the Chinese government, as they have taken control of the Tibetan river source. When these dams are constructed, the flow to

India and Bangladesh will be significantly impacted. Tension is mounting. Assam relies heavily on this water source for survival.

After the bridge, the scenery begins to run together. Parbati is quiet, no longer pointing anything out and my drowsiness gets the better of me. We arrive. The town of Gauripur is bustling, a small town, with improved roads. Anchored by libraries, schools, government buildings, and various shrines and mosques, it seems a cross between a town and an emerging city. We spend the night at a local Ganesh temple and retreat center and, in the morning, drive to Parbati's childhood home.

There she stands, the house that has been a beacon for my dreams over the past two years: Matiabag Palace. I climb out from the car on shaky legs. The sight before me is exactly like the photographs in the book.

Beautiful ruins. The house is an ornate Victorian architectural marvel, even as it has fallen into disrepair. Faded and cracked lemon-yellow paint on the plaster exterior. Black mold grows in streaks, streaming from vents and clustered around windows. Wooden shutters and cut-out trim are accented in parakeet green. White painted filigreed ironwork and white marble stairs lead to a covered veranda to my left. Once an elegant and formal entrance, a heavy-patterned rug now hangs where the front door once was. Above it is Lalji's study, painted entirely in white, lined in Gothic arched windows with a commanding view over a lake and the once-forested miles of land the Baruas used to own.

The midmorning sun streams onto the upstairs veranda, casting warm light on the gray decking, illuminating a basket of freshly picked eggplant and peppers. Empty clotheslines are strung from columns that support the roof and connect the scrolled metal railings.

Lalji's study is in hexagon-shaped room overlooking the front yard and the hilly landscape beyond. The walls are a bright mustard yellow, a color that lends richness and grace to every dust-covered item in the room. Curved window seats line the tall windows, fabric window coverings are tightly bunched on delicate rods to keep the sun out. A massive dark wooden desk topped with glass dominates the space. Black-and-white and sepia-tone snapshots of family members—portraits of women and children, group photos, many with elephants—adorn the surface, along with stacks of papers and magazines. A glass-front bookcase holds the treasures I have come all this way to experience: decades of meticulously kept hunting logs from the early 1930s through 1950s and rows of hardbound books. The bookshelf is topped with a variety of reed-woven hats in various shapes and sizes, hats I have only ever seen in old photographs and caricatures of Indian hunters and men in the field.

"I will leave you to your work," Parbati says. "Do what you need and then we will have lunch. I am going to spend some time with my family."

Here is Lalji—his personality, priorities, his heart and soul.

The abundance is dizzying.

Photographs are everywhere. Parbati's folk singer aunt, Lalji's royal grandparents, young mother, and famous Bollywood uncle. I open the bookcase and read the spines. *A Sportswoman in India*, *The Jungle and the Damned*, *The Diary of a Sportsman Naturalist*, *In India*, *Jungle Trails in Northern India*. Tales of adventure, hunting advice, wildlife knowledge, and expeditions.

Where to start? Reading each book and journal is naturally my strongest desire, albeit wildly impractical. With only two days to spend here, and no clear sense how many hours I have, my plan needs to focus on what I need.

Every book has holes inside, intricate patterns like a maze through the pages. At first it is a mystery, but then I discover the culprit—a tiny fuzzy yellow caterpillar. A bookworm? These books are not long for this world. Cracked spines and worm-riddled pages, disintegrating from the humidity. Who is going to take the time to save these? Book after book comes off the shelf.

These materials are a wonder of lost history, a testament to another era, but what about the bounty of elephant wisdom I was anticipating? Where is it? Even as I scroll through indexes, all the elephant references are about riding them into a hunt or capturing them for selling. What about the medicinal wisdom? I imagined a big ledger full of handwritten observation and tables of medicines that only elephants and the most traditional mahouts know about.

On the lower layers are stacks of handwritten journals. Certainly, these will be the Indigenous wisdom treasure trove. Yet, one after the other, barely a mention of elephants beyond brief descriptions of elephant catching and many references to how well each elephant performed in the hunting activity of that day. Every journal is either a hunting log or painstakingly transcribed book excerpts about various topics such as special guns, leopards, and tigers. Lalji's style mirrors that of the books he loved.

The heat is oppressive and working the camera physically exhausting. Time is running out and my priority is getting footage. Documentation. As much, and as artfully as possible, I begin to arrange the most compelling books in combinations of open pages and covers, illustrations and text atop the desk, with the family photos and sometimes my white cotton scarf as background. Composition. By now the sun is overhead, no longer flooding the room, but if I carefully push aside the tightly drawn curtains, enough light gathers. Lifting books, holding the camera in awkward positions, relying on automatic settings as a painful amateur. Lalji's chair holds my weight as I stand over the table trying to capture the best angle of all the books.

I am an impostor. In the viewfinder, reviewing the images, my computer and phone are visible in many of the frames, ruining the careful composition. What was I thinking? The clock is ticking, my time here is precious, and I am now rushing. Such valuable time I will never get back. Parbati returns while I am deep into the work. She watches me for a bit.

"So, why do you need to spend all the time in here if you are writing a book about me?" she says, breaking the silence.

"This history is an important part of the story," I say. "If I can understand your past, it gives me a more complete picture of who you are now."

Parbati blinks and gives a little nod, as if to say "carry on." Only with hindsight do I understand what Parbati already knows: I will not learn much about elephants by staying in this room. Right now, all I can think about is the bounty before me. Decaying books! I am swept up in their devastating beauty.

16

The next day, we have car trouble and are late getting to the house. Parbati's nephew brings out stacks of about fifteen to twenty photo albums. I am eager to dig in. Parbati looks at the stacks. "First, we will have lunch," she says.

By the time we get to the albums, the light is unpredictable. Shirts, tiny pants, dishrags, undershirts, underwear, and scarves, fresh from the wash, are drying in rows, draped over yesterday's empty clotheslines. Every opening of the archways on the porch has become a visual backdrop of clothing, linens, and moving shadows. A new challenge. We unroll a sisal rug and sit on the porch.

Albums dating from the early 1930s depict a lively and luxurious camp life. Snapshots of hunters lined up in a row atop their elephants, groups posing with large tigers, leopards, one with a now locally extinct gharial crocodile on a leash. Mahouts fixing howdahs so the owners can ride safely into the jungle and hunt from the perch. Elephants being groomed, children swimming and playing. Men gathered in shirts with ties, jodhpurs tucked into boots. Posing with rifles and next to mahouts and other staff who are wearing white cotton lungis. Of course, clothing is one way to distinguish caste, and in this case the divide is extreme. Caste system or not, the class difference is palpable in every shot. This is the era before independence, when the Barua family was acting royalty of the Gauripur Zamindary Estate, Assam.

"What is this?" I ask, pointing to a photograph of a train, with porters, horses, and many carts piled with luggage and supplies waiting at its base.

"It is our camp. My entire family would go into the jungle for eight months out of the year. All of us children had tutors and the school arranged that we would learn while at camp and return only for exams. We would take a train and porters would pick us up. Maybe a hundred people were part of our camp. We had everything, chefs, servants, even a barber. The mahouts and staff met us when we got off the train. Then we traveled to the camps."

Parbati often refers to herself a "jungle person," a term that refers to the Indigenous communities that live off the land, deep in the forests and jungles in Northeast India. These communities lived with captured elephants and sometimes sold them at fairs or leased elephants out for work in timber or hunting. Lalji learned from these men: the patawallas (fodder collectors and apprentices), mahouts, and the elite phandis (skilled in the art of *mela shekar*, the capturing of wild elephants with a lasso). When the government purses to former royal families ceased in 1971, Lalji sought to make a living doing what was once a hobby, capturing, then buying and selling elephants. Parbati chose to follow his path, without dozens of staff, and for a few short years they made quite a team.

But these albums tell a different story, of the years before Parbati was even born. The Baruas in these photographs are not "jungle people," even as they do hire and live among them. They are not living in bare-bones dwellings or eating only what they can gather from the land; even in the forest they have every creature comfort known to the time. *Glamping* takes on a new meaning.

Lalji was a wildly passionate hunter, elephant catcher, and adventurer, who was steeped in elephant wisdom, renowned for his way with elephants, respected and revered by mahouts everywhere he traveled. But the Baruas are elephant owners. They employ mahouts. Parbati and her father retreated into a jungle existence, making a living buying and selling elephants when the family lost its fortune. But they still had paid staff, and they were still viewed as royals, as owners.

The mysterious veil is lifted. Owners can be mahouts, but mahouts are rarely owners. Owners can walk away from their elephants and go on a vacation or to dinner with friends, owners can travel with pesky writers who want to know too much about their lives. Mahouts are tied to their elephants.

Here is a woman who chose not to have children. "The elephants are my children," she is famous for saying as she settled more deeply into the forest, alone. These are not choices women of Parbati's time and culture typically get to independently make. Lalji had many children, he brought them all with him while he went off to the camps for hunting and elephant catching. No one questions a man's right to have both.

At the end of the day, as we say goodbyes and head out to the car, the nephew says, "Would you like to see something?" He puts his hand on the knob of the door beneath the porch. "It used to be a billiards room. Guests would come and play. Now it houses all that we have left of our family history."

The door swings open and we walk in. My eyes struggle at first to see in the dark space. When they adjust, I am stunned by what unfurls before me. Rusted rows of rifles, a big-game hunting rifle, small cannons, and bed-length knives for sacrificing goats. Massive gold ornamental bowls, a howdah with tigers engraved on it, wooden shelves containing curios, tools, and utensils.

The walls are lined with fading taxidermy: tiger heads with glowing yellow eyes, a decaying badger on hind legs with his claws long gone and hands falling off. Curled python skins draped from freestanding doors and cabinets. A black-with-soot greater one-horned rhino, now virtually extinct. The stark white skull of an elephant dominates the corner, so large it reaches my chest. A macabre space. A profound metaphor for the Barua family and, ironically, for me. The ways that the past can take up so much space. Outsiders can see it clearly, the detritus of our past that decays even as we cling to it.

My time with Parbati is over. I have achieved some of my goals: softer images of her and an understanding of how the Baruas' past fits into the present day. I am succeeding on my first solo journey. And my photographs are good. But discouragement starts to creep in.

I am losing my way.

It is two o'clock in the morning at home. There is no one to talk to now, as it is that black hole during the day when I know that my children, husband, and loved ones are all sleeping. Loneliness seeps in and I begin to question myself once more.

I have wound my way into this labyrinth and now stand in the center, confused. The path is only blocked by my inability to see it. The story I have been on a quest to tell, about elephants and people in crisis throughout Northeast India, is still out there. I wrestle with my self-doubt all night and awaken regalvanized and ready to take the next steps to continue. Away from the past and into the present.

17

There are two days left in my trip and my hope is that Avijan will take me to see wild elephants along the Nepalese border. My camera is packed in a day bag and my nerves are steeled for what will be an hour-long scooter ride through Siliguri and out into the countryside.

"The plan is," Avijan says (and I love him for having a plan), "we will go now to visit my former professor. He is an expert in Indian wildlife and the conflict in North Bengal. If you want to understand about elephants here, you should listen to him first."

"Oh," I say, disappointed. "What about seeing the elephants?"

"I do not think they are there yet, maybe next week," he says. "But this is most important for your project."

I am frustrated, but telling myself to trust the process. In my quest to understand the human-elephant conflict history and scenario, I am certainly learning my fair share of the human part. I climb onto the back of Avijan's scooter, and we take off through the city. In addition to the usual barriers of chickens, cows lying in the road, stray dogs, tuk tuks, other cars and honking trucks, we have now added tight alleyways with moving people, large buses, and speed to the elements that already make this journey harrowing. Avijan has loaned me a helmet. But it is little more than a bowl on my head. Closing my eyes, I hope for the best. He makes this trek every single day.

The visit with the professor is fruitful, and I am grateful to meet Avijan's mentor. Much of what he tells me is consistent with what I've learned already. One topic is new. "They say corridors will create a safe and free passage for elephants," Avijan says, referring to efforts such as the WTI's 101 Corridors Campaign, "but everything depends on voting and politics. People come into the country and take up illegal residence along the borders, in the elephant habitat. If people stay there for three years, they earn full rights and politicians count on those illegal residents for votes. They are not even Indian, and they live in the elephant habitats. They do not have the same attitude of reverence that Indian people have for elephants. He is a god to us. The refugees are afraid of elephants and wish to kill them."

We stop at the border between the city and the start of the countryside. Plastic bottles, bags, food scraps, and other garbage is piled in a long line inside the ditch between the highway and the tea gardens. Smoke is rising from the end of the line, where the trash heaps have been set on fire. "This is a problem," Avijan says. "The animals—goats, cattle, dogs, pigs—they come here to eat the easy food. The leopard comes out from the forest, living in the tea garden where she can hide during the day, then eats those animals at night. And see, the human population is right there, but the people do not know because they never see the leopard."

We continue to visit a tea garden that has been abandoned, a common situation occurring throughout India, as the decades-old leases expire, and the owners are no longer interested in running the tea estate. They leave and tea plants become overgrown, clogging the ability for natural vegetation to return. This particular tea garden was abandoned about three years ago. Yet the employees who made this estate their home still live in the village that has existed in the center of the property for generations. With nowhere to go and no income, the residents have been struggling to survive. The overgrown garden, with its ideal sheltering spots, is now a breeding ground for leopards. Most of the residents have lost dogs and cattle to the local leopards, with no income or government compensation to pay for replacement.

When we arrive, the community leader greets us in the courtyard of his home. Flowering trees line the thin dirt lane, thick wooden sticks are tied together vertically to form a fence. Inside is a carefully raked dirt front yard with a tarp stretched out across one section. Tea leaves are scattered over the tarp, drying in the sun.

The house is a combination of corrugated metal, painted blue-green wood, and a cement foundation. When I peer inside, the interior is meticulously tidy; a cot and a broad wooden armchair are the only pieces of furniture. Shelves hold containers of collected rainwater, peacock feathers, stacks of magazines and books in Hindi and English

Avijan introduces me. "This man is the leader of this village. Both of his cows have been taken by leopards, and almost his dog, but he saved it. The leopard came right up to his back porch at night. I am working with him and some other villagers to help them build organic gardens, so they have an additional food source and something to sell at the market. No one is caring about these people."

Behind the house, the man shows Avijan the sprouts that have just started to poke through the soil. The garden here is substantial in terms of what and how much it can grow, and is carefully laid out to make the most of the small space. Behind the fenced and gated yard, the brush has been cleared.

"I told him to clear several feet of land behind him. This way the leopard cannot hide there. It is safer for him. He did all this by hand. We are working to help educate the other members of the village to do this too. People here want to kill the leopards and sneak across the Nepal border to sell the skins. If I can teach them another way to make a living, to help them with it, then maybe they will not be inspired to break the law. It will protect the leopard and their families." We walk out into the abandoned garden, brown and thick with plants that send stickers like small splinters out onto anything that brushes against it.

"Oh," Avijan says after a while. "Watch for your pants, these bushes have seeds."

I look down. My fabric slip-on sneakers, delicate pants, and favorite new dress all look like they have been attacked by a miniature porcupine. Of course. Wrong clothing. Again.

When we return, some members of the community have gathered. We have tea while Avijan socializes with them and they intermittently tell me their stories. A woman with brittle hair, hastily pulled back, and slim gold earrings, is slumped into a red plastic chair. Her young son—reed-thin arms and legs reaching out of oversized shorts and polo shirt—sits on his mother's lap, leaning against her concave body. A grandmother and adult daughter squat behind them, alternating between chatting and listening to what is being said. Across from Avijan sits a man with a beard and an injured eye with scar tissue, which looks off vaguely toward the drying tea.

"This woman's husband," Avijan points to the mother who looks younger than twenty years old, "has had to move to another tea garden for work. Now he can only come home to his family a few times a year. This man lost all his cattle and cannot get new ones. He has poor eyesight and cannot find a job. These people are living with leopards every day. We are trying to help them, so they do not do things like cut wood out of the forest. Illegal things out of desperation."

Avijan has told them ahead of time that we are doing a story about their situation. He encourages me to take photographs. I do, but my heart is not in it. I feel like I am taking advantage of their pain. I am slipping into a vortex of doubt. The foundation of all that keeps me returning, the lure of writing stories that will make a difference, is beginning to shake and crack. As I lift and shoot the camera, talk to the grieving, hopeless families, and walk the scraggly abandoned fields, I know with certainty that even if I write a story about this situation for the best publication in the world, with the largest circulation, little will change in these humans' day-to-day lives.

But it is clear that Avijan is making an impact. Every day, he goes out into the field to document elephants and leopards, to use his photographs to help people understand the landscape in North Bengal. Several times a week, he comes to villages like this, where people let him stay the night in their homes so he can photograph the wild things, the animals that they fear. In return, he teaches them new ways to survive and provide for themselves while ultimately protecting the forest and nature.

We never do see the wild elephants. Again, I have missed the window. Avijan and I say goodbye with promises to meet up in November, when the crops are ready for cultivation. As my plane lifts off above Bagdogra, the landscape is thick with smog, rolling greenery of tea gardens, and pockets of congested towns and cities. I think about the young mother holding her malnourished son on her lap in the red plastic chair, wide, pained eyes fixed on me as I took her photograph. I remember wishing she would smile.

I am a fool.

As I fly home to my daughters, I think about motherhood and our instinct for protection, even when so much is out of our control. All the ways I've struggled to keep the girls' lives stable amid turmoil. And how rooted in the psychological my situation has been. The mother I met is trying to provide the most elemental needs, vulnerable to predators and elements, with scarce access to food and clean water. No matter the circumstances, I think mothers are universally fierce in our primal efforts to protect our children.

I'm frustrated and depleted. Parbati is clear: the story is not about her. I've been chasing an idea, but it seems to have run its course. The abandoned tea garden was the first time I saw people living with and suffering from wildlife, but not elephants. Something is out there just beyond my grasp. I can't stop reaching for it.

18

I arrive home two days before Goldie's moving-up ceremony from eighth grade to high school. From there, summer unfurls in a wild frenzy. I have a soft idea about returning to India in October to see wild elephants eating crops and document Parbati training mahouts. But a fourth trip without any funding or publication interest is a discouraging proposition. David has been very supportive, but he is having trouble seeing a clear path, likely because I am having trouble seeing it too. I keep saying this is a book and then a documentary film but have little structure for either. Jody is teetering about her interest in a return trip.

Then some things happen.

As soon as I get home, we send the new photographs to the *National Geographic* editor. She tells us that, while compelling, the magazine will pass on the Parbati story. They have just run a feature about wildlife abuses worldwide, which includes an undercover spread about emaciated temple elephants in India. This is not exactly the best timing for the magazine to run a piece about traditional mahouts and a princess that used to catch wild elephants to sell them.

The story rejection is big hit to Jody's already waning enthusiasm. She has been receiving a lot of opportunities for paying projects, and this one hasn't gained much traction. I, on the other hand, am not ready to let it go. I feel called to keep trying.

I pitch the Parbati images and unique history to several other magazines. No one is particularly interested, but one of my favorite magazines, *Sidetracked*, tells me they would like to run a story about the human-elephant conflict if I am able to experience it firsthand, on the front lines.

While the story assignment won't be enough to cover the flight to India, it motivates me into action. Jody opts out. Our travel partnership will come to an end.

Some good news: *Maptia*, an international storytelling journal, will feature the mahout story Jody and I worked on during our time at the elephant camp. The article is titled "Keepers of Ganesh: The Lost Art of Mahout." I am grateful that our collaboration comes to fruition in a lasting story that shows the complexities of the captive elephant situation in India.

In June our friend, Tom, a pilot, offers to take Anhwei, Goldie, and me up in his small plane. Both girls have shown an interest in learning to fly someday. David, Goldie, Anhwei, and I drive to his hangar.

"Are you going to come with us, Mom?" Anhwei asks. She is sixteen years old, kayaking increasingly difficult whitewater and just raced her first Super-G alpine ski event at exorbitantly high speeds. She is fearless and has been keenly interested in flight since she was a little girl. Today's focus is to give her a chance to sit in the copilot seat and see how it inspires her.

"Yeah! You should come," Goldie declares.

Small planes have always terrified me. The way they get bounced around like balls in a lottery air machine generates a bad combination of motion sickness and fear of crashing. Wasn't I already proving my courage by letting the girls go?

"I am not sure if there is room for me," I say. This is both true and a stall tactic. My mind immediately goes to my paragliding motion sickness faux paus with Anhwei years earlier, something I don't wish to repeat.

David gives me a side glance and a slight nod to say there is room. I also know that he is eager to go. He loves planes and loves the girls. This is a rare opportunity.

We pull into the airplane lot. Tom's Cessna is already parked out in front of his hangar. The sunlight bounces off the shiny nose propellers, making the plane gleam with a playfulness that fits Tom's personality. His wild shock of gray hair tops a compact body with coiled-up positive energy that leaps out like a spring to all that know him. A gentleman, ruffian, adventure junky, and spiritual seeker, Tom is unconventional in looks and manner. His generosity is widely known and deeply appreciated by the many who love him.

"Ready to fly a plane, Anhwei?" he asks. "I have room for three. Who is coming?"

It is a vibrant morning. Clouds billow to the south and far north. The surrounding foothills are still a pistachio green from the recent rain.

Both girls look at me. David grins and quietly says, "You go ahead."

"I'd love to go if that's okay." I hear the words spill out of my mouth at the same time as I realize that I mean them. The fear I expected to feel is gone.

Goldie and I take our seats in the back, the plane is as narrow as my arm span, a fact that I immediately put out of my head. Tom gives us headsets and shows us how to use them. While we practice and laugh, Tom walks around the plane with Anhwei teaching her some basics. Goldie gives me a tremendous smile and asserts, "This is going to be awesome."

Anhwei climbs in the copilot seat and turns around to say hi. She is radiant with joy, and I want to hug Tom for making this moment happen for her, for us. David becomes a waving dot as we head down the runway and into the sky.

While Tom shows Anhwei various controls and explains what he is doing, Goldie and I each look out our windows. We live in a small community packed into a tight valley, surrounded by foothills that give way to granite mountain peaks. In moments, we have left the rolling hills and silver-specked river and are approaching the Sawtooth Range to the north.

The plane bumps and jostles but I am not afraid. I am spellbound. For all the years we have lived within the embrace of these storied mountains, never have we soared within them. I see snow winding like white streams, still clinging to peaks, crags, and shaded narrow chutes. Hidden shimmering blue lakes tucked into crevices of brown and gray rock, which glint and glow as the clouds pass through.

Tom looks at Anhwei, "Want to take a turn?" He shows her the controls and explains what to do.

Anhwei nods. Goldie and I look at each other openmouthed. There she goes, smooth and supported. Tom takes another look at the radar. "Well done," he says. "We have a bit of weather coming up in a few minutes. I think we should turn around now before it gets too bumpy for you." Tom takes over the controls and we all congratulate a beaming Anhwei. When we lock eyes, no words are necessary. We are sharing this adventurous moment; the shift in me has not gone unnoticed.

As we begin to turn around, the Sawtooth Range telescope out into a wider view of the peaks. I think of the flight to Assam, just a few short weeks ago. So anxious and eager for what lay ahead. My seatmates were two young men, tucked into large sweatshirts with hoods up. In my irrational fear, I was convinced they were terrorists, but they were, in fact, Indian Army soldiers and bought me tea. Midway through our flight, the man next to me reached over his sleeping companion and flipped up the window shade. "Ma'am," he said. "Look!" Out the window with chiseled clarity so detailed it took my breath away was the entire Himalaya mountain range parallel to our view. We strained to watch it for as long as possible, all three of us snapping photos. The most famous mountains on the planet, unfolding before us, in all their history and lure, magic and hardship, firmly anchored to the earth, rising to the heavens. Out my window right now, here with my daughters in this fragile, contained space, I feel the same momentous soulful connection in my own backyard. I had not recognized it until now.

In July we are invited to Washington, DC, for the fiftieth anniversary celebration of the Apollo 11 moon landing. I go with the girls a couple of days early so I can show them some of the places where I used to live when I was a Head Start Fellow.

Because the girls love animals, we take a trip to the Smithsonian's National Zoo. Here, the zoo has poured efforts into animal conservation and recovery. A sweltering day, the grounds are enormous. We must prioritize. Anhwei and I explore the big cat exhibit. She has an affinity for large and fierce tigers, leopards, and lions. It is a thrill to see real ones for the first time. Goldie is crazy for pandas. We watch them eat and play for an entire hour before tearing ourselves away.

As we leave, I notice that we are near the elephant enclosure. The girls are merely patient with me when I talk about India and show them photos of the elephants and my experiences there. When I ask if they would ever like to come with me, both are a resounding "no, thank you." Over time, I stop talking about it so much. I had not even thought to visit the elephants! When I suggest it now, I see the same glazed-over expressions. Goldie is ready to head home. Anhwei says, "Yeah sure, I'll go." I have a strong suspicion she is saying this only to please me.

We trek over to the elephant trail, winding through a large natural enclosure. As we turn the corner Goldie says, "Mom! Look!" Her boredom and fatigue disappear. Two female elephants are drinking from the watering hole. One dips her trunk in and, with a flick that immediately transports me back to the Murti River and the Dhupjhora elephants, she sprays a shower over her head. Both Anhwei and Goldie yell, "Did you see that?!" We watch as she does it again, then again. I stay quiet to let them experience this marvel on their own. We continue into the enclosure, where a caregiver is filing the nails of a large male Asian elephant. We press our faces near the glass.

Anhwei says, "Mom, were the ones you saw this big?"

"Yes," I say. "Some bigger and some smaller. The mahouts file their nails like this, only they use the kukri knife I have at home on my dresser."

Anhwei stares a little longer. "That's so cool you got to do that. They are amazing."

End of August. Goldie begins high school. Anhwei and I take her to school on her first day, then sneak in to wander the hallways, taking photos and placing sticky notes with inspiring quotes all over her locker. We hope to give Goldie some of the encouragement that she always gives to us.

Still lost about where to go from here, I spend my free time wistfully reading the *Asian Elephant Digest* and following Instagram accounts that feature Indian photographers and wildlife biologists documenting elephants. This leads me to some other sites; one is a tea garden owned by a woman. On her feed is a remarkable video of a wild elephant herd peacefully moving through her tea garden. In her caption, she spoke about the conflict and how important it was to give elephants space to travel without interference. These fragments are not enough to satisfy my curiosity—instead, they tease and taunt.

Mid-September takes us to London, where David is giving a talk about recovering the Apollo F-1 rocket engines at the Royal Geographical Society. Afterward, we take a brief trip to Wales to visit friends. Over breakfast, David asks our host, a filmmaker and one of the most innovative storytellers on our planet today, if he would be willing to look at my photos and hear about what I have been doing in India; if he could give me some advice on where to take it from here. I am unprepared to succinctly articulate what I am attempting to accomplish with all this material. It is getting difficult to justify a return to India in a month without a clear plan. Anthony is patient, listens carefully, and is intrigued. He gives solid advice about putting my energy into writing a book, telling me that only then will I fully understand the story, and only when that is honed should I put energy into a film.

Later we three take a hike behind their stone house, up a well-traveled sheep trail that winds up the hill, through a dense forest of trees and along a creek rushing around moss-covered rocks. An enchanted landscape where I fully expect to see an elf or fairy any moment. At the top of the ridge, we stop to take in the view. This morning's rain has abated, and low-hanging storm clouds drift across the horizon. A sweeping panorama of undulating emerald-green hills. Anthony has a small camera and is avidly taking photographs. I had not even seen it at first.

"You should get this camera to take back to India with you." He shows me. "It's small, so not as alarming or intimidating to people when you want to take their photos. The shots will be more natural. It does everything well with the automatic setting, easy to take it with you anywhere, and shoots 4K film. Don't use your phone."

I record the specifics of the camera in my phone notes.

"Also," he says, "don't try to write field notes while you are over there. You get too tired; it is hard to keep up. Just use your recorder. I use mine all the time, everywhere. Take all your notes and reflections with voice recording, even as you are in the moment, so you don't forget the details."

"What a brilliant idea." I say. "My written notes always start out so robust, but midway through they are scant and illegible."

The wind picks up and the hillside grows blustery, whipping tall grasses into a frenzied dance. Clouds have blended, creating a single dark gray sky. Fat drops begin to plop on the earth around our feet. Our rain jackets fill with wind, sounding like flapping parachutes. Just as we start back down, Anthony says, voice rising over the impending storm, "Don't worry if you don't have it all yet, Kim. Sometimes you have to fight for the story."

In early October, Avijan starts sending me texts: *When are you coming? The elephants are already here.* It is decided that I will go alone again. This time I am going to experience the conflict in real time and I already have a magazine editor who is keen to publish the story. Avijan will shoot the conflict photographs, and I have a new small, but mighty, camera that promises to deliver for the rest of my time there. Only, I do not have a plan for what else I want to achieve. Avijan is only available for four to five days and I do not know how to fill the other two weeks. It takes so long to get there, and to acclimate, I cannot possibly go only for four days.

At first, I feel completely deflated. Then something shifts. Instead of wringing my hands, I tell myself to think more broadly: What do I want to accomplish while I am there and who can assist? Experiencing wild elephants in the field with Avijan is a key part, but maybe there are other entities who can show me other facets of the conflict and coexistence work while crop season is at its height? Upasana Ganguly, director of the WTI Elephant Corridor Project I met with when I was in Delhi last May, connects me with two of their Corridor Project sites that would be a good fit and they will let me shadow their work for a few days. With this loose arrangement, I determine this will be the trip that I will trust to fall into place when I arrive. Even the wild elephants will be unpredictable. Days before I leave, Parbati's niece reaches out to me to let me know Parbati has returned from the field and will meet me at the elephant camp for a few days if I pay her a per diem and the cost for lodging. The per diem and lodging is a fair request as I am likely taking her time away from critically needed paying work. But we have already worked together in the elephant camp, and there is nothing more for me to do with her there. I ask if she would meet me in Assam, to document her elephants. But this is the only plan that could work. I am worried about saying no, but I do.

Knowing that I will be riding on the back of scooters and motorcycles throughout the night and busy traffic days, David buys me a low-key but safety-rated helmet. He and Anhwei decide to paint it. Anhwei studies drawings of elephant heads, deciding on a spectacular Ganesh head, which she re-creates in jewel tones with a set of special waterproof art pens. She spends hours laboring over the elephant, which is displayed in all his brilliance across the top of the helmet. For extra luck and protection, she creates an elaborate third eye on the front. A labor of love that takes days. Each day, she comes home, does homework, and sets to the task of creating this helmet. When she is finished, David adds an Indian truck–style design along the back, in bright chunk letters that say HONK, PLEASE.

I put the helmet on my head and wrap my arms around Anhwei while David takes our picture. "It's your 'Scooty Beauty Helmet,'" he says. A motorcyclist's joking reference to the scooter I will be riding. We set the helmet on top of my luggage to finish drying as I continue to pack.

Later, Anhwei hands me a folded paper with cartoons drawn on the front and the words *Mom, Mama, Mommy* dancing around the paper with swirling designs. "Don't open it until tomorrow," she says.

When I say goodbye this time, it is with new, and even more intense, fears. Now I am afraid of death by a wild elephant, getting hit by a bus while on the back of a bike, being kidnapped and tortured, getting raped or robbed while we are out all night, and having to go to the bathroom when there isn't one. For the second time in less than a year, I am embarking on this journey alone. But this time, no one is greeting me at the airport and driving me in their car. This time, I have made no in-country flight arrangements or hotel reservations beyond my first five days. Instead, I am applying all the lessons I have learned so far to take each day as it comes and find the magic. For the first time in my life, I am traveling somewhere with entire stretches of days completely unaccounted for. Whatever it will be, I am open and ready.

An early morning departure is always the rawest. The girls are still asleep. Anhwei and I said our goodbyes last night when I tucked her into bed, but Goldie asked that I wake her before I leave. This worries me because her separation anxiety has always been most acute in the wee hours. Her room is lit with a polar bear night light, helping guide my way. She sleeps on the top bunk of a loft bed, so I must stand on tiptoes and reach high for her cheek. As is our routine, she lifts her hand in the air, searching for my fingers before lifting her head. I clasp hands with hers and squeeze. "Good morning, muffin," I say. Goldie sleepily sits up in her bed, not tall enough yet to hit the ceiling. She reaches into one of the baskets she has rigged up along the outside edges, digs out a homemade envelope with the word *QUOTES* on it, stars and comets swirling around the letters. "Here," she says, voice thick with dreams. "I made these for you to take with you." She hands me the envelope and inside are a stack of handwritten inspirational quotes. The writing on each card varies in size and style, artfully organized on the paper. I read the top quote, fighting not to let my voice crack:

Create the highest, grandest
Vision possible for your life,
Because you become what you
BELIEVE

"These are incredible," I say. "They will help me so much. I will read them every day." We hug and this time I am the one fighting to walk out of her room and into the dark predawn without tears. "Brave Mouse," we say almost in unison. Referring to a book I used to read to her when she was young, about a mouse who must stand up to his terrific fears, and eventually prevails. We now use it as code to help each other gather the strength we need to get through a particularly challenging moment, which this is.

David insists on driving me to the airport, even though it is 4:30 A.M. He slips an Explorers Club flag patch into my backpack. This is not a flag expedition, but it could be. The former head of Flag and Honors is subtly letting me know that this trip is a worthy exploration. I discover it as I reach for my passport when we pull up to the airport.

"I am proud of you," he says. "Good luck, I hope you discover everything you need."

We kiss goodbye in the car, he helps me with my bags, then we wave until his car is out of sight. Inside the terminal waiting area, I find a quiet spot to open Anhwei's letter.

> *Mama—I love you so so so (soo) much. I hope you have fun in India. I am sure you'll learn and see lots of awesome stuff. Please know that I fully support your trips and work because it's your passion and you worked hard to achieve freedom and flexibility. It's so cool that you have these opportunities, it is something to be proud of. I love you and may your trip be safe and amazing. Love, Anhwei xoxox*

Now I am crying in public. I press my lips to the letter, then hold it to my heart before texting my daughter a thank-you. After all these years of being cast out as a "couch potato" for reading and writing, for failing to paraglide without getting motion sickness, after all these years fearing my children will be emotionally damaged if I travel to build a career that I love, lying awake at night worrying that my family and my community think I am a neglectful mother, after all these years of wondering if my actions today will destroy something fundamental tomorrow, this.

Anhwei's letter, her work-of-art motorcycle helmet, Goldie's quotes, and the Explorers Club flag patch. These will be my guardians and force fields to keep me safe.

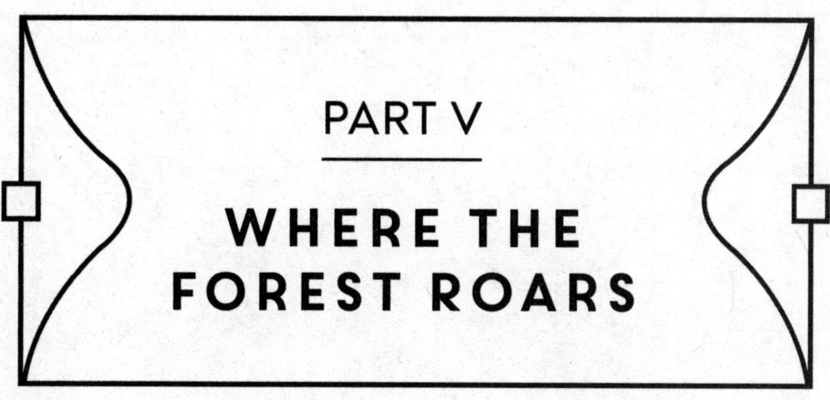

PART V

WHERE THE FOREST ROARS

What we are doing to the forests of the world is but a mirror reflection of what we are doing to ourselves and to one another.

—Mahatma Gandhi,
Collected Works of Mahatma Gandhi vol. 13

19

Siliguri is particularly congested and polluted when I return five months later, more than I have seen before. At the Saluja Residency, I have a smaller room, trying to conserve money. The room is stark, bare-bones, with the type of stains you can never clean, like smears of blood, on my comforter. This is the last trip I can afford to take without any kind of outside support. When I pull the drapes back to see the reason for the commotion, there are bars, the only view a cement wall. A now-familiar sight. My family would be surprised if they saw this, and when I see how other people are living, I know this is relative luxury. There are people living under the overpass bridges. Makeshift houses of corrugated metal, garbage piling up all around. Cows and dogs eating trash. But I also see community, men talking over tea and newspapers, women shopping, socializing in clusters, children playing. People speak of India like it is a throbbing, pulsing massive beat of the same sound. It is more like all sounds at once. But who am I to know what India is? I only know this one little part and hardly that.

Music blares from speakers out on the street. Loud bursts that sound like cannons exploding outside. It is six o'clock in the evening on a Saturday. The sounds come in rhythmic succession, like drumbeats. I challenge myself to go fetch provisions. Out into the night, the cacophony becomes clear, a parade with firecrackers, singing and dancing, and all ages lining the streets waving flags. Only men are in the parade, but women follow along on the sidewalk. It is the Muslim holiday Mawlid, the birthday of the Prophet Muhammad. The chanting shifts as the floats go by. Sometimes it sounds like religious singing, other times more like a protest rally.

Much like the chanting crowd during my drive with Parbati after the election, there is this experience filtered through my own lens, rather than facts. My instinct feels celebration mixed with tension. Back in my room, thanks to the local newspaper, I learn that yesterday, after decades of dispute, the national court ruled the 2.2 acres of Muslim temple grounds is the birthplace of the Hindu god Ram, and the property will be returned to the state and transformed back into a Hindu religious site. The *Hindu Times* speaks to the ruling and how the timing has affected the tone of today's celebration. Many areas have canceled their celebrations fearful of a repeat of the deadly Gujarat riots of 2002, where 790 Muslims and 254 Hindus were killed.

From the very beginning, I was compelled to understand the nuances of culture and spirituality, politics and relationships in this region. It's astonishing how our instincts can sense the essence of emotion: anger, fear, joy. But without facts and history, all we mistakenly use our unique lens to interpret what we see. With all the competing demands, our attention span is growing shorter. We react to sound bites, clips, and micro stories. From these, we form our opinions. I fall asleep studying the history of Hindus and Muslim relationships in India, how it's playing out today, and wondering how it affects the elephants.

A creature of habit, I wake at 4:00 A.M., ready to go. Only Avijan will not be picking me up until late this afternoon, which means I am stuck in this depressing box of a room for hours before the day begins. This is maddening, but one of my strongest lessons from these journeys is practicing the art of patience. Somehow, I can be patient here in a way that I cannot be at home. Here, when you force things, you pay for it. When you yield to the flow, whatever that is, you are given gifts. It is up to me to see these gifts, look for them, and trust the process. My goal today is to be open to whatever come. To let beauty win over menace. India is rich with energetic opportunity. You can draw in what you want. If you are fearful, you perceive everything through fear and suspicion. But if you create a bubble of love and kindness, you will draw in love and kindness.

Finally, Avijan arrives. After an enthusiastic reunion, we set off. I am shocked to see that the sun is already low on the smoggy horizon. The light is dull and flat. As the cityscape falls away to a pastoral countryside, Avijan shares his view of the range of issues facing elephants and the local people.

"All the corridors are fragmented. Whenever the elephant comes out from the forest and wants to move into another forest, they must go through the gaps, which involve barriers like highways, train tracks, housing developments, army barracks, and tea garden estates. The gaps are being referred to as 'corridors' by the NGOs and trusts, but that is just a word, nothing else," he explains. "If the forest is connected, we do not need corridors. If connected, it becomes a habitat for wildlife. Most of the forest is now made up of tea plantations—that is not a habitat. 'Habitat' means the place where animals live and thrive.

"If you simply connect the forests, that will not solve the problem because there is no food left in these forests. The elephants have learned that they cannot depend on forest food. But the nutritious food from the crops, the manmade foods and planted fruits in the village, these foods are extra nutritious and fibrous. Elephants need them because they know if they eat these foods, they can eat less to get the same level of nutrients. They have strong reproductivity from eating these foods. The bulls become more sexual to attract the females, elephants can mate, and population grows."

We are on our way to the village where Avijan does most of his photographing, where he has identified most of the regional bulls over the past few years. It is located along the India–Nepal border. The World Bank and other wildlife organizations have built a large wall there, blocking the elephants' traditional migration route. This is the area where the elephants used to pool, the spot where Jody first saw the selfies three years ago. The border area between Nepal and India in North Bengal is the birthplace of this storytelling quest. I have written about this spot for the *Explorers Journal*, with Avijan, even as I have yet to see it with my own eyes.

Avijan tells me that wall was new when he first took Jody there, and the elephants pooled because they were confused. "Now they have figured it out, they have made new pathways."

We pull over at one of the tea garden villages and walk around the crop fields. Avijan is looking for evidence of elephant herd activity. We see large prints crossing a river. "They have been here," he says, "probably last night."

Out into the field and he points out the different types of rice stalks, which are most nutritious for the elephants, those they prefer. All cultivated by hand, and as we talk a farmer walks past with a newly picked bundle hoisted onto his shoulder.

At a small town outside of a tea garden, we pull over. On the corner is a food shop with two small tables outside and a Nepalese cook working a flaming wok in a galley kitchen behind the counter. The menu features Chinese, Nepalese, and some Indian snack food.

"This is my restaurant," says Avijan.

"What? This is yours?"

"Yes. It is very near the village where I do most of my photographing, so I opened it to help give some local people a job and a different option for food. Then I come here too. We'll wait here for Tufan."

Avijan orders dumplings and noodles for us, along with masala chai from the table across the road. We have been out of Siliguri for almost four hours now and I have to use a bathroom. Of course, there is no bathroom or even any place to squat and pee without people seeing me. I did bring a special device called a She Pee that is made of plastic and allows you to discretely pee like a male, off in the bushes, without exposing your butt to the world. None of that even seems possible. So, I will the need away. I have never traveled anywhere else in the world where it is so impossible to find a place to relieve myself.

A year from now, I will read an article about how sixty percent of all India's population defecates outside, sans bathroom of any sort. And that women in particular often struggle to hold it in because of modesty to go in public like men. Perhaps that is the reason you never see many women active at any one time. This is a problem that also contributes to the human-elephant conflict. Many of the human deaths that occur at the hands of elephants, happen early in the morning when men are having their morning poop, often at the edges of forests where elephants are startled.

Tufan is the unofficial "mayor" of this village community. He is unusually tall and muscular, with thick hair and well-dressed in a navy button-down shirt tucked into dark jeans with dress shoes. His entire presence commands respect. He reminds me of the saying "Speak softly and carry a big stick." For his is a quiet strength. No one is going to mess with Tufan.

He is going to guide us each night, and I think that he offers protection to Avijan. We are now a group of four and it is getting dark. We walk to an open-air shop to buy a chicken for tonight's dinner. The chicken is walking around, then it is lifted into the air in front of us, neck twisted swiftly, and chopped with a cleaver. The butcher's wife plucks the feathers, and the chicken is boiled, placed in a bag, and handed to us for our dinner.

We gather in Tufan's brother Kishor's house. He has a wife, two daughters the same age as Anhwei and Goldie, and a son. Tufan's mother lives in the house as well. While the women prepare dinner, the men drink tea in Kishor's bedroom, sprawled across floor and bed, talking about the elephant activity and other things that I cannot understand. The women will not let me help them and I feel grateful to be included, as if I am one of the men. A picture of Mahatma Gandhi hangs on the cobalt blue wall. "Do you know who he is?" asks Kishor, who is even taller than his brother, but lanky with a cool air about him. He seems like he could have a career as a social media influencer or a Bollywood star.

"Yes," I reply, "Gandhi."

"He was a great man, Gandhi," Kishor says, then laughs as if he is playing a joke on me.

After dinner we go out into the closest field. Clusters of farmers, mostly men, are standing around. Forest patrol vehicles with sirens and lights atop the truck drive through. In the distance people are shouting and firecrackers pop. "The elephants must be there," Avijan says. We stand around in the dark waiting and listening. "Look, look, you can see them!" Avijan points into the trees, there is some movement, a blur. Flashlights are flickering to light up the spot. After a while, things seem to die down. Tufan is taking constant calls on the phone, people are telling him where there are sightings. It is late; at 11:00 P.M., Saluja closes its gate. The front desk staff said the guard would let me in after hours, but I am worried. We decide to return now, as we have an hour-long drive ahead of us. We will go again tomorrow, and the next night. "You cannot really see it unless we spend the whole night," Avijan has told me. "We will do that tomorrow maybe."

A plan is starting to come together. Upasana Ganguly from the Wildlife Trust of India has connected me to a group in Dooars called SPOAR (Society for Protection of Ophiofauna & Animal Rights) who are working on creating safe passage for elephants throughout the identified corridors there. When I have completed my time in North Bengal, they have agreed to take me with them for a few days while they do their work. They work near Riverwood, and we agree that I will stay there; it is close enough for them to pick me up. All my work so far has been in North Bengal and Dooars, along the Himalaya range and India–Nepal and Bhutan borders. I am eager to move out of Saluja, but I am feeling overwhelmed at the idea of spending the night in the village.

This afternoon we take the scooter, and I proudly wear my helmet. Avijan is explaining scenarios to me the entire way. He keeps turning back to tell me stories, but I worry that he is not keeping his eyes on the road. We seem to be spending a lot of time waiting around, departing midafternoon when the light is dull and gray. Winter light that I do not associate with this place. The sun sets early, an orange ball against a smoke-gray sky. The saris seem less bright, the tea gardens less verdant. I am useless as a photographer in this light because I have not yet learned how to properly work my manual settings. The iPhone is taking better low-light photos, but I will rely on Avijan. We are doing the *Sidetracked* magazine piece together, and I will need terrific images because the photography is an important part of the magazine. Already, I am thinking of shot lists and telling him what we need. He says, "Yes, yes, okay." Dubious.

We wait for almost an hour at Avijan's restaurant. Tufan finally arrives on his motorcycle and tells us that there is a herd moving through a tea garden. The decision is made for all three of us to all get on Tufan's bike and ride.

We arrive at the entrance where there is a guard station and a tea estate sign that reads NUXALBARI TEA ESTATE 1894. Nuxalbari? The name sounds so familiar. We wait at the gate while Tufan makes a phone call to his contacts regarding the whereabouts of the herd. Avijan says, "Sonia Jabbar is the owner of this garden. I tried to call her today to see if we could come here. Many times, the elephants will come through here. She offers them safe passage."

My memory is jogged. Nuxalbari? Sonia? I quickly check my Instagram account. There is the clip of elephants walking through the pathways with my supportive comments below. The sign is the same. Somehow, I am now standing at the entrance of this exact tea estate that I've been following for weeks, about to go inside to see my first wild elephant.

Avijan picks up his phone and calls. "She is not answering," Avijan says. "She may be out of town."

Tufan and Avijan have a conversation trying to determine what to do. The sign says NO TRESPASSING, but the guard knows Avijan and waves him in.

We ride the dirt road until we get to a bridge over a trench. Just beyond are signs on trees that say ELEPHANT FRIENDLY CROSSING. There appears to be a route and, while people are gathering at the bridge, no one is going to the other side. Somehow the news has spread, and a crowd is rapidly forming along the road. All young men, no girls or women. They talk among themselves; the mood is festive and anticipatory. Avijan begins to set up his camera. Tufan waits in the background.

Suddenly, I hear a distant roar, constant stream of honking, and a booming female voice rapidly coming toward us. A petite but solid woman with short black hair is shouting and beeping from her open jeep. Dust kicks up from the back as the vehicle (a stunningly restored Kaiser, British racing green with camel leather seats) comes barreling toward the entire lot of us, as if she is a bowling ball and we are the pins.

"Get out! Get out! All of you!" She slams the truck into park and jumps out. Her sweeping and constant hand gestures create a largeness well beyond her physical stature. A wispy, pale young man, ashen now, remains in the passenger seat, apparently here for a tea tour. Most of the crowd has dispersed. We are still standing.

"Avijan?" she says. "You know better! What are you doing here?"

"I tried to call you," Avijan says, "So we could get permissions . . ."

Before he can finish, Sonia sees me. "Who are YOU?!" she yells, pointing in my face.

I love her immediately; admire her from the core of my being. This woman who is practically spitting on me with fury. I am desperate to be her friend.

"I am a huge fan of yours. I follow you on Instagram." I hear myself sounding like a crazed groupie. She has already discounted me with disgust and turned back on Avijan, berating him for exacerbating the stress on the wild elephants.

"Photographers are part of this problem. The elephants need to be left in peace. You know better. I can't believe you did this!"

I step forward, realizing that it is up to me to fix this. "It is my fault," I said. "I am a writer and I have been working on a book about humans and elephants in India for two years. I still have not experienced the conflict firsthand and I am here so Avijan can show me. I am so, so sorry. It is because of me."

She looks me up and down.

"Come on, get in the jeep," she sounds exasperated but softer. "Come in for tea."

I look at Avijan and Tufan, hesitating. "Avijan," Sonia solves the problem for me. "You both come. Meet us at the house."

With that, Sonia tears off down the road, hitting every bump. She looks like a character in a wildlife television show from my youth—full khaki outfit—pants and short-sleeved shirt, sneakers. I cannot believe my good fortune. In my social media universe, Sonia is a conservation rock star, fighting for elephants using her tea garden as a sanctuary. I have been following her Instagram account for months. It is so rare for a female to own a tea estate. I sneak some photos and video when I am certain she is not looking, terrified of her catching me.

We pull up to a gate on a curved road leading to a large white office building and an enclosed plantation house. A white painted clapboard built in the 1800s, with low-slung, pale green metal roofing, artful iron grills on open leaded glass windows with large white shutters, and wide French doors. The house is surrounded by grass and gardens, well-kept and beautiful.

I am having trouble getting over my shock at this strange turn of events.

The young male passenger who was ashen at our first interaction has recovered a flush to his cheeks. We follow Sonia through the latched gate to her home. Sonia yells out some instructions into the house. "Go, have a seat out on the garden." She points to me. She says to the passenger, "I'll check in with you at dinner time. Be back by 7:30." Looking at me again, she says, "Go on. I'll be there in a few moments."

By the time Sonia returns, an uneasy Avijan and Tufan have arrived and are sitting with me. They are a bit distrustful of the transformation of Sonia's ire into hospitality. I can sense Avijan simmering still with anger over being publicly reprimanded.

"Why are you here?" Sonia asks.

"I want to see the wild elephants because I am writing a book about the human-elephant conflict here. Avijan and I are working together on a story for a magazine in the UK, so he is teaching me about the issues."

Sonia looks at Avijan. "You need to show her the Hathi Sathi [elephant education] program that we do with the children. We teach them not to be afraid of elephants, to want to protect them. It is too late for their parents; we need to educate the next generation."

Avijan nods his head back and forth, agreeing and not agreeing.

Sonia says, "Why do you want to disturb the elephants? You should leave them be."

"I do not want to bother them," I reply. Taking a sip of tea and trying to figure out how to articulate my motivation, "I just want to understand, to see it for myself so I can tell others at home. Most people in the West do not know what is happening here."

Sonia asks me where I am staying. When she discovers I am alone in a hotel in downtown Siliguri, she is horrified.

"I am hosting an artist's retreat next week," she says, "otherwise I would invite you to stay here." She thinks for a bit. "Actually, I think this front room could be available. Here is my number, text me tomorrow if you would like to stay for the next three days."

When we gather to leave, Sonia sees that we have all come on a single motorcycle. "What is this?" she asks Avijan. "She cannot ride with you boys like this. I will have her driven back."

"No, no," I exclaim, trying to come to Tufan and Avijan's rescue. "We are only down the road and we have proper transportation there. I'll be fine. Thank you, though."

We return to Avijan's restaurant and retrieve his scooter. Bidding Tufan goodbye, we decide to head home early.

"Tomorrow night," Avijan says again on the ride home. "If you want to see the elephants, you must stay overnight in the village. It is the only way. I think we should do it tomorrow."

Back in my room, I research the Nuxalbari Tea Estate and Sonia. The estate was founded by Sonia's great-grandfather, the nawab of Jaldapara, a Muslim royal who had a passion for tea. The website has the stories of each of the three women who have led Nuxalbari, a rare circumstance among Hindu or Muslim communities. I can barely sleep, hoping Sonia's offer to move in with her tomorrow still stands.

In the morning, I send Sonia a message asking if the offer of accommodation is still open. She says yes and texts the specifics for room and board for the next three nights. The rate is reasonable, and I cannot believe my luck that after two years of never even seeing a wild elephant I am about to live in the middle of the tea garden where the elephants come for respite each night. I am moving out of this room that has felt like a cell and headlong into a compelling new story.

20

This morning I wake to songbirds rather than pigeons fighting, and the sunrise floods my room through a picture window that looks out onto a garden instead of cinderblock. A room that is spacious and clean. Decorated in simple but elegant style, with a four-poster bed and mosquito netting that I tucked under last night. Yet last night, instead of feeling safe and grateful, I was up at 1:00 A.M., imagining a gang of armed men coming into the house, knowing I am staying here, kidnapping me. Eyes wide open and stricken with sleep-confused fear, frozen in place like a young child afraid of the dark. Thinking that the bars on the windows were too delicate and why where they there in the first place? Remembering the story of Sonia's mother, Dolly, and her facing the hundreds of angry workers as they threatened to destroy her and her home in the Nuxalbari town uprising decades ago.

I had thought about this when walking with Sonia yesterday, as we passed the workers who live at the tea garden's edges in houses with no running water or toilets. They greeted Sonia with respect and smiles. She enthusiastically greeted everyone. But I understand these power dynamics and recognize the platitudes.

I am just going to say it: I do not want to stay in the village overnight.

I have seen the situation at night, do I really need to see it all night? Can Avijan ensure my safety? Honestly, I am having a ridiculous bathroom-based fear. I hold it for hours and hours, because there is nowhere to discreetly relieve myself. Yet I do not have enough content for a compelling *Sidetracked* story. What will I write? *I stood in the dark and heard crackers and pipe guns. I saw one elephant move along the shadows.* I am in this thing on my own now. Making my own decisions.

"Sometimes you have to fight for the story," I hear Anthony tell me while the storm blew in over the top of a hill in Wales. I must make this story happen and stop obsessing about peeing or safety beyond my control.

At breakfast Sonia says, "You don't have to be a hero. The elephants should be left in peace. Not chased all night, not even by the photographers." She is firm, and in her tone I hear how she is long used to directing and commanding. Still, there is an underlying softness to her—the way she brushes her short hair from her eyes, the lilt of her voice when speaking of her daughter, of the garden. The way I can almost see her heart when she mentions her mother, the grief still lingering in every fiber of her being. I am here during a very tense time, an intersection of decision-making. She is not popular among the local community, nor is there any love lost between herself and the Forest Department officials, but still she persists.

I say, "I think it's important to document it. It helps people understand what is happening here. It will help me write about it. The Western world has no idea how urgent the situation is. They think African elephants and Asian elephants are the same, with the same problems."

"Do what you have to do. But I do not share your opinion. The elephants are visibly relaxed when they move through here. The stress that the villagers put on them with their lights and crackers, sirens, and shouts, it is too much. You'll see," she says. "I will have the kitchen prepare a sandwich for you. You can take it in case you get hungry."

I spend the morning working on the computer, photographing the garden, sipping tea on the veranda, bathed in sunlight, surrounded by sounds of nature, the whirring of a ceiling fan, thinking again about Mark Shand and his tea garden stay. The way I felt he had sold out to comfort.

Avijan seems annoyed by my move to Nuxalbari. He may view Sonia as overly aggressive, loud, and full of privilege. He is very attached to the village situation, the plight of the farmers, their right to a bountiful life. It seems everyone in this area relies on Avijan for something. He is contacted regularly by the Forest Department and often goes with them out on patrols. Wildlife Trust of India has given him the honor of Green Corridor Champion for his work on documenting elephants in this region. Many of the photographs they use for fundraising are his, and they have published his book of his years of work, identifying all the male solitary bulls in the region. Still, this trip he seems frustrated with all but the villagers. He sees the urgency and also sees that the political situation often interferes with the solution. In his opinion, no one is working together as much as trying to gain notoriety and funding for themselves. Avijan does not appear to be getting paid for his work, yet he is in the field every single day, building relationships and helping others. Even Sonia relies on him for photography and help with her Hathi Sathi programs that she runs for the children on the estate, to help dispel fear of elephants and instill a love of protecting wildlife for future generations.

The situation here is heating up. The elephants have been marauding through the crops in the region every night for weeks. Then they come back and sleep, uninterrupted in the sanctity of Sonia's tea garden. Sonia feels this is good for the elephants, this peaceful place to rest. The villagers, however, are increasingly upset that the elephants have not been driven out of the area. They see what Sonia does as harboring criminals.

This is a job that falls under the purview of the Forest Department, and the people of North Bengal believe that the Forest Department is wholly responsible for the elephants' behavior. When people are killed by elephants, they are incensed at the department for not preventing it, even angrier that the government does not provide a higher rate of compensation, or in some cases, no compensation at all, or remediation for destroyed property. Every night for weeks elephants have been coming into these communities, destroying crops, often trampling people early in the morning or crushing them in their homes while they sleep at night. The Forest

Department has patrols that work all night to drive the elephants from fields as they come in, but the elephants have become wise. Using an old military strategy, the herds, who typically travel in groups of thirty to fifty, split up into smaller groups and spread out over a variety of crop fields. The Forest Department does not have enough staff and vehicles to cover all the fields at once. Eventually, the entire region is saturated, and elephants seem to be everywhere at all times. Each night during crop season they come back together as a full herd when they have eaten enough and travel to Nuxalbari, where they know they can sleep and be protected.

Now the Forest Department is getting pressure to drive the entire herd into the nearby forest, but they must pass through Nuxalbari property to do it. Sonia has been resistant because drives entail chasing the herd with loud crackers and sirens. The villagers, who are eager to see the elephants leave the area, all come out with their own noisemakers, shouting and throwing rocks, taking selfies, and harassing the herd as it goes. It is a highly stressful event, particularly for the mothers and calves.

The Forest Department needs Sonia's permission to conduct the drive through Nuxalbari, and so far she has said no.

"I am having a meeting here with the Division Forest officer," she says. "Will you sit in and maybe take some photos? They want to do a drive but need my permissions. The drives are hateful. I have an idea for a way to do it peacefully. I am trying to get the department to agree to it."

"Of course," I reply. My luck is starting to feel like more than luck.

"The farmers in the area are getting very heated. They will have my head, blaming me for their crop failures. I am not the problem! I have been working on setting up crop insurance. Don't you think if people were paid if their crops were damaged, they would let the elephants pass through? My idea is to start a pilot program with the local village, and if it works we can raise the funds to cover the conflict areas."

"That seems like a terrific idea," I say. "Are people open to it?

"It is hard for others here to accept a woman who is leading, it is always a struggle. There is some support, so I will keep trying."

The Division Forest officer arrives, and we sit in the side garden, surrounded by a small stream and wood bridge, well-tended flowering plants and a gazebo. In a circle of mismatched lawn chairs, Sonia and her estate manager, the Division Forest officer, and the Forest Department officer who will lead the drive discuss the situation, while the house caretaker serves sandwiches and tea. I take photographs of Sonia impressing impassioned pleas for a quiet drive, hands in the air, body leaning to the edge of her chair. I take photographs of the officers sitting politely sipping tea, an air about them that seems as if they are wishing to get this over with, hoping something miraculous will happen, such as the elephants retreating on their own. They are caught between the angry villagers and this headstrong woman whose permissions they need to move the herd through.

They agree to meet again tomorrow morning before the planned drive at one o'clock in the afternoon. Sonia will show them the route that she believes the elephants will take, unprodded, to the forest. Her plan is that if the department can drive to the border of the tea garden, the elephants will naturally move through to the forest. That the animals will understand what to do without sirens and crackers, without crowds of people and aggressive yelling. This has never been done before, and the men seem dubious even as they are deferential. There is no other option; Sonia is a shrewd negotiator. They may not appreciate her style, she is far from sweet and subservient, but she knows the power of her position and uses it deftly to protect the elephants.

Meanwhile, my anxiety about tonight builds as the day progresses. Avijan was supposed to be here at 3:00 P.M. and he is over two hours late. It is almost dark, and I am pacing, fear welling. I have spent the day trying to teach myself manual settings on my camera so I can take photographs in low light. I cannot rely on others to enact my own vision. The last few nights, I have been asking Avijan to take certain photographs that I feel we need for the magazine. But he is distracted by his engagement with the farmers and patrol officers. I am worried we will not have the right photos for *Sidetracked*. I am not thinking clearly, treating him as if he is a professional photographer who knows how to do a shoot with a writer and editor, or who instinctively knows what to capture. He has his own idea in his head of what he is trying to capture—an elephant eating crops in the full moon, for example. He has his settings for that image. Asking him to start taking photos of Forest Department patrol vehicles and me in the field does not make sense to him. But I do not see that right now, all I see is my own frustration building as I sit around waiting for him to pull around the corner.

Avijan has been silent all day, with no responses to my texts asking to confirm tonight's plan.

The last thing I feel like doing right now is getting on the back of a motorcycle and riding off into the dark, placing all my trust in someone I am angry with, spending the night with strangers, running around until dawn in a landscape with no women and a bunch of intoxicated rabble-rousers, then going to sleep in an exposed house, all the while having nowhere to pee. It suddenly sounds ridiculous, dangerous, and stupid.

What will I learn that I do not already understand? Why am I going through with it? Because it is an adventure? Because those extra overnight hours mean something for understanding the conflict? I really need to ask myself, why does sleeping in a stranger's house, in a village where everyone is in an epic struggle to survive, constitute exploration or adventure?

My backpack is stuffed: change of clothes, snacks, camera, water bottle, light sleeping bag. Avijan finally arrives. We drive off to the village, waiting for Tufan at Avijan's restaurant. There is a plan. We will have dinner at Tufan's brother's house again, then afterward set out. Kishor and Tufan will join on Tufan's motorcycle, I get the sense it is for our protection.

At 9:00 P.M., we are ready to leave. A full moon is overhead and Avijan is disappointed that it is orange. He wants to photograph the elephants against the moon, but this one will look like the sun.

My backpack is fat and full, and I begin to put on my helmet.

"You have too many things," Avijan says. "What is in there?"

"A sleeping bag in case we end up sleeping in a field somewhere," I say as I adjust the straps on my Ganesh/third-eye helmet. "And Sonia packed some sandwiches for the morning."

Avijan's eyes grow wide. "Kim, you cannot lie down on the ground for a minute, it is way too dangerous. Also, do not carry food in your backpack, an elephant could smell it—it is very unsafe."

I move the food to the side case on Avijan's scooter. My backpack is still full, but on my back it feels like a buffer, a soft landing if I fall. An odd security.

"Can you run fast with all that?" Avijan says. "You must be able to run very fast if we need to."

This is news to me, until I remember that elephants run much faster than humans. There is no way I could outrun one, no matter how fast I am. A fresh wave of fear settles in.

"You should leave your helmet too." Avijan is always telling me to get rid of my helmet when we are on the country roads, where it is no longer required by law. He wants me to experience the freedom of it, and likely, feels like I make him look decidedly uncool.

"Oh, I am wearing the helmet. I am a mom; I am not taking any chances."

Of course, I am already taking extreme risks by embarking on this foray, the depth of which remains to be revealed.

We launch off into a trail system that runs along dense forest on one side and crop fields on another. Avijan shouts out at me to shine my flashlight left then right constantly, and not to disturb his line of vision. "Tuskers are often in the woods and fields. They can come charging out and crush us," he says. "We must be extremely careful. They are everywhere, but you cannot see them. Masters of disguise!"

We are chasing Tufan along a tiny trail, the scooter no match for the motorcycle, and we are alone. Avijan is worried because we are so far behind, which puts us at greater risk. Tufan and his brother are important to us, we are safer in a group, more vulnerable solo to animals and men.

Up ahead a collection of people appears. We stop. Tufan and Kishor are there. We wait for a while. The farmers are standing around, waiting. It is a clear, cool night. Cold for those who live here; they wear layers, sweaters and jackets. A few have made small fires, both as an elephant deterrent and as a way to get warm. An elephant is spotted. A small group of mothers and calves approach the paddy crop. The crowd roars to life. Taunting, yelling, angry, and scared. The crowd grows as farmers start shooting firecrackers, everyone shouting. One young man runs straight into the field, arms flailing, screaming as if the elephants were simply cows in a road. As the noise and crowds grow, the elephants slowly and patiently begin to move away. Thwarted from the nutrients they need, mothers moving their calves along while the crowd jeers at them, as if they are the most hideous predator on earth. Ashamed to be watching, ashamed that I am doing nothing to stop this. Shameful to be human. Tears fall silently down my cheeks. I yell out at the guys as they begin to chase the elephants, my voice drowned out by the crowd. Trying to remind myself that I am here as an observer, to tell the truth of this story. I feel for the farmers whose crops and lives are in jeopardy, but this crowd is more than that now. An angry mob for whom this is simply the evening's entertainment.

I am horrified. The emotional outburst is so full of hate and anger. Looking around, I see that there are probably about thirty men and teenagers standing about; some are drunk, clearly there for the sport. The malice is intense and amplified by the contradiction, the soft tranquility of the elephants, a surprising gentle, peaceful energy. They are committed to eating, presumably desperate to feed themselves and their young, yet their desperation does not manifest in anger and fear. Instead, they stay unruffled, focused, and strategic. These elephants have the power to attack at any time. They could kill half this helpless and unarmed crowd with one charge or grab with their trunks, yet they choose not to.

The first fifteen minutes of our all-night journey, and I am completely over it. Furious, sad, disgusted, in tears. *What kind of hell is this?* I have seen more than enough. But there is no going home, no home to go to. I am stuck here for the rest of the night. *Get your nerve back, stay strong.* Tufan has people updating him throughout the area about elephant sightings. We climb back on the bikes and tear off into the woods; the trail is so tight and Avijan is racing to catch up. He is nervous and yelling at me to direct the flashlight better than I have been. A rich earthy musty smell clinging in the air along the forest triggers my nerves. It permeates the area as if you could see it, surrounding us.

"Do you smell that?" Avijan asks. "It is the musth. There is a bull here in musth right now."

We speed up. Musth is the regular hormonal change that occurs to male elephants, creating sixty times more testosterone than normal in a black, sticky secretion that oozes from the temple. Elephants in musth are nothing to trifle with. They have been known to kill their mahouts, and even young calves, in their heated, sexualized frenzied state. A musth elephant is mythically violent. One who is being harassed while he is trying to eat is a recipe for certain rampage and death. My fear reaches its zenith. But I am stuck here.

The trail is rough and uneven; we take a turn too fast and tip the bike. By the time we arrive to the next open area, I am certain that we are doing something so dangerous we will not survive. There is a yoga kundalini mantra, a protective chant song that has been giving me comfort. It may sound strange, but it does soothe me. While the others are waiting around, I plug into music, play the mantra "Aad Guray Nameh" on repeat, take deep breaths, and try to envision a protective bubble of safety around me.

At first, I cannot see the elephants. Only flashlights strobing through the open field from the trees and darkness. Crackers and sirens ring out from over the far side of the woods. Smoke from homemade pipe-gun noisemakers linger, its drift illuminated by our flashlights. This the frontline of a battleground, from where one can hear the action like a drumbeat in the distance. A cacophony of voices ringing out from multiple places. Suddenly, everything goes quiet—the voices, the bombs, the sirens. Momentary silence. The crowd around me is murmuring. From the dense forest to my right rises a noise I have only ever heard in a movie. An earth-shaking full bellow trumpet of an elephant. Then, from within another section of forest, a responding trumpet, accompanied by a steady and thunderous rumble that rattles to my core. It is impossible to tell if this elephant is on the move toward us or away, or simply standing his ground.

Eventually, most of the young men move on, to find more action. Now, only we and the two farmers whose crops are near, ready for cultivation, remain. They have been standing out here every night, for more than two months, protecting their livelihoods. These men do not have illegal pipe guns or even crackers, only big dull flashlights and their own voices. Each morning they go into the fields to work, each night after dinner they keep vigil. Once their rice is harvested, they break for only a month or two before the maize season requires them to keep watch again. Then, the monsoon. It is a bleak existence. These men are exhausted to the bone. They rely on the trained patrols who do rounds throughout the village in vehicles paid for by the World Wildlife Fund (WWF) to help drive the elephants away so the farmers can get some rest. But this is not enough. The herds are so intelligent and strategic, they spread themselves out in small groups and lone bulls, over many areas at once. No match for the farmers. Particularly when the elephants understand that noise is the only deterrent they will face.

Unlike most countries, India does not permit wildlife-management strategies that entail killing the unwanted visitors. In my own community, bears that come out from the forests to forage human trash at night are "euthanized" by the Forest Service. Most states in the United States currently allow predator-hunting contests to kill as many foxes, bobcats, wolves, and coyotes as possible, with no limits. It is easy to point a finger at the behavior of people when confronted with wild elephants, but we need to take a close look in our own backyards before doing so. Many can argue that India's no-kill policy sets a standard for wildlife preservation around the world. Of course, this is only one part of the complicated puzzle. For there are a myriad of other ways to force a species into extinction. Conflicting policies, corrupt leaders, lack of resources allocated for conflict mitigation, shrinking habitats, and human obstacles that encroach on, and kill, hundreds of elephants per year; all combine to create a time bomb for Asian elephants throughout India.

Just as I am finally calm and growing hopeful that the activity has settled for the night, Tufan gets a call and we are on our way again. We speed up the dark trails into the unknown, turning off the dirt and onto a highway.

A field on one side and the forest on the other. A crowd has gathered here. We stop along the road with them.

Avijan explains, "The elephants are so smart. At night they cross the highway at the bend, they know that headlights will see them in this place, in time to stop. They always cross in this exact place."

True to his word, a herd comes up the embankment. The sweetest line of mothers and their babies, trying to make their way. The crowd roars and shouts, flashing their lights. The elephants stay steady and calm, as if they do not see or hear the angry mob. No longer do I feel like an objective observer. My presence makes me part of the problem. I know this with certainty.

The first elephant in the line suddenly stops in the middle of the road while the others continue past her. A matriarch, ensuring her group is safe. She stares directly at us, not moving. She seems to be reading us, assessing the possibility for danger. I panic, certain she will charge; this is the moment of no turning back.

"Go, go!" I yell to Avijan, who has been in this situation almost nightly. "She is going to charge!" Avijan knows she will not, for there are clear signs for a charging elephant. They typically mock charge first to scare people away. Obviously, I do not know this. We back away and watch from a distance as she turns around and walks with her herd into the woods.

My first wild herd.

Terrifying and beautiful, powerful and shameful, all of it at once.

As they disappear into the forest, we immediately set off to the other side, hoping to see them as they come out. For years I have been reading accounts of people getting killed by elephants. Now I see how it happens. Half the time they are making poor judgements, as we seem to be right now. It calls into question the quest for wildlife photography. In this case, we are chasing stressed-out animals inside what feels like the trauma of a war zone. Yes, we are documenting the conflict and I have faith in the power of stories like this to raise awareness and make change, but in this moment everything feels wrong. There is no time for further contemplation as we arrive at the next site and there in the field, chomping peacefully on long grains of rice stalks, is a massive tusker. We are close enough to have a grandstand view when he is lit up with flashlights. Kishor assures me that the bull will not run our way because we are standing on a raised ditch and elephants struggle to climb steep hills. This does not put me at ease.

Avijan is ecstatic. “It is Lama!” He recognizes him from his bull-identification project in this region. “He is in musth, look—by his eye. Can you see it?”

Yes. I also see that this is the photographic opportunity that Avijan has been seeking. Lama is munching away at the rice and grasses, seemingly oblivious to the hysteria that surrounds him. His sense of control is astonishing to me. No raging and charging, just calm eating. He clearly knows what each of the players on this field are capable of, including him.

Right next to me, someone shoots a large pipe cannon. The farmers make these, illegally, out of metal pipes stuffed with firecracker-style explosives that make a booming sound and generate an impressive trail of smoke, but do not cause injury or death. I almost drop my phone. I am trying in vain to film, but only getting blurred flashes with frenetic shouting and yelling in the background. Lama looks up and around, as if he is hearing the mayhem for the first time, and begins, stalks still in his mouth, to saunter back into the forest.

“Let’s go!” Avijan is on a mission. Lama will likely cross through the patch of trees and the road at the same curve the elephants always take to reach the field on the other side. With luck, Avijan will be ready to get the shot.

Returning to the highway, we park near a house and a small shack next to it, lit up in pink and purple lights, sending an eerie purple glow out into the air. This is likely so trucks and cars can see the house at night. The structures are fragile, an illusion of safety. Standing next to the buildings, I can hear a woman sobbing inside; her voices rises to a scream, as if she is being forced to do something she does not want to do. My nerves are already shot, now in addition to worrying about elephants, I am picturing a woman in danger in her own home. Her pain seeps through the cracks in the windows and corners. I feel her. But I can do nothing.

Trucks and cars careen around the bend. Those of us in the street flag them, tell them to slow down, elephants in the area. For a moment, our presence becomes useful, possibly saving elephants' lives tonight. Now we are simultaneously protecting elephants as well as chasing and stressing them. The trumpeting and rumbling continue within the forest. Likely they are doing what we are doing, calling out commands and directions. Advising the rest of the herd where people are and are not. They are also on a mission; the elephants need food. This is a battle over resources, and lives are at stake on both sides. Nothing anthropomorphic about this, the elephants' strategic action and behavior shifts are clear. The calm nature of the elephants as they move is so peaceful, it feels as if they are setting an example with the juxtaposition. No need to panic, stay calm.

A crowd has gathered in search of Lama. Avijan and the others are getting impatient and move closer to the bend in the highway where they are certain he will appear. Avijan is setting his camera to get the shot. I have had enough. A bull in musth is unpredictable, this is where I follow my instincts and stay behind.

Avijan says, "Okay, stand here and if an elephant comes, slip into the crack between this house and other building. Then you will be safe."

In the glow of purple light, I wait. Listening to the protection mantra. Nothing is calming me down. I text David and tell him what is going on.

I am not proud to be here.

He replies: *Mark this date on the calendar. You've passed a one-way gate—you are no longer just an observer, someone who has shaped other people's words but has not seen for themselves. You are now a participant who has done something terrifying and seen it with your own eyes. You have earned your stripes. It is the difference between seeing the world through weary eyes instead of through wide eyes. Your storytelling will have to be very deft.*

I reply: *Well, my eyes are wide all right. I'll be so happy when this is over. But the feeling of gravity and responsibility . . . I never want to disturb the elephants in the wild again.*

The crowd, with Avijan at the lead, is running back my direction. Is Lama chasing them? Avijan is flashing his light into the field to my right.

"Kim!" He is out of breath. "Lama just moved past you! Just now, directly behind you." The crowd is searching the field. Sure enough. The elephant in musth silently tiptoed behind me from the forest to the field while I was texting and listening to protection mantras, expecting that any danger was up ahead. Completely oblivious.

"You cannot be on your phone. The elephant will see you. You are lucky to be alive right now. Put it away."

Duly chastised, even as I know that the elephant had already seen and smelled me from a distance. Lama chose this path because he knew the others were waiting for him. That he did not crush me or toss me as I was standing in his path, with all his raging testosterone, is a miracle. One never to be tempted again. Now I am dizzy, swaying with adrenaline and confusion. Why did he spare me? Did Lama instinctively know why I was there?

No time to process this either, we are back on the bikes to a new location. This time Tufan waits with me at a culvert while Kishor and Avijan leave the scooter with us and hike directly into the dark forest in order to reach a section of village on the other side where WWF vehicles are three across, sporting floodlights and sirens, trying to drive a herd cluster of approximately twelve elephants out of the rice paddy. There is no way I am walking through that section of woods. All I want is to get home safely. We wait and wait. Five farmers are sitting around a campfire. Tufan watches videos on his phone. It seems safe to check my phone again. It is past midnight and a text comes through from Anhwei's dermatologist reminding me of her appointment today. She cannot afford to miss it, but is with her dad and he is not always reliable about these things. Morning there, and if I do not let them know, they will likely forget. I text them. Successfully managing part of my duties as a mother from this great distance relaxes me. Like I am able to exert some small bit of control within an outrageously out-of-control situation.

I am desperate to relieve myself. It has been almost six hours. Open fields and roads are too visible in the moonlight and there is no way I can take a chance peeing in the woods. Willing it away, we have been sitting here now almost an hour. It is almost two o'clock in the morning. Tufan is getting weary, waiting so far from the action. We decide to get the other two and head for home.

This requires me riding on the back of Tufan's bike, which does not have much power. We chug along roads and highways, not taking the shortcut through the forest. After almost twenty minutes of travel, we arrive. It is a scene here, so close to houses, the elephants are not budging. Bright lights, cannons, firecrackers, voices yelling until hoarse, nothing is working. The elephants continue to eat methodically and with great calm. The energy they radiate is so strong, so remarkably peaceful. They could handily kill every person standing here, decimate their homes and eat the food stored within. Their decision not to can only be part of their strategy. There is a palpable force, this feminine energy radiating from the matriarchal herd. Only one or two young bulls are in their midst. Calves and mothers, older sisters. Their elegant patience amid such chaos illuminates the base vulgarity on the other side.

At last, we are all together. My bladder can barely make it a minute more. We head back to Kishor's home, where we will sleep for what is left of the night. There has been a dramatic change in perspective, as the house I was once dreading is now a beacon for security. I cannot wait to be inside. As we turn the corner toward the house, an enormous tusker is blocking the path, trunk up and plucking fruit from the neighbor's front yard tree. We surprise one another and he turns to face us.

There are scenes in movies where mere mortals find themselves face-to-face with beasts that dwarf everything around them. Motorcycles, humans, even trees look like they exist in miniature up against the massive size of the creature. In these movies, the giant King Kong, T-rex, or fantasy space monsters loom so large the human peril is clear. This feels like one of those moments, only it is not fiction. Kishor leaps off Avijan's scooter, with a cracker and flashlight, and lunges for the elephant, making a terrific sound. If he had planned to charge, the bull now determines it is not worth the trouble. With a dead-on eye-lock stare that lasts a second but feels like minutes, he turns and moves toward the field behind Kishor's house. He is walking slowly, as if to communicate that he is leaving on his terms, not because of the irritating sound. Everyone kicks into action, waking the neighbors, shouting for help to drive the bull from their backyards. Tufan takes me to Kishor's house where I run into the outhouse with both relief and the terror of knowing the tusker is just behind these makeshift walls. When I come out, Tufan shows me a section of the house next to the privy. There are only remnants, a cement foundation, and an irregular edging. A pile of mangled metal roof in a corner.

"Last week, late at night, an elephant crushed this part of the house," Tufan says. He leads me to the blue painted room with the Gandhi portrait where earlier we had tea. I have my backpack and my sleeping bag. "We'll be back," he says.

Another perspective change. Now the eagerly anticipated shelter is as dangerous as sleeping in the forest. A dramatic difference between research and experience. I knew that houses got crushed while their inhabitants are sleeping, but only now does the reality of that vulnerability sink in. The situation here is this: you are not safe in your house. There is no protection. The elephants need food. They do not have food. That is the root problem. There is not enough food for everyone.

We can say "peaceful coexistence," but honestly there is not much peace in what I just witnessed. Peaceful coexistence is the vision, but we are further away from it than I thought. Out there it is a conflict, a full-blown war in a fight for survival.

The shouting and crackers have died down. The others return to the room; excitement and accomplishment fill the space with fresh energy. Eventually, we tuck in and sleep, me on the raised platform bed, wrapped in my sleeping bag, while Tufan and Avijan quickly fall asleep on the floor next to me. I am thankful for earplugs as the snoring booms. For a few short hours, I drift into deep sleep. A kaleidoscope of dreams: yelling boys chasing sauntering herds, thick black oozing from the eye of the tusker, sirens, flashing lights, explosions, angry trumpeting.

I wake before dawn to a powerful foreboding, feeling a charged energy, certain the elephant from last night is roaming nearby. This is the hour when people are killed, as they venture out half asleep to relieve themselves or gather wood for the breakfast fire. In stillness, with a full bladder, I wait, my male companions still passed out on the floor below me.

When the light becomes more pronounced, I peer out. Framed directly through the window, etched in white against a milky blue sky, is Kanchenjunga, the highest mountain in India, third highest in the world. To the left of it, Mount Everest. All these days, I was within full embrace of this range, but only now does it appear. Before me stands proof that just because we cannot see something does not mean it is not there . . . or it is not true. The moment is holy. My helmet lies on the bedside crate beside me, a talisman. Across the planet, my daughters are falling asleep, nestled in blankets of privilege they cannot yet understand. The full weight of my growing sense of responsibility is crushing.

21

After breakfast at Kishor's house, we say our goodbyes and Avijan rides me home on his scooter. Nuxalbari Tea Garden appears as a surreal oasis after what I witnessed that night; Sonia is out having tea on the veranda when I am dropped at the gate. Her six-year-old daughter is leaving for school, lunch pail in hand and wearing an adorable outfit that reminds me of the joy I took in dressing my girls, before sweatpants and sweatshirts dominated their wardrobes. Sonia gives last-minute instructions with the nanny and covers her daughter in kisses and hugs, waving as they go out into the world. Joolie, the family's new boxer puppy, is ecstatic to see me and wriggles at my feet.

"Join me," Sonia says.

I want nothing more right now but to crawl into my room and sob, to record these thoughts and experiences in solitude, processing, to shower and sleep for the rest of the day.

"Okay," I reply. "Let me put these things in my room."

Birds are chirping, enclosed in a shroud of green gardens, flowers bloom in pots on the patio, rare bright sunlight warms the space. Masala chai tastes like nectar of the gods and I feel unworthy to drink it.

"How was the night?" she asks.

"Terrible," I start, and the floodgates open. Through tears, I say, "I understand what you meant. I never want to disrupt an elephant in the wild again. It was one of the most upsetting scenarios I have ever experienced. Last night, when you asked me what was more important the photographs or the elephants being left in peace? I insisted the story and photos are most important. I still believe that documenting the truth so others can learn, and change their views, is critically important. But, honestly, where do we draw the line? Every person out there wanted to experience it. So many are driven by the desire for popularity on social media, not crop protection. But how are we filmmakers, photographers, writers different? Just because we are 'professionals.' Isn't that one secret selfish motivation, recognition for our work?"

While many were legitimately protecting their food source, others, particularly groups of young men, seemed to be doing it for sport. Their bloodlust was palpable. If elephants were not protected with the highest legal standards, I am stricken to realize that a mob could easily turn and become killers.

Sonia nods and hands me a tissue. I can smell myself, unshowered, fear sweat clinging to last night's clothes. I cannot stop now that she has asked.

"It would be one thing if it was just Avijan and his guys taking photographs quietly in the dark forest, but giant crowds form. I mean, it is stressful for humans too, but I was so ashamed because I stood by while these elephants struggled just trying to survive right in front of me. They do not even have food." I bury my head in my dirty hands, dirt-encrusted fingernails grip into my tangled hair. And I choke out the last words as the full truth of what I experienced last night reveals itself. "They are desperate, they are so desperate."

"I am glad to see you crying," she says. "Now you understand."

Nodding into my hands, snot smeared across my face as I try to clear my nose, I swipe at my eyes to stop the tears from falling. The tissue soaks through with tears. I try to catch my breath.

Sonia says, "At four in the afternoon today, the department is going to drive the herd up here. They have agreed to let the elephants pass through

Nuxalbari without interfering. It will be peaceful. The DFO and his team are on their way here now, so I can show them the route. You won't want to miss this. I suggest you come with us; you can photograph. Go clean up."

My brain can barely switch gears. The news is on the farthest end of what I think I can put myself through right now. I am delirious with exhaustion, emotion, and utterly filthy.

But what are the chances of this? That on the exact day they are conducting an experimental drive, moving the herd out of the area, I happen to be staying on the very property with all the action? One I had followed just weeks before on Instagram?

As terrifying as last night was, I did experience, nonstop, the full spectrum of this conflict. An impossible coincidence? There is no time for rest or recording of the events. Only a quick wash off of my face and some deodorant, a quick snack, and water refill. Before I can even change my clothes, I hear the men's voices. Sonia calling me, "Let's go."

We climb into two cars, the Division Forest officer and Sonia, with me and the tea manager in the backseat, in one vehicle, while following in the other, more Forest Department officers. Nuxalbari is much larger than I realize. We drive across the various areas and stop. In each location Sonia explains where the elephants will cross, based on her knowledge of their passage in the past. The tea garden estate, in its entirety, is stunning. We stop high along the ridge, overlooking the property. A delicate mist hangs above a dark green meadow below, with the forest entrance beckoning like an enchanted kingdom thick with trees and lasting as far as our eyes can see. That forest is the end goal. And people will be stationed along the ridge to confirm the elephants' movement. Sonia has employed many individuals from the tea garden village, employees of hers, to stand at various points to assure passage. They have been given strict instructions to only communicate to others via a walkie-talkie and not to harass the elephants in any way.

We complete our task at almost 2:00 P.M. There are only two hours before the drive.

"You should shower and take a nap," Sonia says. "There is a rash all over your face and neck. Probably from bedbugs." In the mirror, my reflection is shocking. Tiny red bumps cover my left cheek and down my neck on that side. It dawns on me that this is where my face was not on my own sleeping bag. After a hot shower I fall into a jagged sleep, worried that I will miss the drive, still jumpy from the experience the night before. When I wake the light is dim; it is almost time. Now I have some sort of eye infection and a cold in addition to the rash, which is unchanged from this morning. But these things will pass. As long as they do not interfere with the work I am trying to do.

Tufan and Avijan are here—Sonia has invited them to stand watch and photograph. Her contradictions are much like Parbati's, in this case, decrying the wildlife photography, yet also relying on it to showcase her business and promote her commitment to conservation. My hair is still wet, so I am wearing it down. I only have one item of clothing left that is not dirty and damp, a sundress. I put flip-flops on because my white sneakers are encrusted in dirt.

Sonia greets me as I come out of my room. Her bold brown eyes get wider as they look me up and down before sending me back to my room. "Do not wear your hair down when you go into the field," she says, "You look too glamorous. This is traditionally a man's job. To be a woman out here means you must look and act like one of them. This is why I keep my hair short. Also, you need sneakers in the field, always."

Sonia is, in many ways, alone here, far from Delhi or Kolkata—without her network of friends, far from the life she once lived filled with adventure and intellectual stimulation. Determined to carry on this family legacy, even if it means standing rigid and fierce in the center of a storm. A vestige of another era—her friends ask if she is still living her "colonial" life. Devoted to an ideal, the tea garden has become a cause, a model. Where once Sonia wrote and filmed about justice and human rights, now she is a gentleman farmer, trying to show another way, create positive change in the best ways she can see how.

I have no idea what to expect. Everything is rushed and Sonia is growing more agitated, bordering on frantic. "Get in," she says, and I climb into the Kaiser, her restored open jeep that I am obsessed with photographing, not that I can enjoy it fully at the moment. She is on the phone yelling nonstop until we get to the bridge crossing where Avijan and I had trespassed just a few days before. "Okay, you get out," she says. "The herd will cross here, and you can photograph them." Off she goes.

There are two men standing with walkie-talkies at the bridge. I try to explain what I am doing there. We stand together and wait. In the distant village where I spent last night, shouts, sirens, and firecrackers begin to explode into the air, the noise dissipating when it reaches us. The setting sun casts light on the endless shelf of tea leaves, turning them into emeralds. Filtering through the shade trees, sun in variegated light. At last, we find ourselves in silence. Then, along the very path with marked signs on the tall barks of trees that read ELEPHANT CROSSING, the herd appears. Slowly, as last night, but this time the energy is wholly different. There is no sound but our breathing, and the periodic trumpets of the elephants as one by one, in a gentle and peaceful line, they begin to pass. A large female stands guard at the one end of road, two calves by her side, as her herd makes their way. It strikes me only in the moment of this writing that she did not need a guard on our side, trusting that we were doing our job.

The evening sun creates a warm glow on their dusty backs as they wind their way between the rows of tea plants, not trampling a single one. What I thought was ease last night was only a mask, a disguise in the form of seemingly calm outer physical movement. Now I feel their serenity. Their internal calm. It radiates into me. I relax in their presence. It is as if they reach into my deepest core, my innermost sanctum. They know the intentions of this place. If science does not prove this, it is only because we are not yet evolved enough to discover the evidence.

After they are out of sight, the two guards and I smile at one another. They seem to have felt it too. Someone far afield calls out. There is a lone bull with piercing tusks, standing in the tea garden. He is almost invisible, camouflaged within the trees. I wonder if he is the bull from last night, plucking the fruit trees. One of the men signals to me, "Sonia wants you to go to her," he says. The other man has a motorbike and offers to take me. There is some confusion and excitement, as if I have been summoned by the queen and they are chosen to assist. I get on the back of the bike, and we take off through the garden paths, taking a shortcut. We stop for a moment because the man driving the bike does not know where Sonia is. While we are trying to figure out what to do, we hear shouting. The men across the field are yelling and pointing ahead of us. Craning our necks, we can just make out the tusker as he moves through the tea leaves ahead, toward us. When he hears the commotion, he stops and turns. For a third time in less than twenty-four hours, an elephant is staring me down. This time my driver is as frightened as I am and we rapidly turn around, tearing back the way we came. When we get to the road, Sonia is gesturing from her jeep.

"Wasn't it enough?! You couldn't be satisfied with what I gave you, you had to seek more. You put people in danger!" She is screaming with a voice already hoarse from an afternoon of barked orders. "Why did you leave your station?!" she yells and points at the bike driver. "You had strict instructions."

"We were told that you wanted me to meet you," I reply. "He was only following what he thought were orders from you. We both were."

"Why on earth would I call for you? How could you even know where I was? I was driving around. Who told you this?" She is shaking with fury. To the driver, "Take her to the office and wait in there."

Like children who have been caught breaking the rules, even though we are wrongly accused, we head back to the office. There we sit, waiting, as if the principal would return any moment to deliver our punishment. My driver is very concerned that there will be consequences and he is hoping I can fix this. I am also hoping to fix this. We did put ourselves in great danger, we were likely overexcited with the sudden call to action, but it was an honest miscommunication.

It is almost an hour before the jeep returns. The sky is warm, a glint of light remains. Sonia is exuberant, cheeks flushed and ruddy. "We did it!" she says, "You should have seen it. They walked right in front of me, straight past me. They directly followed the path I showed the department yesterday. Come, we will celebrate!"

We are forgiven. The man returns to his family, and I follow Sonia into the house. Darkness settles as we gather with the others, several Forest Department officers, Tufan and Avijan. There is an air of festivity, accomplishment, but also a prevailing, crashing fatigue. Post-adrenaline exhaustion.

Only Sonia and I sit down for dinner that night. In candlelight after the meal, in my memory we are enjoying a glass of wine, but more likely it is tea.

"I did not know if this was going to work today," Sonia tells me. "Last night I dreamed of it, the elephants were so strong in my sleep as if they were communicating to me. I woke up and began to pray, continuing the communication, in hopes they could hear me. I was worried because the department had proposed a more direct route that they would drive, but I made the condition of the circuitous path so they could go peacefully. It was a huge risk. When I was showing the path, I sent out strong energy. When the elephants arrived, I sent out that energy again. They did exactly as I hoped. I believe the elephants were intuitively knowing my mind. They understood that if they went peacefully, it was going to help them in their survival for the future. Now the Forest Department can consider that there is another possible way to move them."

What she is saying resonates so strongly; I felt it out there both last night and today. We talk about the female connection, the female-led herds, the women who are trying to make change in a country dominated by conservative male oppression and opinions.

"It seems there is a strong female force," I say. "The elephants exude it, like they are trying to teach us a lesson through their calm behavior. And you. I think the solutions for these conflicts will require women to lead. Like you are."

"The men don't like it," she says, "they resist. But we can prevail. We are the ones in tune with nature. She is female."

Sonia tells me of her desire to be a mother. How she arranged to get pregnant outside of wedlock, so that she would not have to wait for the right relationship. How she feels that because of her strong personality, no man in India will want to be partnered to her. "Too difficult for a man to manage," she says, laughing sadly. We talk about motherhood and how we dream for the planet to be a healthier, more equitable place for our children. About prejudice, her Muslim-Hindu heritage, my Chinese daughters, how these checked boxes present both barriers and opportunities.

She tells me how she came to make a documentary about women's rights in Kashmir, how she was supposed to be the writer and photographer, but the filmmaker canceled at the last moment, so she had to go alone and learn the camera as she went.

"This is how we learn, she says. "We create ourselves out of need. When you leave tomorrow, stop worrying about whether you are a writer or a photographer. You will be exactly what you need to be. Be confident as you go out into this next part of your studying the elephant problem. You have seen both sides here now. You have witnessed the worst of the human situation for elephants, and you have experienced the peaceful possibility. Go with courage."

As I climb under the mosquito netting and slip into crisp white sheets, the bars on the windows no longer seem weak or a harbinger of danger. Above my head the ceiling fan spins slowly, its rhythm creating a *gunk gunk gunk* sound. Fresh, folded laundry on the chair next to me, a pitcher of water on the bedside table. It is almost ten o'clock, the time at which we set out last night. Almost impossible to reconcile those harrowing events with the utopia witnessed this afternoon. Floating now, in that space between wakefulness and sleep.

A new feeling emerges, the bright lightness of euphoria. Fear faced and conquered, I am firmly standing on the other side. For every hope dashed with disappointment over these past three trips, for all the seeking and failing to find, through all the insecurity and self-doubt, I have finally experienced the truth. I have confronted the horror and witnessed the beautiful possible. As I drift toward sleep, I am reminded of something that happened to me many years ago.

I was running along the beach, listening to an orchestral piece of stirring and triumphant music. I became aware that the physical separateness of myself had disappeared. For the briefest moment, I was the simultaneously the ocean and each grain of sand. I had become the oxygen I was breathing and the molecules of every single living being around me. In fact, there was no me. I was one with the clouds. Time as I knew it ceased to exist; every minute from past, present, and future swirled and merged as mere perceptions. As this was occurring, I understood two things without having to think. First, the essence of our being, our energy, exists eternally; death is not finite. Also, we exist in forms that shift and morph, but essentially everything is one—pulsing and interconnected.

As with most precious things, this experience was fleeting. I did not emerge as a reborn Buddha, enlightened spiritual leader, or with any profound contribution to theology or physics. Death still terrifies me, and I continue to act as if my body and actions are not constantly affecting and affected by everything that surrounds me, whether I see it or not. Yet I do not forget. The memory is enough to secure my faith that everything is possible. Now, just a speck at the base of the Himalaya, these seemingly uncanny coincidences and opportunities feel part of a grand design. My last knowing thought before falling asleep is there are no happenstances along this journey; I am being led by an unseen force. And all is interconnected, just as I felt one with the oxygen, ocean, and grains of sand in that moment by the sea.

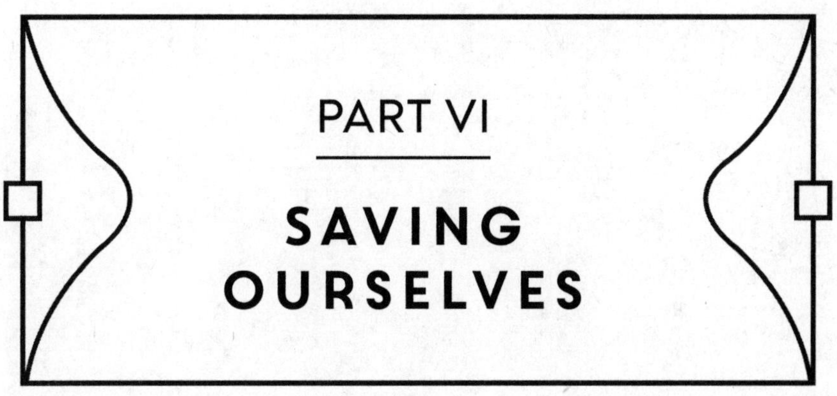

PART VI

SAVING OURSELVES

Another world is not only possible; she is on her way. On a quiet day, I can hear her breathing.

—Arundhati Roy, *War Talk*

22

S.P. Pandey is a self-taught snake handler who has rescued king cobras with his bare hands, although one of those hands is missing two fingers now, after a leopard-relocation effort went awry. A scar over his left eye makes his eyebrow appear always raised, as if questioning all that you say. There seems to be another scar on his forehead, though I do not stare hard enough to determine whether this is an indent or an old injury. Though receding a bit, there is still ample hair from the thick black shock on his head to provide subtle sideburns to a moustache that connects to a scruff of a beard. It is a look that suits him, that looks natural and ungroomed, even as the shape and placement of his facial hair seems only possible with regular maintenance. In any event, S. P. Pandey's stocky, tall physique is made even more formidable with his daily uniform: camouflage shirt, camouflage pants, and short hiking boots. He is a man who clearly has stories to tell.

Devoted to "protecting, nurturing, conserving and restoring the sub-Himalayan region through science and legal measures for future generations," Pandey is the founder of the Society for Protecting Ophiofauna & Animal Rights (SPOAR). SPOAR is one of the organizations working with Wildlife Trust of India to secure safe passage for wild elephants throughout eight identified corridors in this part of the West Bengal region.

Pandey and his partner, Anindita, are picking me up an hour after I arrive at Riverwood. For the next few days, I will be shadowing them as they do their corridor-related work.

Anindita comes into the office to collect me. She is in her twenties, energetic and bright, her English is terrific. Dressed in jeans, blouse, and sneakers, with long thick hair and a quick, broad smile. I like her immediately. There is a young female intern in the backseat, Arpana, who is spending a semester working with SPOAR and studying wildlife conflict in this region. We climb into the car, and Anindita begins to tell me stories as Pandey drives.

"I have seen many things since I began working with SPOAR two years ago. Once an elephant got hit by a train. She had some bruising and was slowing down the herd. There were maybe thirty-five, forty elephants. She stopped by the edge of the forest and was picking out some vegetation to eat. Just standing still and trying to recover. The Forest Department officers arrived on the scene with a tranquilizer gun and a vet on standby in case the elephant needed care, and we came as well. When we arrived the herd had split, and the mothers led their calves to a nearby teak forest where they waited. A few elephants, the strongest-looking ones, stayed with the injured one. Four were bulls. When the department officials arrived, the bulls got in a line. I have never seen anything like this in my life. They formed a line and charged the humans, to chase them away from the injured elephant. The people ran for their lives, then waited a safe distance away, watching in case they needed to help save her. We would not tranquilize any animal if they are recuperating on their own." Anindita pauses. "Isn't this what we do for our loved ones? We stay behind to take care of them."

"We got word that a crowd had formed around the elephants in the tea garden. The people were harassing the elephants and had surrounded them. We went there to help out. I do not know why, but many of the people were very intoxicated. They started lighting some crackers. The intention of the mob was to agitate as much as possible so they could photograph and video. A stupid person took a bet that he could touch the tail of an elephant. He could not even stand properly. His friend was videoing and the man walked into the herd to try and touch the tail. From the side another elephant came in and gave a sweep with her trunk. Simple sweep. I saw it with my own eyes. The person flew in the air and landed on his back, screaming, in tea garden bushes. The ambulance came to take the person to the hospital. We had to stay there to try and control the other people."

"Only at night could the elephants safely move. At 11:00 P.M. that night, we went back to the injured elephant where the Forest Department was waiting. The bull elephants escorted the injured elephant out of the forest. They crossed the road and joined the rest of the herd. The complete herd moved together with the injured elephant and the watchers into the forest. We later heard from a SPOAR member who is a doctor at the hospital that the man who tried to touch the tail for a video selfie died from burst lungs. This is what happens here."

Our first stop is to visit with a local Forest Department officer, named Raj. We file into his empty office. Pandey makes a phone call.

"He is asleep," he says.

When Raj appears he is apologetic, hair a bit mussed but enthusiastic to meet with us. He is laughing when Pandey teases him.

"I sleep whenever I can," he says. "There are two small patches of forest, with a paddy crop between them, where a herd of maybe thirty, thirty-five elephants are staying. We are trying each night to drive them back into the bigger forest, but they make their own plan and trick us. They get to the road, then turn around, come right back and eat the paddy."

This has been going on nightly for a week. The villagers demand that the Forest Department responds, but the elephants will not obey.

"The government has a provision to compensate people for lost crops, but the farmers in this particular area do not own the land, it is recorded as forest land," Raj explains. "So, they are angrier when the crops are damaged, because they do not receive any compensation. We have already had a death this season. A person was operating a bulldozer; he went to work around 5:00 A.M. He did not see the bull at all. It came and smashed his head."

Raj has only been at his station here for a little over a year, but is already seeing so many incidents that he is writing a book of collected stories. Likely in the tradition of P. D. Stracey's *Elephant Gold*, a book that references Lalji Barua, which Parbati told me to read if I wanted to understand the life of elephants and humans. Stracey had been an elephant catcher for the Assam Forest Department during the 1940s.

"The other day I received word that an elephant had injured a little girl in the village area," Raj continues. "I was a bit fearful of the public's agitation because it was a little child. With my staff, I reached the spot as early as possible. A huge public gathering was there. We all feared great trouble from the villagers. I was surprised, though, to find the crowd was silent and standing normally. I asked what happened. They told me that early that morning, one tusker had tried to damage the hut. The father and mother managed to escape but could not carry the girl child. When the elephant saw the girl, he took the child by his trunk and put her aside at a safe distance. Later, he returned and totally damaged the hut. Because of this behavior the public was so surprised that they did not show any agitation. Later I sent the girl to the hospital, and after one day's treatment she was fine."

Pandey's phone rings in the sound of a delicate bird call, and each time it happens, I am certain there is an actual bird nearby. He is in high demand. We say our goodbyes and Raj returns to his sleep; there will be no rest for him in the coming hours.

The road is lined by tea gardens on both sides, for as far as we travel. So beautiful to look at, until you consider what used to be there, thick nourishing jungles stocked with wildlife. From the backseat, Anindita fills me in on SPOAR's corridor project work:

"Here, we have eight identified corridors, passages that connect the forests. Each has a number of obstacles in the way, such as tea garden fencing, train tracks, and human settlements. Our task is to make those linkages safer for elephants to pass through, and also safer for the humans who live there. We have over sixty members and about fifteen to twenty volunteers who survey the corridor area with us, looking for dung and other evidence that elephants have come through. We have divided the corridors into grids and cover them regularly. We record with crib notes. It can be very difficult because there are a large number of rapidly growing refugee settlements. There are also boundaries, with Bangladesh, Sikkim, Nepal, Bhutan . . . China is also very close. The migrants are coming for the increase in opportunities, settling in areas that used to be forests. Every day, every minute, more and more people come. The cultures are also different. The people from North Bengal have lived with elephants and leopards, but the people who are migrating from Bangladesh have rarely seen these animals. They agitate them. We have seen people getting killed right in front of us."

We pull into a tea garden. There is something so serene about the layers of green, the pops of the women pickers' colorful clothing. Such aesthetic beauty that belies the complicated situation. The work is painstaking and physically backbreaking, wages are low, and benefits often nonexistent. There is much to say about the power dynamics found on a tea plantation. But this is not a story specifically about the lives of tea garden workers, owners, and managers, though the complexities are interwoven throughout the human-elephant conflict in this region.

"We have a computer program with GPS of the Teesta River area," Anindita continues. "We survey each grid twice a year. There are four seasons: paddy, maize, monsoon, and dry. In the dry season there is much less movement. Paddy is August through November, four months. December to March is Maize. Then March to May is Dry. The monsoon is June through September. This means there are eight months of elephant conflict. October and November are the most intense because the paddies are cultivated. Then, people cut it and stack it. They dry it on their roofs and store in their houses. This is when the bulls come. The herds come to the crops, the lone bulls raid the storage, destroying the houses, breaking all the walls to get to the supply—oh, look," she says.

Ahead of us a handful of people are standing at the edge of the garden, pointing. More people are riding bikes and running along the road to join them. I know instantly what this means.

"The elephant herd is ahead. The manager told me," Pandey says. "They are seeking shelter during the day in that forest."

"You must be good luck," Arpana says to me. "I have been here almost a month and have not yet seen any elephants in the wild."

We pull over. At the edge of the tea garden, along the trees, are approximately fifteen elephants, older females, and calves, eating leaves and milling about. It is rare to see them during the day. People are gathering; the crowd has doubled since we arrived. We step outside, joining the others. I am again part of the problem.

At first, we collectively stand in awe of the elephants. Clusters of women, groups of young boys, standing a respectful distance along the road. Craning necks to see the herd. Some young men arrive; when they become the majority, the energy shifts. Where first those who gathered seemed honored to be graced with the elephants' presence, now some are making noises. The young men call to one another, trying to film and photograph with their phones, but discovering they are too far away. Now some are edging closer, walking into the bushes so they can get a better shot. One man strides through the garden, toward the herd, as if he does not even know they are there. More people arrive. This is how it starts. The chatter increases, people begin to take more risks. What began as a reverence has turned into a challenge to see who can get the best shot. I asked a group of schoolgirls what they think of the elephants. Pandey translates their reply for me:

"We don't like them. They destroy houses and kill people. We wish they would go."

"I love to see elephants, but I don't want to see elephants," Pandey says on the way out. It is getting dark and we are headed to the Forest Patrol headquarters. "My presence in front of any elephant means that other people will come."

"Do people still revere elephants as a god here?" I ask. "It seems like those girls certainly do not."

"Depends if someone is Hindu, if they have a belief," he replies. "The new generation, though they are Hindu, are not depending on faith. They are not devoted. The new generation believes in taking photographs over praying before Ganesh. They think, 'I will take a selfie with that calf because I want attention from girls. I have to put it on a Facebook page, send it through WhatsApp.'" Pandey talks with his hands as he drives, deftly weaving in and out of traffic. "I am not a photographer. I know how to take photographs and have a DSL camera, but you noticed that I do not bring it. We can document with our mobile if we need. If everyone came and tried to photograph, what would happen? If an animal is not feeling disturbed by us, then we have already influenced the elephant's behavior. I do not want to disturb animals for my photography, by any means."

"This is one of the many incidents that I have seen during our work," Anindita says. "People came to see some elephants bathing in the Murti tea garden. There were calves there. The villagers began to discuss getting a photo. They did not have a good camera for distance. A man walked right into the river. An elephant takes two steps and smashes him to the ground. He died. She did it to protect her calf. They had very small calves."

I flash back to a car ride with Parbati, when she'd talked about the media reporting the death of a person by elephant, but rarely saying what the human was doing when it happened.

"It is a sport," Anindita says. "They do it for social media. It is the most pathetic thing I have ever seen. Selfie cameras do not take an exact distance. Elephants can be ten yards away and silent in the leaves. I have seen them move without any noise. Sometimes they are right in front of you and you cannot even see them! I tell Pandey that people have to be able to see the areas. They do not have lights or electricity; at night they cannot see the leopards and elephants. They have planted elephant apples, jackfruit, and bananas. Why wouldn't the elephants want to visit the houses? We are trying to teach them. Do not take down the trees, get the fruit before it is smelling in ripeness. We try to outfit them with a torch and encourage them not to go out at night. But they do. After the day's work. They sit down and drink hard liquor and then get on social media. It is a relatively new phenomenon, proving to be one of the most important causes of human casualties."

The phone rings and it is Upasana Ganguly from WTI. They are confirming plans for the upcoming meeting with a local village; someone was attacked by a leopard walking down the lane to a neighbor's house a few weeks ago and they are eager to secure some lights and set up a local patrol. Anindita tells her we saw elephants.

"What?!" Upasana is now on speakerphone. "I was just there for a week and never saw any elephants!"

The rarity of what I am witnessing, day by day, minute to minute, impresses on me an enormity of responsibility. I must create something meaningful with this. That I have two more days full of opportunities, visits, and interviews injects a fresh burst of energy and purpose. Darkness falls and envelops the car as we make our way to the regional Forest Department office. Rising to the challenge, I push all lingering fear and exhaustion into the background, ready for whatever comes next.

In the driveway of the Forest Department office, an old Land Cruiser with a broken green roof and cracked windows is parked under a tree, branches and vines growing over it. A dim light streams out from the front window of the office signaling someone is inside. The office is a cement box with a cheery interior of butter-yellow walls and faded blue-green doors; thick pea-green fleur-de-lis–patterned drapes hang in front of the open doorway and windows. Behind a massive glass-covered square desk sits the district officer. In uniform, three brass stars on each shoulder like a hardened army general, chiseled features softened only by a moustache, sunken eyes that betray his weariness, an African-print turquoise towel draped over his chair. The items on his desk are meticulously organized, walkie-talkies charging, lists of names and places with dot stickers next to them. Stacks of files, two-hole punches, a few small brass plaques. On the wall behind him is a wooden chalkboard with numbered officer names and times. To his left a plain black-and-white wall calendar displays each month of the year. The green door to his right has a large metal padlock on the handle and another lock above. One can only imagine what lies behind it. This man has clearly seen it all.

We take seats around the desk and Pandey makes the introductions. The officer has been with the Forest Department since 1979 and working in the elephant-conflict scenario since 1986. He is considered the most experienced elephant driver in the region. As we begin our conversation, a truck pulls into the driveway. A newer truck, specific for elephant drives and patrols. This one has bench seats in the back where officers can ride in a group like a military vehicle. Four men spill out, in full khaki uniforms. They flood the room with animation, eager to share their story.

Pandey starts. "There are a few categories of elephants. The male bulls, 'Makna'—no tusks, and tuskers, with tusks. But then some have only one tusk. We call them Ganesh."

The men are talking over each other, excitedly, relaying the story to their leader. Anindita, sitting next to me, translates: "They got a call and had one minute to mobilize. A Ganesh bull in musth was in a village and a crowd had formed around the tusker. It was a very delicate situation. When the department arrived, they had three teams, cars in two directions, but actually one team had to drive the elephant on foot. It was very hard to guide on three sides, trying to move the elephant back into the forest and control the crowd. Keeping the people out of the way is the main difficulty. The bull was agitated, trying to chase people more than once. People do not understand musth and the mental condition of the elephant. They want selfies."

At this the stern man behind the desk, who has been listening without wavering his expression, lets out a chortle. "Ha, selfies." Tone thick with disgust. The men are speaking rapidly. Some English words float by: "twelve rounds," "rockets," "cannons."

Anindita looks over at me—generous with her spirit, and determined to help me understand, she continues her translation: "During this time there was a trolley filled with children nearby. The elephant suddenly charged towards them, but the children all managed to escape. Twenty-five children. This is common. When mothers are plucking tea, they cannot safely leave their children alone on the ground to play, because of leopards. So, they put them on an open trolley where they are above the bushes and can play in there."

The men have wound down, adrenaline edging away.

"They were finally able to drive the elephant back into the forest, so for now it is over," Anindita says. "But, who knows how soon until the bull comes back? There is no pattern. It could be in a half hour, or he could travel to another place. If they are lucky, he just goes deeper into the forest. They are getting ready now to go back to a different location. For another bull."

It is only 6:00 P.M., but their work is just getting started.

The head officer speaks. His voice is deep, and while I hear English words, I cannot fully make them out. Thankfully, Anindita whispers to me, "He is saying that he got a call the other night and was on his way immediately, but when he arrived an elephant had already killed someone. It was by the teak forest I was telling you about."

At the mention of teak forest, Pandey speaks up. "All the trees, plants, and fruits inside the forest have been taken by people. Ninety percent of elephants want to stay in the forest. But they do not have food there. I am going against the Forest Department to tell you this. There is an order, a cycle of sixty years to replace forests. In the 1980s and '90s the department made a big mistake. In an effort to replace forests, they planted teak and mahogany trees, but those have a side effect that do not allow for undergrowth. The elephants do not like those leaves. So there is a forest, but nothing to sustain elephants. There is a plantation of single-species trees, planted years ago. It looks like a forest, but there is nothing there for them. Now the department understands their mistake. They are trying to replace it, but it will take another sixty years to completely convert them back."

I am not certain how much of what Pandey said was understood by those in the room. They do not register much of a response. On the shelf, inside a protective thin plastic cover, is an award from WTI for this department's work as a champion of elephants in this region. When I ask about it, they beam. It is the size of a large dinner plate, golden and engraved. The group proudly poses with it.

"How are selfies are affecting your work?" I ask. "And what kind of changes have you seen in the conflict, from the beginning of your time until now?"

"For the sake of the photo, people are risking more, they are touching more," the head Forest officer says. "The main problem is the flash, it is agitating. Overall, the conflict has become tougher. Everyone wants to take photographs. This trait motivates people to get much closer to take pictures, this is what raises the risks. People used to be afraid of elephants, now they treat them like a horse or cows."

A man enters the room; others get up and offer him their seats. Tall, balding, and moustached, his physical stature and air of authority commands the room. Someone brings him up to speed. There are side conversations as the head officer waits.

The new officer weighs in. "There is an increased population, but decreased food in the forests. The elephants are in more places at once. The herds are splitting. It seems like the elephant numbers are increasing, but actually they are splitting so they can be in multiple crops. It used to be a herd of sixty to seventy, now it is ten to twenty in smaller groups. And then you have the bulls on top of that."

"What do you think could solve the problems? Is there a solution?" I ask.

The head officer makes a joke in Hindi. Everyone laughs. They do not tell me at first, then they do. His answer is a meant as a joke but reveals the deep frustration and helplessness they feel: "If we could shoot them."

I am not even sure who he means by "them," the elephants or the people.

Pandey worries I will misunderstand the context. "What he means is that this is the general population's feeling. Many villagers and farmers wish the department could just kill the elephants."

The officer gets his straight face on again. "We need to evacuate the corridors. The government should relocate the people who have settled on the elephant's pathway. Also, bridges or flyovers for highways and trains, so they will not disrupt the movement. That could be a solution."

Another officer adds, "We need more staff. We have only twelve people in the entire region. It is impossible for us to drive away all the elephants. The problem is that the public has become so intense. Who do we look after, the people or the elephants? During the day is the worst. Everyone is out. People lose their minds. Fifty percent of people here are illiterate; it is a rural area and they do not understand at all. If the elephant comes out, they say, 'Why did you let this elephant out?' They act as if the Forest Department has locked the elephants in a cage and then we release them into the villages. They yell at us, scream at us, 'Why are you not keeping them in the forest?' That is how they think. We are dealing with angry elephants, no staff, no sleep, and angry people, and we have only old British guns."

"What keeps you going?" I ask. The entire scenario seems impossible.

"We are connected to the forest." It seems as if every man in the room is speaking in unison. "We are connected to the animals. That is what keeps us going."

Imagine green as far as your eye can see—tall waving grasses, tea leaves planted in pleasant rows punctuated by leafy trees, a single road embraced by subtropical forests, green vines dangling from twisted barks with pockets where streams of morning sunlight push through. If you are lucky, the distant mist will clear, and you may catch a glimpse of the rising peaks of the Himalaya. Compared to India's cities, this landscape is rich in natural beauty, with Gorumara National Park almost fifty square miles and nearby Jaldapara eighty-three, less than an hour away. Together these parks offer protection to several species of wildlife, including the endangered one-horned rhinoceros. In the dry season, wild elephants take shelter here. There is no recorded human habitat in Gorumara, and the villages that surround it are Indigenous, made up of several tribal communities. As we drive it is tempting to believe that this is a nirvana for wildlife, but the truth is hidden. Man-made barriers exist everywhere, hidden death traps, and apparently I have been driving straight past them trip after trip, lulled by the scenery and never seeing most of them.

"We found that all the tea gardens are using razor fencing, wires with blades attached to them," Anindita says. "They use fencing to keep cattle and goats from getting into the garden. But the elephants see the tea gardens as still a forest. There used to be bigger trees, and now they are smaller, but they are still green. So, when the tea garden areas are empty, it seems like a safe passage for movement. But these fences surround three sides of the garden, with one side open. The elephants come in and get trapped. The whole herd cannot get in but some members are there. They either have to try and smash down the fences, or they move into the tea garden labor lines because their movement is blocked. We, the culprits, are actually driving the elephants through human habitation. This is our most important plea to the tea associations. Elephants do not eat tea leaves. So, fence the nursery, but fence on all four sides, and fence the labor areas. This is small enough to fence. People and elephants are much more protected if they do this."

"Are they doing it? I ask. "Is there funding to help them?"

"There are some who have already changed their fencing," she replies. "When nothing changes you get morally down, so this is inspiring. Most tea gardens can roll up the old fencing and move it, so the cost is minimal. We are also advising them to try lemon trees, turmeric, chili peppers, and ginger. These are productive and can sell in the market. And they repel elephants. What works in other parts of the world, such as bees or big cat urine, does not work for us here because of the monsoons. So, we try solutions that are a fit for this climate."

We are driving now to meet with a tea garden manager in one of the identified corridor zones. They are hoping to convince him to let the WTI/SPOAR build a Quick Response Team (QRT) there and also educate on some new strategies that will help elephants without hurting the tea or people living there.

Pandey interrupts, pointing out of his window. "That is the train track," he says. "It is responsible for many elephant deaths and injury."

The track is raised and lined by a tea garden on one side, then a highway edged by forest on the other. From this perspective, the road seems the greatest barrier and it is far less crowded than any I have been on recently. Avijan had told me that in Nuxalbari, there is a track where elephants wait before crossing, having memorized the schedule.

"If elephants have tremendous hearing and can sense vibrations along the ground from kilometers away," I say, "why do they get hit so often?"

"When the herd crosses the track, the matriarch or bull will try to protect the other members of the herd. They stand guard. If the train comes through, that elephant will try and stop the train or sacrifice themselves to protect the herd," Pandey explains.

"For example," Anindita adds, "right here on this section of track, on July 18, a mother died trying to protect its own calf. It was morning, around 8:00 A.M., the train was coming. The mother had already crossed but saw that the calf could not get up over the track because it is so steep. So, she came back. The train hit them both at that moment. The driver thought that the elephant had crossed and did not see the calf. I visited the spot with our members. It was devastating. The calf died immediately; the mother tried to reach the calf but could not because she could not move. And then she died."

"On June 13 this year," Anindita continues, "a male got hit by a train on his right side. His brain was not completely damaged. The right part of his face was completely smashed, but the left part was completely working. He was trying to gasp for air wherever he could. He died slowly on the track. This was the most devastating. It died in front of our team."

Anindita is in tears, as are Aparna and I. Pandey interrupts. "Tell Kim about the last incident."

"Oh, um, yes." Anindita struggles to continue. Her voice is soft and full of emotion, but her desire to please Pandey or follow his direction prevails and she quickly recovers. "Recently a female got hit by the train and dragged for a hundred meters. She lost the skin and flesh from her chest and hind legs. She could not move and sat beside the track for a few hours. Later, when she gathered the energy, she moved toward the edge of the forest and the tea garden. She tried to eat. A full medical team was there. They tried to put some medicine on her, and she accepted it. She did nothing to stop them, understanding that they were trying to help her. She died the next day at 5:00 P.M. People were taking video of that elephant while she was trying to enter her own habitat by dragging her body. They could see her organs visible from her ribs. It was . . . it was just horrible. When she took shelter in tea garden and forest, people came to see her, as if to enjoy her pain. People are sadistic. They enjoy witnessing the macabre."

"Let me show you the track situation," Pandey says, and he pulls over by a small path that leads up to the track. Standing at the bottom, it is shocking how high above the tracks seem from this angle. "Elephants do not like to climb, calves especially. They are learning for the first time. Here, there is a constant trench along the road, then a hill up. So steep. The trains are often late, so you do not know when or which way they are coming. The highway movement masks the sound."

Together we hike up the path. The top of the tracks is lined with small stones on each side. Two women carrying overflowing bundles of tea leaves on their heads, hands raised to keep it in place, are making their way down the path; not only is it steep, but the vegetation is thick enough to tangle with their harvest. At the top, the actual platform of tracks is much narrower than I imagined. There is similar steepness on the other side, with another trench before the tea garden.

"These trenches are built purposely to keep elephants out," Pandey says, "often the calves fall into them."

A woman with a shopping bag is walking from the tea estate with her daughter. They seem so small as they hike up from the other side to cross the tracks, passing us and making their way back to the other side. On our way down I struggle on the soft dry dirt, slipping on the stones underfoot. When I look up, there is another woman in front of me. She is likely my age, wearing a lemon-yellow long sundress and a red-and-green scarf wrapped around her head like a turban. On both wrists are red-and-white bangles, and in her ears are gold earrings in the shape of a horse or dragon's head, with a brilliant ruby-red stone in the center. Her bindi faded, likely from the day's heat. A withered plucking bag affixed to her back. She pauses in the middle of the path as I approach, raises her hands in a traditional namaste greeting, bows slightly, and gazes directly into my eyes. *The light in my soul sees the light your soul, we are one. We are all part of the same.* If you have ever place your hands together, with the intention of this greeting behind it, you know the feeling of energy and heat that forms a spark within the space between your palms. We hold another's gaze at the same moment, together honoring the light within one another. No males in this place, where elephants die crossing the tracks, only females, many mothers and daughters, plucking, then crossing and seeing each other for the ways in which we are the same, rather than how we may be different.

Back in the car Pandey gives me space to let all this settle. We are quiet as we begin our drive. In mere seconds, a train is passing, exactly where we were standing just minutes ago. I did not hear it coming, I barely hear it from the road. No warning, no sound. No whistle.

"When you ask the railways to make an underpass or reduce the steepness," he says, "they respond, 'It is not our duty. It is the responsibility of the Forest Department to take care of wildlife.'"

"Yet," Anindita says, "the Supreme Court has set new laws, ordering a whistle all the way through the elephant corridor areas. Also, they have identified hot spots where the speed must be reduced. This is directed by the Supreme Court of India. Conductors will want to maintain their good credentials and chances for promotion, so they will likely start to follow the rules as it is in their self-interest to slow down."

"We will see," Pandey replies. "I have gone again and again to request that the steep grade is leveled, that could make a real difference. But still nothing is happening."

The tea estate meeting is a success. With Pandey, with charisma and dynamic presentation, proposing the ideas, and Anindita following up with natural empathy and details for next steps, the two make a dynamic duo. While initially resistant to the costs, eventually the tea garden manager agrees to allow SPOAR to conduct training on the estate, and within the villages, outfitting with lights. He also agrees to remove his fencing, to consider other options, to fill in the trenches. The trenches are particularly egregious. A few months ago, at another tea garden, a calf fell into a trench. The mother tried to pull it out, and in the process, the calf was badly injured. Ultimately, the calf bled to death.

The meeting lasts for about two hours. Afterward, I congratulate them on the success. Pandey says, "We used you as a prop, so thank you!" Never seeming to celebrate any result, I get the feeling that these two have seen so much and are so committed, they cannot help but think each win is a drop in quite a large bucket. I am surprised to discover that the husband-and-wife team are also full-time teachers. They travel great distances from their home near school every afternoon and each weekend, to do their wildlife conservation work throughout this region. The grant from the WTI is a significant help, but it does not cover the breadth of other work they do.

At the end of the day, we stop at a gas station with an outside café. Here, Pandey shows me the computer programs they use to monitor the grids that map all the corridor areas in their region. We are on call, as the Forest Department said they will notify us if there are any incidents happening. If yes, we will go there and assist.

"I will tell you a story," Pandey says as we eat grilled-cheese-and-tomato sandwiches and sip masala chai. "In 2017 the National Highway Authority initiated a highway over a railroad track, within a forest area. I, along with others, tried for days to change the decision. We realized that we needed to beg the court. So we went to high court in Kolkata. We successfully helped them understand the problems and the court minimized the space that could be destroyed. Still, they allowed destruction of a significant part of the forest. We protested while they cut the trees. When we were there, we saw that many trees were marked illegally for cutting. That night, I received a call, threatening me not to protest or we would be arrested the next day. The next day, the entire area was covered by hundreds of police officers. Most of our supporters were too afraid, only eight of us stayed and protested anyway. They arrested us and took us very far away. They did not keep us overnight; I think they were also afraid of agitation. That evening, they drove us in their own vehicle to Gorumara National Park.

"There is a place, in the middle of the forest. It borders the highway, and the forest is again on the other side. We call it the Mahakal Temple. There are small boulders set up in piles and a clearing, an outdoor temple made from nature. There are flags and candles; people mark the rocks. It is a religious place, for honoring Lord Shiva. The police stopped the car there to let us out. At the temple, a large Makna (male, no tusks) was standing there. After seeing the vehicle, he just paused, like this."

Pandey begins to cry. He tries to hold his body up and puff out, to show me what the elephant was doing, but he is crying too hard now.

"He was guarding. That Makna. They say that elephants come to that temple and stay for some time as if having a conversation with the god there. The path is frequently used for elephant crossing."

Pandey is composing himself, apologizing, but the tears do not matter; we are sharing them.

"There have been some incidents. Once a herd was there and people were running away, a baby girl fell on the road among the elephants. They did not hurt her; one of them guarded the baby as her own. There are things no one can understand. A bull came into a village, he was searching for rice beer and drying paddy. Other bulls were with him. Sometimes they gather together instead of staying solitary, like a teenage gang. Families ran from the house. In one house there was an old woman in bed, she was disabled and could not walk. The elephant stood over her to protect her while the other bulls destroyed the house. Elephants seem to guess the intention. Animals in general have a much more acute sense than we do."

Pandey stares off over the highway, the gas station is beginning to grow more populated, like a destination hangout rather than a simple rest area. The constant honking has become so familiar, I barely hear it now. Riveted by every word, I can only hear these stories, this wisdom.

"I think there is only one way to completely stop this conflict," Pandey continues. "Within a few hundred years, *Homo sapiens* will be extinct. That is the only way. If someone is rushing to the peak, they cannot stay balanced on the point, they have to fall down the other side. It is not only about elephants; it is about all the species, including flora and fauna."

The Forest Department does not call, and it is late. Back at Riverwood my room feels, for the first time, like just a room, not a bastion of security and solace. Tonight, my heart is so heavy, my sense of connectivity so acute, the walls seem impermeable, as if they do not exist. My bed seems temporary, not for comfort and rest as much as a brief reset before the next day begins. Tomorrow morning I return to Dhupjhora, to visit the mahouts and elephants there, to see if I can capture a connection between them with my camera, to feel what has changed, and to face my fear from the last experience I had there. Tomorrow evening will be my last with SPOAR; I will join them for their training and patrol recruitment at a village quite far from here. Sleep tonight is simply a passageway to get me to tomorrow.

23

Today is a test. What will the elephant camp feel like now, after all this conflict and wild elephant immersion? Will I see things differently? My last time here, I watched a mahout strike his elephant with excessive force and it called into question the captive elephant situation. Are captive elephants truly one solution to the human-elephant conflict or, more importantly, to the larger vision of peaceful coexistence? A wise friend put it so well, “There are not enough forests for elephants to survive in; this forces people to make complicated choices. We can only do the best we can do, given the circumstances.” When we published the mahout story in *Maptia*, the editor could not see the emotional bond between the elephants and the mahouts. Yet, I was certain I felt it there. Today, I have a goal of photographing with eyes wide open and seeing if I can find that synergy demonstrated on expressions and nonverbal communication, or if this emotional connection was a mirage, a layered misperception, something I hoped to see.

With all my focus on mahouts, I have always viewed the Dhupjhora beat officer, Roshan, as a barrier to my ability to get closer, to go on patrol. In my ignorance, I did not even know he spoke excellent English until this visit. When I expressed surprise, he said, “You never asked me.” It pains me to think back and see how bumbling, how preoccupied I was with how I felt the story should be, what opportunities I may have missed. After learning so much more about the Forest Department, my conversation with Roshan is so much easier this time.

His office is raised on stilts, to protect from monsoon flooding, and out the window is the elephant pilkana where he has an uninterrupted view of the mahouts and elephants as they come and go. Roshan manages the schedule for patrols and rotates the elephants so that they have consistent rest and free time each day. He and his family have a house next to his office in the compound, where some mahouts, Forest Department staff and their families, and elephants all live together.

This morning we are talking about bulls. The solitary bulls roam around and often make the villages their destination for food and fun. I have learned from Avijan that they will often gather and roam in packs, but they do not stay this way. The bulls are the most troublesome for the Forest Department staff.

"The Maknas are the biggest problem. They often have a stronger, bigger head. They do not have tusks, so when they try to attract females, they are not as attractive. They are the ugly ones. This makes them frustrated. When they do not get partners, they get more frustrated. Tusks are a beautiful thing; the elephants have something to show. Apart from us, most male species in nature have some embellishment—horns, colorful feathers to make them beautiful to the other sex. The Makna has nothing. They are sad. The females always chase him from the herd, so they often live alone. They create havoc everywhere in the jungle and villages. If I compare, the Makna is more problematic than any other elephant."

"I have heard that in some parts of Asia, male elephants have a higher percentage of Maknas than tuskers," I reply. "There is a theory that to protect themselves from poaching, the elephants are breeding the tuskers out. Maybe then the Maknas will be redeemed."

I apologize for not having sought out more of his wisdom, for only understanding now how difficult his job is. "With such few resources," I say, "how do you manage?"

"The more work I do, the more I feel it is never finished," he replies. "We are trying so hard to give everything, but the other side does nothing. I tell the crowds, 'Once I was like you. Then I got a job. I am trying, still I am trying, I am not perfect. You have to help me.'" He chokes up as he tries to keep talking.

"Does anyone listen?" I ask.

"Point one percent."

"Point one percent listen?"

He nods. "Wild animals are no one's property, but people think they are Forest Department property. NGOs might be helping, but I am not sure how much impact they have. In this tea garden area, most people are tribal. At night, they drink. That is a big problem, and during that time we cannot explain to them, they do not understand. So now at night you are dealing with intoxication. You cannot explain to an intoxicated. Sometimes I feel that there is no end to this problem. I have been doing this for ten years, day in and day out. Still the problem is growing. Still, I try to give my best."

Faridul, Suriya's mahout, the original owner of my khukri knife, greets me at the entrance of the pilkana. He gives me a wide smile and lets me take several pictures. In each, he poses with a fixed gaze and radiant expression of love that goes through the camera into my heart. We share a special bond, even as we can barely speak to one another. Suriya's tumor is much worse. He can no longer go on patrols or fulfil his role as a koonkie. Faridul bathes Suriya with the others but tends to his illness privately, and with great care. I follow them to the tool hut, where Faridul is putting compresses on his beloved elephant. Suriya keeps lifting his back leg to his other, a sign that I understand means he is uncomfortable. Faridul asks me to leave, and my sense is that Suriya wants his space. He is in pain and this transition is likely confusing and difficult. Later, Faridul retrieves me so that I can photograph Suriya eating.

There is a strange tension throughout the camp. Most of the mahouts are new—the ones who are still there from my former visits greet me as old friends, still asking after Jody, laughing and welcoming smiles all around.

The new mahouts are open and friendly once the others explain who I am. They invite me to feed the elephants, help with bathing, and take my time with the camera. Still, something has shifted. Gone are the three female elephant friends; they have rotated to another camp.

This time there is a mother and her calf. The patawalla keeps pushing the calf with a stick to keep him from reaching his trunk to me, so curious. The mother lies on her side in the cool water, while her mahout scrubs and bathes her. When the calf isn't exploring me, he is drinking milk from his mother. Every few seconds she lifts her trunk, just enough for the tip to reach toward him. I crouch down and try to capture their interaction on camera. She opens her eye and her gaze bores right through me. I set down my camera. She somehow communicates to me as if we speak the same language. And we do. The language of mothers.

In that eye, I understand that we do our best, that we can't always change the conditions we find ourselves in. That we struggle on regardless. Her eye tells me that she knows her calf will be taken from her in a few short months, and she is resigned to this. In her eye I see that my children will be who they are, shaped by me and their father for better or worse, and there is no undoing. I must be resigned as well. Her stare is unwavering and cause tears to stream down my cheeks. I understand that there are no romantic solutions. That captive elephants do not have it better than wild elephants. That wild elephants are also undergoing extreme stress. She closes her eye and turns her body slightly, slipping deeper into the water. I wipe my own eyes and walk back to the pilkana.

Later, I learn from Roshan that a mahout was killed during the training session at Jaldapara, just a few days before my arrival. The same training that Parbati Barua was originally scheduled to conduct, but the funding was not there to support it. Likely the mahout got frustrated and did not have the patience or proper skills. Parbati's wisdom is about the nuance, and mahouts must learn that bonding and synergy is the foundation of a successful working relationship between human and elephant. Both must be gaining something valuable. This dance of communication needs few words but requires utter devotion. Without it, deaths occur.

After lunch, as I am preparing for the evening's meetup with SPOAR, Lama texts me. In an inexplicable twist of luck, Ravi Kant, chief wildlife conservator of West Bengal, the man Jody and I met in Darjeeling, who encouraged the organizer to let us in, and who is in charge of granting our Forest Department permissions to film and photograph within the elephant camps, is staying at the resort and having lunch right now in the dining room. I laugh out loud. Of course he is. I set out immediately, with nerves and tears of gratitude for the opportunity to thank this man who has paved the way for so much.

At the head of the table facing a row of windows that look out to a pond surrounded by pink flowering trees sits Mr. Kant. A woman is on his left, opposite a couple with their backs to me, and there is another woman facing me who smiles as I approach.

"Mr. Kant," I say, suddenly overwhelmed. "I am Kim Frank; I met you in Darjeeling at the elephant corridor meeting. You gave us permissions to study the mahouts and elephants here. I just wanted to say thank you so much. I am so grateful."

He looks up and smiles as if he is a movie star and I am an earnest fan bothering him for an autograph (at least this is my perception).

"Yes," he says. "I remember. Let me introduce you to Nisha G."

And there she is, the woman who smiled as I approached, Nisha of the begging, Nisha of the patrol permissions. She breaks into a big, knowing, grin.

"Hello," she says. I want to hug her. It is taking everything I can not to cry.

"And—" Mr. Kant waves his hand over to the man with his back toward me, who has turned round, looking up at me even as my eyes cannot focus on him, I am so overwhelmed. "This is Mr. G. I believe you know each other."

Mr. G, whom I met with Animesh, with whom I spent hours in the HNAF office having tea, conversing together. He gives me his typical, slight smile.

"Come sit, join us," Mr. Kant's wife offers. It is the polite offer, but one I feel is made out of obligation and Pandey is picking me up any minute.

"Thank you," I reply. "I would love nothing more. But I am going with SPOAR to a tea garden meeting. They are creating a patrol there and offering lights. I just wanted to tell you all how much I am learning; how grateful I am for your support and encouragement."

Honestly, I do not even know what I am saying, mostly I stand there flabbergasted and blathering. They watch with some amusement.

Have you ever seen a movie in which all the important people who made something possible show up at the end? The characters that died, who have been guiding you like angels, invisible but intentional, show up and reveal themselves? This is how it feels. These two weeks could not have been scripted to produce such rich learning and experience. I half expect Parbati and Animesh to come through the door.

It is twilight when Anindita and Pandey pick me up; Aparna is with them. We drive almost two hours to a remote tea garden village. Dotted throughout the tea fields, perched high in the tree branches, are plywood platforms with makeshift blue tarp-covered tents on top. "These are watch stations," Pandey explains. "People spend the night up there to guard the elephants." A slim ladder leans against one tree. The structure is so precarious, an inadvertent bump of an elephant's body would send the whole thing crashing down.

Every person in the village has shown up to the meeting. Several SPOAR volunteers wearing Wildlife Trust of India T-shirts have set up wooden tables, a plastic tablecloth and silk bouquet of flowers laid on top, and several mostly white plastic chairs, their backs stained brown by hours of sweaty sitters. Large banners that show what to do around elephants and why we need to get along with them are strung up around the cement pillars under the metal roof overhang of a dugout-style building. All the children, maybe fifty of them, gather on a large tarp laid across the ground, and Pandey transforms into the Greatest Showman as he dazzles the crowd with colorful stories, weaving in why we should respect wildlife and how to be safe. I am given the job of passing out candy at the end.

After his presentation, Pandey speaks to the adults about establishing a patrol and what they could do. The crowd is eager and agitated. They lost a community member to a leopard attack just last month. They want proper lights and are incentivized by the promise of getting them. They want immediate help. First, they must be trained, Pandey explains. Then they can be given the tools. Several men sign up to serve on the patrol. The meeting is a wild success. With the enthusiasm brought to the event by the organizers, it is impossible to see how the outcome could be any different. As I talk to other SPOAR volunteers, I am fascinated to discover that many have impressive day jobs: teachers, doctors, even a city administrator. They are all young, in their twenties and thirties. On the drive home, the mood is buoyant, festive. I ask Aparna what inspired her to study this conflict.

"There are so many things at stake here. Now that I have seen this conflict unfold, I feel much more emotionally connected to what I am doing. We created this terrible situation. People of our generation do not deserve good things." She laughs with a quick burst. "Where I grew up, there used to be so many spotted deer. We used to get stuck on the road with elephants crossing, but now they do not cross anymore. There is a market where they used to go. All this loss, in such a short time. In my family, we used to talk about how things are changing so fast, how trees and animals are disappearing. My uncle would compare the places that twenty years ago used to be here. There were so many more trees, but now it all is gone. Drastic changes. In the early period, when environmental depredation was starting to come up as a subject, I learned that people in congested towns were collecting garbage and dumping it near forest areas. The forest villagers could not breathe because of city and tea gardens dumping in their environment. This is what I wanted to focus on. Animals have the right to fresh air, water, everything. At first, I did not have the proper channel to focus on making change. But now I am studying on my own, for a PhD, studying environmental rights and the northern states of India."

With every answer comes more questions. The sand in my hourglass here has almost run through.

"What do you think about crop banks as a possible solution?" I ask, thinking of Sonia Jabbar's proposal for crop insurance.

"WTI is trying to build the crop bank. One without compensation money. Instead, they would offer crop for your lost crop. If an elephant damages a certain amount of paddy, then the crop bank offers the paddy itself. This way the people can still feed themselves," Pandey replies. "Another aspect. There are middlemen who are trying to work their way toward compensation money. If farmers are given crop against crop, they won't try to enter in as much. The middleman's self-interest is money, but they do not value the actual crop. They say I will do this paperwork for you, and they charge a fee. Often, they take all money. The idea is to create an actual crop bank from the field. Storage is an issue still, but this is a strong idea."

It is very late, but everyone is still energetic. That flush of energy and hopefulness that accompanies a successful advancement toward the goal of making a difference. We stop at a food truck and I search everywhere for a working ATM so I can make a cash donation to SPOAR. Over and over the small banks do not give out cash from my card. SPOAR's work is extraordinary, so many volunteers giving all that they have. I give my remaining cash, frustrated to not have a mechanism to give more. I vow to myself that someday I will find a way to get them more support. Saying goodbye to Anindita, Pandey, and Aparna is painful. They've welcomed me so deeply into their work, I have become completely immersed. I feel like an imposter as I shut the car door and set out to return to Riverwood, with its gates and gardens. In a few short days I will be home, surrounded by comforts and far from this conflict. As I walk away, each of these everyday heroes remains, fighting the clock, determined to heal their part of the planet.

24

I wake to darkness, but inside all is light. While physically fatigued, my time with the volunteers and leaders of SPOAR plugs me in to the enthusiasm and energy I had as a young and determined leader of Stand for Children. The satisfaction of being utterly spent from teaching and inspiring others, traveling, sleeping in strange beds, barely sleeping, preparing with others who are committed to a beautiful vision of a better world, yet waking renewed and ready to take on more. As if I have been sent back in time. All these trips, searching for answers. Now I know. Intervals of despair and doubt, all cleared away. There are still no simple answers or fix-all solutions, but now I see that there are solid answers and multiple solutions being employed throughout all of India, earnestly and urgently.

I'm starting to finally understand what Parbati Barua was trying to tell me and how all the fragments fit together. On our drive back from her ancestral home a mere six months ago, I could barely grasp what she was trying to say. Now, since experiencing the situation firsthand, it is clear. She was impatient and distrustful with my questions, making me write them down so she could review ahead of time. With tea gardens on either side of the highway for miles, we sat in the back seat, bags of natural pumice stones for the Dhupjhora mahouts to scrub the elephants piled by our feet.

She read aloud, with irritation in her voice: *How do you see your role in the conservation/protection of elephants?*

Hearing my question come out of her mouth is embarrassing. "It's a big question," I said apologetically. "These are big questions."

"For me, it is not a big question," she replies. "Because I am trying and giving my all for the conservation and protection of elephants."

I settled into my seat, ready to hear how Parbati sees herself in the movement to save the Asian elephant from extinction.

"Now people are becoming more conscious that we should have this animal. They are becoming more aware. The younger generation is helping take care of that. Also, the Forest Department is doing so many things to help raise the consciousness. People are finally trying to understand what wrong we have done before, so we do not do it now. Slowly, slowly, it is working. I hope in the long run it will work."

Parbati stared out the window and I imagined she was assessing this altered landscape, having driven this road for a lifetime, maybe wondering how much longer she can be hopeful. What happens when hope runs dry?

Risking irritation, I added a follow-up question. It was still not clear to me what work Parbati actually does. "So your work is training the mahouts?"

"That is an important part of our conservation. We keep elephants in captivity, so we should take good care of them. The department is also keeping elephants. So, they should be trained how to keep them well and must give good training to the people who are working with elephants."

She paused. Thinking. "Captive elephants are very important. They can help with science and patrol the parks. But they must be treated with respect. We have written guidelines for mahouts and the department to keep elephants safe when riding and about the materials used to take care of them safely."

Now I understand that given the thousands-year-old relationship between humans and elephants, the keeping of captive elephants is an evolving practice. One foot stands in history; the other strives toward the future of best practices. Just as the US government has a practice of culling wild stallions and horse trainers are increasingly taught to use positive reinforcement and ethical training, there exists high standards for mahout training. Only, with the generational mahout families dying out and Forest Department resources tapped, the entire system is suffering. Now I understand that Parbati may be antiquated with her beliefs, but she is absolutely correct that while captive elephants still exist in India, mahouts must be trained and supported to bond, love, and deeply understand the elephants in their care. There is an opportunity to enhance and overhaul this part of human-elephant coexistence structure.

I wondered how often Parbati has been asked questions with traps, accused of abusing elephants, misunderstood. She has been through so much change. As if reading my mind, she added, "People will think differently about these things, at various times, but I am the same person I have always been—whether I am famous or not. I was raised to care for elephants. I know elephants better than anyone who criticizes me. I love elephants more deeply than anyone who looks in from the outside. My behavior does not change. I will do my level best, for the entirety of my life to save elephants. I do not care about what the media says, I know what is in my heart."

Is there a solution?

"Solution? Yes. The solution is that we must grow their habitat. We should not disturb the elephants. Even in the beginning, elephants need a big jungle. Trees, forest, grasses, fruits—good jungle. Also, trees, give oxygen for *our* survival and good health. We must conserve this, for elephants, but also for humans."

I asked about selfies.

"It is a craze," Parbati replies. "But people take risks. When they are curious, it kills the cat. You can take a selfie with people, it's okay. But a wild animal, you cannot go near. You should take care of yourself because the animal will not take care of you." She laughed. "The elephant will be irritated. That is why they charge."

For once, I do not say anything.

"We say that we are the best creatures of God," she continued. "There is a question mark—is it true that we are the best creature of God? We have reasoning. The animals do not have reasoning. Who says they do not? They are more well-behaved than we are. Much more. We make the law, and we break the law, then we also break the law of nature. We are always blaming the animals. I do not know. There is no reasoning. Long, long ago, God created everything in this world. Every living thing has the right to live properly in this world. But we act as if animals have no right to live. God created me; God created them also. God has given the right to live peacefully together. We are always poking them; we are always irritating them. This is not good."

What she said is so beautiful and true, I did not want to breathe for fear of stopping her.

"We only hunted once a year for tigers. And only in those areas where the tiger was creating trouble for people. The government asked us to hunt because we had elephants and guns, we had everything. When you are hunting animals that are abundant, you are hunting for food, and that is part of a natural ecosystem. But in those days, there were less people. Now the population of our state and country is far more than the land."

"So it is imbalanced," I said.

"Imbalance. That is why there is conflict. People greet the elephants with yelling, pelting with stones. They yell, 'They're coming!' and chase them, instead of just letting them pass. People are always disturbing, disturbing, disturbing. So, the elephant becomes irritated. When the elephants resist, people say the elephant is doing harm to us. Yes, the elephant comes to the paddy field, but those areas were once forest, that is their home. Long, long ago there was elephant, there is elephant, there will be elephant. We are encroaching on their area, not the other way around. Did you see that?"

At the time, I had not yet seen it. I only knew the captive elephant side and stories from what others had shared. I was leaning on Parbati to be my guru, and like any good teacher, she was trying to push me out of the nest, out into the wild to know it for myself.

"What do you want people outside of India to know about Asian elephants and the situation here?" I asked.

"I request that people study the situation. Come to India and see what people are doing with their elephants. It is not true that we are torturing elephants, being cruel to them. We are giving them good lives. Even in the wilderness we try and keep them well. If anyone has the wrong idea, they should come to India, travel here, and study the situation. Then they will understand what we are trying to do. People need to know that."

What is important to you that I communicate out into the world in this book?

"Many people read books, but do not travel to the place. You need to show people that their idea about India and elephants is wrong. You have seen, they have not seen. You must try to make them understand. They should have an experience through your words. I do not want any publicity for myself. This is not about me."

Outside the window the countryside is green and lush—primarily tea gardens, military barracks, and crop fields. Sporadic villages. In the distance are the foothills before the Himalaya, dense with trees, mist clinging. Parbati signaled that this conversation was over by leaning back against her pink travel towel and folding her hands in her lap, maintaining elegance.

I was left to my thoughts, struggling to understand this woman and what she means to conservation in this part of India. Parbati Barua is a keeper of experience and wisdom from an era long gone. In many ways, Parbati mirrors the elephant. She *is* an elephant—adapting to a rapidly changing landscape that no longer supports her the way it once did. She is flawed, human. Like all of us. She does not try to hide this. The times may change, but she is fierce in her beliefs. She trusts her opinions, even if they have fallen out of favor. As an Indian woman who makes her living in a man's world, she is extraordinary. Her assertiveness and cold manner make me uncomfortable, but would it seem so abrasive if she were a man?

I arrive early to the elephant camp for patrol, my final opportunity to experience the working team of mahout, Forest Department, and elephant. Just before dawn, I climb to the top of the riding stand with its latched gate that swings in so you can easily climb aboard an elephant's back. On this bench, overlooking the pilkana, I interviewed Parbati for the first time. Here in this spot, so often empty and private (people rarely look up) I spent hours journaling and watching Suriya, whose space is nearest to the opening, eat his breakfast. Two years and four trips ago. It is my last day in the Dooars, fitting to spend part of it perched here. The sound of raking disturbs my thoughts. In the growing light, Faridul is alone, cleaning the pilkana and distributing fodder. Suriya is helping move the grass. This is a job typically allocated for a patawalla and other elephants. Suriya has spent most of his life as a koonkie, akin to a warrior. He is noble and strong. If not for his tumor, he would be my guide for patrol this morning. But now the two of them are reduced to the most basic, albeit most important, job. Their lives have both changed because of Suriya's disability. Yet I am certain Faridul would never leave his elephant's side, even if given an opportunity to return to their former more daring and adventurous work. *If Suriya is sick, I am unwell too. I will be with him for all my life.* If I was seeking the truth of devotion and connectivity between captive elephants and their mahouts, it has been here all along. Interdependence plays its last note for effect in the solitude of this moment.

We do not make eye contact, Faridul and I, even as we are well aware of each other's presence. A feeling of shame washes over me, and I cannot tell if it is coming from Faridul, Suriya, or me. The officers arrive, old wooden-stocked rifles slung over their shoulders; they load along with me on the perch, and the mahouts driving the elephants pick us up. At the end of the line is Satish on his sweet and tiny elephant, Saboney. He is the one familiar face, and we exchange big smiles.

The rangers during patrol are alert, and quietly search the undergrowth with a tense anticipatory edge. But, while the tone is marked by seriousness, patrol is also a peaceful time of camaraderie. No tourists or selfies, no loud chatter, the mahouts, officers, and elephants seem to be lost in their thoughts, at one with the landscape. The captive elephants are key players in the conservation efforts here, and even Pandey, who is adamantly against riding elephants for tourism, concurs that some of his snake rescues were only possible because of the elephants who delivered him to the injured reptile.

Later, I will meet with a scientist who is using GPS collaring technology to track the wild elephants, with the goal of creating early warning systems to help mitigate the human-elephant conflict through prevention. Studying the movement patterns of the herds and bulls will help conservationists and Forest Department officials enhance habitats through strategic placement of rewilding projects and increased corridor identification. The scientist tells me, "The concept of elephant reserves can be found in one of our ancient texts on statecraft, *The Arthashastra*. Kings had elephants for war, so it was of high value to conserve them. Elephant killing was illegal as early as the fourth century. When the British came, they hunted for elephants for trophy, and introduced firearms. This was a major contributing factor to declining elephant population. With the 1972 Wildlife Act, elephant hunting was banned, and some recovery was documented. But now, with so much deforestation and population increase, the populations are rapidly declining again. People mistakenly believe that the populations are increasing because the herds are splitting and interactions with people are much greater, and so it seems as if the elephant is everywhere, all the time. But this is not supported by data."

This scientist can only collar the wild elephants for tracking by using koonkies like the one I am riding on right now. They are trained to manage the wild herds, to help isolate the identified elephant so a team can tranquilize, then collar. A painless procedure that is frightening, but over quickly. The elephants have not tried to take the collars off, and that makes me wonder if they somehow recognize this effort to save them. They are quite adept at dismantling almost any fencing, including electric fences. Nothing seems to stop them if they want to do it. Removing a collar would be a simple thing.

As we wind our way through the brush, the patrol team splits up, fanning the area. A significant part of patrol is to regularly check on the greater one-horned rhino population within the park. With horns highly sought after by poachers, the rhinos are now endangered. This park protects some of the last rhinos in India. They tend to live deep within the forest core, where only patrols and their elephants can go to confirm their ongoing health and safety. My permissions do not allow for core entry. But I have seen the rhinos. They are often by water, in water, or hiding in plain sight within the tall grasses.

In Jacob Shell's *Giants of the Monsoon Forest*, he makes a compelling case for captive elephant keeping under a certain set of circumstances. He even shows scientific and anecdotal evidence that supports the theory elephants may be participating willingly in their own captivity as they, at some level, understand this is one way to continue the survival of their species. After all I have experienced witnessing the stress and plight of wild elephants—harassed, heckled, electrocuted, hit by trains and cars, desperate for fast nutrition and fighting to survive—and then comparing it to the lives of working elephants in the camp, they are both dismal. Yet within these circumstances, taking in and training orphaned and problem elephants that cannot be relocated offers a far greater advantage than euthanasia. While elephant sanctuaries are certainly an ideal vision, achieving that requires substantial natural and financial resources. Lek Chailert's Elephant Nature Park in Thailand is an extraordinary model for what is possible. The elephants have been freed from working situations and live unchained, unridden, and cared for by mahouts who are retrained to use only positive reinforcement. The elephants sleep in pilkanas during the night and are let out for most of the day. People can visit and volunteer. The sanctuary is supported by tourism and a wide range of international funds. For now, in India, captive elephants can make a big contribution to conservation if a commitment is made to replace negative training with positive incentives.

The light is ethereal, a low-hanging mist, so common here during this time of year. The sky appears white, as if you could step into another dimension. The sounds in the jungle surround me: the caws of birds overhead, invisible but vocal like spirits swooping; branches snapping; the elephant's munching of leaves; the gentle commands of mahouts, their voices trailing like the low-hanging clouds that shift and move. And all this green, so bright it seems imaginary. This landscape, the soul home of Parbati and Lalji. An abundance of nature. Here, it is easy to feel our interconnectivity. In this forest, lulled by the rocking cadence of this elephant I am riding, with a protected view out across the grasslands, through the river as it shrinks and swells, it is easy to understand how all of our actions have a ripple effect. Here, in the jungle, where peaceful coexistence is not a troublesome problem to be solved or even a vision to be attained, it is simply accepted. Only humans have not obeyed.

Jungle people don't like to talk. This statement, oft repeated by Parbati, floats into my consciousness. For the first time, I understand what she means. If you want to deeply understand the laws of nature, you must be acutely aware of every detail that surrounds you, including sound: the slightest tremor of leaves rustling, missed while chattering with friends, could cost you your life—a startled python, a stepped-on venomous spider, an unexpected encounter with a leopard. And not simply for your own survival, but to let your ego dissolve into a sense of oneness. Only when you are completely attuned to the abundance and variation of scent, sound, taste, light, movement, and even energetic shifts can you understand what coexistence means. Interdependence is visceral here. Parbati Barua, who suffered our ignorance, our questions, and our bumbling attempts at trying to understand—in her absence, in this biodiverse forest, her truth is revealed.

When I return from patrol, breakfast is waiting. Lama finds me and asks if I would like to visit the local village later today. "You can take photographs, it is market day," he says. "This village is maybe 250 years old. They are a tribal community." It sounds like a lovely way to wind up the trip, and to spend some quality time with Lama (my friend, not the musth elephant. Remember, no coincidences). Around 3:00 P.M., we leave on his motorcycle.

As we drive past the fields, skirting the usual tied cattle and scurrying chickens, random dogs, and goats, I think back to my early visits. How scared I was of everything, everyone. The way I viewed each encounter as a threat. What a difference. Right now, on this bike, proudly wearing my talisman helmet that my daughter and husband painted, I am giddy with freedom. Damp, warm wind, sun low on the horizon. Savoring every mile, and, for the first time, utterly fearless. Lama tells me that he loves this village because it reminds him of where he grew up. It is payday at the tea garden community. Women have weighed the leaves and are in a queue picking up their paychecks. Children dance and play alongside and in the surrounding dirt. Just steps away is an impromptu setup of colorful textile squares, spread out in two rows with a walkway between. Each cotton fabric displays wares, spices, fruits, chickens, fish, eggplants, and utensils. Lama leads me into the entrance of the community where a man dips a bucket into a well, the only water source here.

An elderly man, bald but bearded and wearing a long lungi, greets us. Lama explains what I am working on. The man becomes animated, beckoning for me to follow him. House after house with crushed walls, collapsed roofs, and large tarps covering gaps and open spaces in buildings.

Lama translates: "This house was destroyed by bull elephants. All of these homes along here have damage. The elephants come in through this path that connects the forest to their crop field and leads into their village. 'Every night,' the man says, 'they have problems here.'"

A woman with a toddler slung on her hip peers out at us from a lone-standing, three-quarter cement wall. Around her, tarps and ropes stand in for doors and windows, even a partial roof.

"An elephant destroyed this part of the house," Lama translates. "There has not been compensation to fix it. Everyone here is worried about the monsoon. When it comes, if their houses are not fixed, they will be rain-soaked and completely unlivable."

Banana and mango trees grow in front of most houses along this dirt lane. Along the trail to the crop field is a home with a roof full of drying paddy. This village is not on the identified corridor list, even though it is in SPOAR territory. Later, I will tell SPOAR about it and hopefully they can do some needed education and support here. It is clear why this community has been hit so hard by the bulls. The people here have a history of living in concert with elephants, even willingly sharing some crops with them. But, as the forests are stripped of nourishment, the bulls are increasingly raiding their fruit trees and food supply with a frequency never seen before.

A young man and his wife come out of their home next to the path. He tells us that around 9:00 P.M. a few nights ago, an elephant came straight into their kitchen while they were sleeping. They escaped by running to a neighbor's house, but the elephant destroyed all their rooms in his search for rice beer that was being stored in a back room. The bulls drink the beer, get drunk, and then pass out in the crop fields before they can make it back into the forest. By morning, they are hungover and surly.

The couple explains that the tea garden owns the property, but they do not repair the houses because they expect the Forest Department to fix the damage, as elephants are within their purview. I can imagine the situation. The Forest Department can compensate the owner, and here is where it gets tricky—middlemen are often corrupt. Additionally, many families live in the tea garden areas but are not working for the owner, nor are they registered with the county. This makes compensation a frustrating battle for those who slip through the cracks.

Clusters of children keep chasing each other to reach me, then run away. They make a game of it, and I play along. As I hear them approach, I quickly turn around and wave. They scream and run, scattering away. A couple of the boys stand close to show off their bravery. Every time I see children like this, I think of my daughters, who likely have relatives living in villages just like this. It makes me wonder what their lives would have been like. The playfulness and joy seem no less than that of my girls at this age. We cannot assume we fully understand what constitutes wealth. I can see my daughters here, in this very group, laughing and thriving, but with a more precarious future.

As we walk down the road to leave, the community comes together at the end of the dirt path behind me. I happen to turn around, and there they are in a layered line, boys and girls, young men and women, elderly grandmothers and grandfathers. All of them. Two guys in the middle with arms crossed, the women close together as if metaphorically holding each other up. When they see me see them, one man holds up his fingers and makes a peace sign.

After dinner, I meet Lama and his family in the office, pay my bill, and say goodbye. Tomorrow, I leave early in the morning to have breakfast with Avijan and his family in Siliguri before beginning the long haul home. Walking along the flowered paths to my room, shouts float across the open fields next to the resort, along the road where I ride my borrowed bike. Then, crackers and flashing lights. The voices sound less angry than North Bengal, more routine, as if a tool and not much more. The telltale sign that there is a herd or solitary bull in the crops. They are attempting to drive them out, into the forest. The forest directly behind my room. From the second-floor window I shine my flashlight into the trees, knowing that it will be impossible to see them. They may not be visible, but they are definitely there. Falling asleep, surrounded by elephants, wild and captive. I can feel them, and now I know they feel me too.

The next morning, Avijan shows me a picture of a man who was killed by an elephant last night in the village where Tufan and Kishor live. It was a tusker, not in musth. Avijan, who has seen many conflict casualties, is agitated and upset, which is unusual for him. It turns out the tusker not only trampled and killed the man, but then proceeded to rip his abdomen and body apart. The incident happened at 5:30 A.M., likely when the man was defecating outside. An unusual occurrence, Avijan wonders if it is a vengeance kill.

The tusker's behavior is understandable. The North Bengal situation is so intense, it feels like the front lines of a war. This is a microcosm, a large-scale warning, where resources have become depleted enough to incite battles over the scant supplies that remain. In this fragmented landscape, money is useless. People cannot buy water that does not exist. Neither elephants nor people can eat or drink cash. The elephants seem to understand that for all species to survive, we must recognize our interdependence, but humans have long forgotten this knowledge. While the female herds continue to peacefully move from crop to crop out of the need to protect their calves, the bulls are losing their patience.

The clock is ticking, in a tangible way. Rice and maize crops provide three times the nutrition in one tenth of the time it takes for a herd to eat it. And where there are crop fields, water sources are also more likely. If elephants are reaching their dietary needs in half the time, why would they return to a replenished forest? Perhaps it makes more sense to grow crops in designated rewilded habitats. A crop bank will work for a farmer, but it is not going to stop the marauding humans who want to take video and photos of the elephants for social media. In fact, it could have a negative effect. If the farmer is letting the elephants come, and the Forest Department is not intervening to drive them out, then the crowds will be unchecked. The mobs themselves will be destroying the farmer's crops. More teasing equaling more deaths.

Some encouraging projects include partnerships between NGOs and the Forest Department to allow rewilding projects inside of the deep forest, farther from human habitat. Here, volunteers clear invasive weeds, prepare the soil with elephant dung, and plant the wild grasses that elephants love to eat.

Ultimately, it is a race against the clock as mothers are teaching their calves new habits. In this scenario, the knowledge of how to eat in a naturally replenished forest could get lost through the next generation, much in the same way as Indigenous cultures are rapidly losing their traditional wisdom and language.

These are the thoughts racing through my mind. I am far from alone in my thinking. So much effort and creative solutions, new laws, accountability, and wider awareness are contributing more resources and the political will to enact changes. There is still time and hope. What Parbati Barua, Mark Shand, Elephant Family, and Wildlife Trust of India began has blossomed into a greater understanding about the plight of Asian elephants throughout the Western world and is making meaningful contribution toward peaceful coexistence. But more needs to be done. Quickly. The Asian elephant struggle in North Bengal and Northeast India is all of our struggle. The human-elephant conflict in India is a real-time example of what happens when we disrupt the balance of nature, when we foolishly and wildly expend our finite resources. The fight for survival does not end with elephants and the humans that live with them. Each and every one of us can, and will eventually, find ourselves in these very situations.

"Frankly speaking," Pandey said on our last day together, "I am not trying to save elephants, I am not trying to save snakes or any one animal. I am trying to save the next generation . . . of humans. This is my motivation."

If the elephants die, the humans die too. I began this odyssey in hopes of understanding the complexities of the human-elephant relationships in this part of India, to raise awareness throughout the Western world, where so many misconceptions abound, thwarting efforts for international support. This last trip was the grand finale in a fireworks show, the entire gamut displayed in a constant stream of extraordinary surprises.

Nearly thirty years have passed since *Queen of the Elephants* was written and filmed. So much about this landscape has changed, worsened, the resulting book and film's warnings unheeded. Yet there is great progress too. More funding and awareness have inspired an energetic new generation who care about the environment, using their brains, creativity, and might, their endless youthful energy and indomitable spirit, to create solutions. Maybe they cannot reclaim the forests their grandparents tell of or turn back the clock. But they have faith that the possibility for a brighter future exists. There may be crowds of ignorant, frightened, and selfie-motivated people harassing the elephants, but there is a force for good of all ages, actively righting the ship. So many wise elders who are teaching and mentoring, never giving up, passing down the effective tools of community organizing, old-school relationship building, and encouraging newly developed science to forge a path of meaningful solutions. This is how change happens, when we draw on lessons of our past and act in the present to forge a better future.

25

We do not conquer our fears; we must act within them. By the time I return home, the protective layer that I created to emotionally manage this trip is in shards. The effort of giving everything of myself to this task, to building these relationships, maintaining the endurance and stamina necessary to devote all day to learning, listening, navigating exhaustion, panic, scrutiny, while constantly in the spotlight, has drained me.

It is after midnight when David brings me home from the airport. Three wrapped gifts are set on the kitchen counter. One is in a piece torn from a brown paper bag, reminding me of his phone number that I carried around in my wallet all those years ago. His handwriting looks just as it did in the old birthday cards tucked into my trunk, marching forward and leaning back, much like the boy I knew and the man he is today. *Kimberly, To My Intrepid Explorer, Dave*, and a drawn red heart. Inside is a watch from his collection, delicate and long admired by me, it is a very old watch that has kept time for decades. The company named it The Explorer to honor Sir Edmund Hillary, who wore one like it on his ascent to the summit of Mount Everest. This is how the past can enhance our present. With cherished memories, symbolic meaning, and a useful guide as we navigate our present into our future.

Now I am home with Anhwei and Goldie, in a solid house with heat and prepared food. Embraced within David's arms. Home to computers and espresso machines, clean water, and fresh air. To school bus stop drives and ski races. To going to the bathroom whenever I need and not holding it for hours on harrowing roads in the deep dark of night.

Several days pass. Still, I am struggling. My sleep is interrupted with the wild movement of dreams that make me toss and turn. All that did not happen to me: getting kidnapped, losing my way, crashing on the back of a motorbike in chaotic traffic, being killed by elephants. The weight of the responsibility grows heavier, stifling, and confusing. What gives me the right to drop in and "bear witness," then go back to a life of extreme comfort? So many people have placed trust and support in me, I cannot let them down. I cannot fail. The Forest Department employees are reduced to tears when they recount how thankless their jobs are. Sonia's frustration and elation. Pandey's exhaustion and tears. Yet still they continue. In India, right now, families are sleepless with fear. Elephant mothers risk their lives to save their children.

A month goes by. My life begins to resume a normal cadence and I start to notice how these experiences have shifted the way I am in the world. Over these past three years, I have learned there are no easy answers. Anhwei and Goldie are teenagers now, not the babies and little children in the photos on my phone. These intensive trips have helped me grow stronger, more confident, and self-reliant. The perspective shift has helped me better protect myself by setting firm boundaries with FH. And when I model strength and boundary-setting, my daughters have a path to lead them toward healthier relationships too.

Once upon a time, I left a successful career to stay home with my baby daughter, traumatized from her time spent in an orphanage, because I feared I would not achieve perfection in my career or as a mother if I attempted to do both. In fact, I was striving for perfection unattainable by mere mortals. I am a flawed human who forgets people's birthdays, ignores emails, is preoccupied with what I wear and what others think; who feeds just myself when I am hungry, and chases my curiosity relentlessly. Goldie and Anhwei are rapidly becoming young adults. There are times that I fail them and times I make a positive difference. This is okay. Parenting is messy and difficult; it will drop you to your knees in humility and lift you to the heavens with exhilaration. Being a mother is the most profound, gorgeous, painful, guilt-ridden, satisfying, doubtful, brilliant job you will ever not do perfectly. There is no right way. I think of the mother elephant standing on train tracks while her calf struggles up the hill and the rails as the train careens toward them. We can only try every day to protect our children by adapting to new barriers, just as the mother elephants are doing as their obstacles grow greater each year.

Being a writer who seeks stories across the planet, hoping to make a difference with my stories does not mean I cannot also be a woman who cares deeply for the people I love. Faridul and Suriya have taught me that devotion is not something to be ashamed of, to hide so people will know how strong you are. The very nature of their synergy shows how that physical strength, hard work, intelligence, and loving care can coexist.

Animesh, Avijan, Jody, Parbati, Sonia, Upasana, Tufan, Anindita, Pandey, Goldie, Anhwei, and David have helped me understand. Although daunted and afraid, overwhelmed and doubtful, I stood up and walked forward. It may not look smooth, it may be controversial and complicated, others may not understand, but if you want to fix something, you have to act.

I begin by editing the many photographs and writing the *Sidetracked* story. Then, I talk about the book I aim to write, but do not begin writing. I tell people stories, but do not begin writing. I watch video clips and transcribe interviews, but do not start the first chapter. I keep waiting to start. One morning, I wake at 5:30 A.M., infused with the same undeniable sense of elephant presence as I had at the base of Kangchenjunga that November morning, after the musth tusker named Lama did not crush me. My dream is vivid, as if I am still standing in that field at midnight. Only it is the middle of the day. Sun high overhead and all around me a dusty barren landscape. In front of me is a single mountain made from rocks and trash. I stand at the base of it, knowing I must climb. The shale slips out from under my feet and garbage clings to my shoes. My hands cannot locate a firm surface to grip. After a while, not gaining traction, I look up at the top. There, balancing with grace and elegance, is a female elephant. Her ears are in repose, jagged along the edges. The top of her head resembles two hills with a valley between. Her trunk stretches to her feet, gentle curve inward. She is lean but powerful in her stance. Her eyes are not amber marbles like her sisters, but white, as if carved from alabaster. They stare straight out onto a horizon only she can see. The matriarch does not look down at me, but I can still hear what she says:

"We cannot wait."

Further Reading

A La Recherche des Elephants Sauvages by Gabrielle Bertrand.

A Trunk Full of Tales: Seventy Years with the Indian Elephant by Dhriti Kanta Lahiri Choudhury.

Caring for Elephants: Managing Health & Welfare in Captivity edited by Parag Nigam, Bilal Habib, Ramesh Pandey.

Composing Worlds with Elephants: Interdisciplinary Dialogues edited by Nicolas Lainé, Paul G. Keil, Khatijah Rahmat.

Elephant Company by Vicki Constantine Croke.

Elephants and Kings by Thomas R. Trautmann.

Elephant Gold by P. D. Stracey.

Elephants on Edge: What Animals Teach us about Humanity by Gay A. Bradshaw.

Giants of the Monsoon Forest: Living and Working with Elephants by Jacob Shell.

Queen of the Elephants by Mark Shand.

Right of Passage: Elephant Corridors of India edited by Vivek Menon, Sandeep Kr Tiwari, K. Ramkumar, Sunil Kyarong, Upasana Ganguly, and Raman Sukumar.

Shakti: An Exploration of the Divine Feminine by Nilima Chitgopekar.

Silent Thunder by Katy Payne.

The Asian Elephant: Ecology and Management by Raman Sukumar.

Elephants: Birth Death and Family in the World of Giants by Hannah Mumby.

The Vanishing: India's Wildlife Crisis by Prerna Singh Bindra.

Acknowledgments

The foundational message of this book is "If you want to fix something, you have to act," but that never happens alone. Long before the germ of the idea for *Elephants in the Hourglass* began and through to the moment it was published, so many have shared their powerful gifts, now woven throughout these pages.

To Anthony Geffen, who told me, "sometimes we have to fight for the story," then never stopped fighting with me to tell it. This book exists because of you.

To Avijan Saha, guru and guide. Thank you for sharing your photographs with the world so all can experience what is happening with the elephants and people in this part of India.

To Ravi Kant Sinha, former chief wildlife warden for the Government of West Bengal, who said, "we have nothing to hide" and granted the permissions that made this book possible.

To the West Bengal Forest Department and the mahouts of Dhupjhora Elephant Camp for patiently and enthusiastically showing me the scope of your work.

Vivek Menon whose organization, Wildlife Trust of India, is making a considerable impact on preserving wildlife throughout India. And Upasana Ganguly, who helped me connect to the boots-on-the-ground groups, for teaching me the very complicated landscape that make up some of the 101 elephant corridors. WTI's work is literally paving the way for elephants' survival.

With gratitude to Parbati Barua for taking a chance on me and to the Barua family for graciously letting me into your home and the history within it.

To Sonia Jabbar and her daughter, Tara, for welcoming me into their home, to their table, and their lives. May Nuxalbari Tea Estate thrive for generations to come.

To my other colleagues and friends in India, patient teachers, thank you for trusting me with your stories and welcoming me into your lives: Kishor Biswakarma and his family, Tufan Mallick, Riikjyoti Singha Roy of the Jumbo Troops, S. P. Pandey, SPOAR leadership and volunteers, Anindita Das, Animesh Bose of HNAF, and Rhea Ganguly.

Thank you, Birendra Lama, for your enduring assistance. You are a big brother to me, from the first mango drink to translations to taking me to see it all. And, for all the staff at Riverwood Forest Resort, thank you for being like family, creating my home away from home.

To Sourav Mandal for your gifted eye and wise soul.

My deepest appreciation to the elephants of Dhupjhora Elephant Camp, Gorumara National Park, and all the wild elephants I encountered, may your strength and grace lay the groundwork for next generation of wildlife everywhere, with hopes of peace and freedom.

Mark Shand for your guidance beyond the grave.

My enduring gratitude to Captain Don Walsh, who championed my exploration storytelling and helped me to see the possibilities within myself.

I am grateful to the Explorers Club for acknowledging my work and providing me with a platform and network to share it. Special thank you to Lacey Flint Thorp, the glue holding it all together.

Thank you, Jody MacDonald, for taking a chance on the most timid version of me. For your friendship and tough love when I needed it the most.

To Gather Yoga Studio, maintaining my sanity through all the storms.

For *Hippie in Heels* founder/writer, Rachel Jones, whose blog on India travel and style made me feel like she was a trusted friend. Rest in peace. May your blog keep your spirit alive.

For Susannah Waters, who reminded me how to reconnect to craft and gently coaxed my personal story of motherhood and loss out from a tightly protective heart.

Thank you to my early readers: Nancy Nenow and Antonia Wise Stewart.

To my agent, Felicia Eth, for your faith and tenacity.

Jessica Case of Pegasus Books, for believing in this book and guiding its birth into the world.

Thank you to these publications for printing articles that grew into this book:

John Summerton and Martin Hartley, *Sidetracked* magazine: "Where the Forest Roars: Elephants in Crisis Along the Himalaya."

Angela Schuster, the *Explorers Journal*: "A Sacred Covenant at Risk."

Dorothy Sanders, *Maptia*: "The Keepers of Ganesh: the Vanishing Art of Mahout."

Caroline Coin and Dermot Concannon for sheltering us on Inishbofin, Ireland where I finished the final edits on this book. Ferrying for provisions and gifting fresh loaves of bread on our doorstep. Such kindness and care.

Thank you for being there for my mind, body, and/or soul: Danielle Fuller, Hanna Curran, Chris Fadden, Karen Dolphin Heppler, Kartiki Gonsalves, "Badass Women Explorers Group," Amber Herzog Lyman, Emily Miller, Sarah Brooks Matthews, Book Architecture, Cathie Caccia, Leah Warshawski, Todd Soliday, Kate Schutt, Nikki Giacobazzi, Alexander Parsons, Lisa Day, Trevor Wallace, Matt Draper, Gaelin Rosenwaks, Bretton Hunchek, Rolf Yngve, Gretchen Peter, Tawni Baker, Erin Pfaeffle, Bhavita Karma Bhumo, Marney Sullivan, Beth Stuart, and Natasha Mago.

A special shout out to Wendel Wirth, our creative friendship is one of the most grounding and encouraging in my life. And to Dana Menlove, a force of fierce love, always sending me strength.

With deep gratitude to my family for your unwavering love, support, and encouragement: my parents, Tony and Cricket Frank; my sister, Tory Frank Canfield; Miles and Berkeley Canfield; Megan Elizabeth; and Ian and Shawna Concannon.

Thank you, Goldie and Anhwei, for all of the above *and* permission to share my perspective of our story. I love you with all of me.

To Dave, there is not enough space within the pages of this book to adequately express the vastness of my gratitude for you. My great love, best friend . . . and finest reader. For all the things written here, and more.

And to Drishti, the elephant in my dream, who graces the cover of this book. For guiding me always.